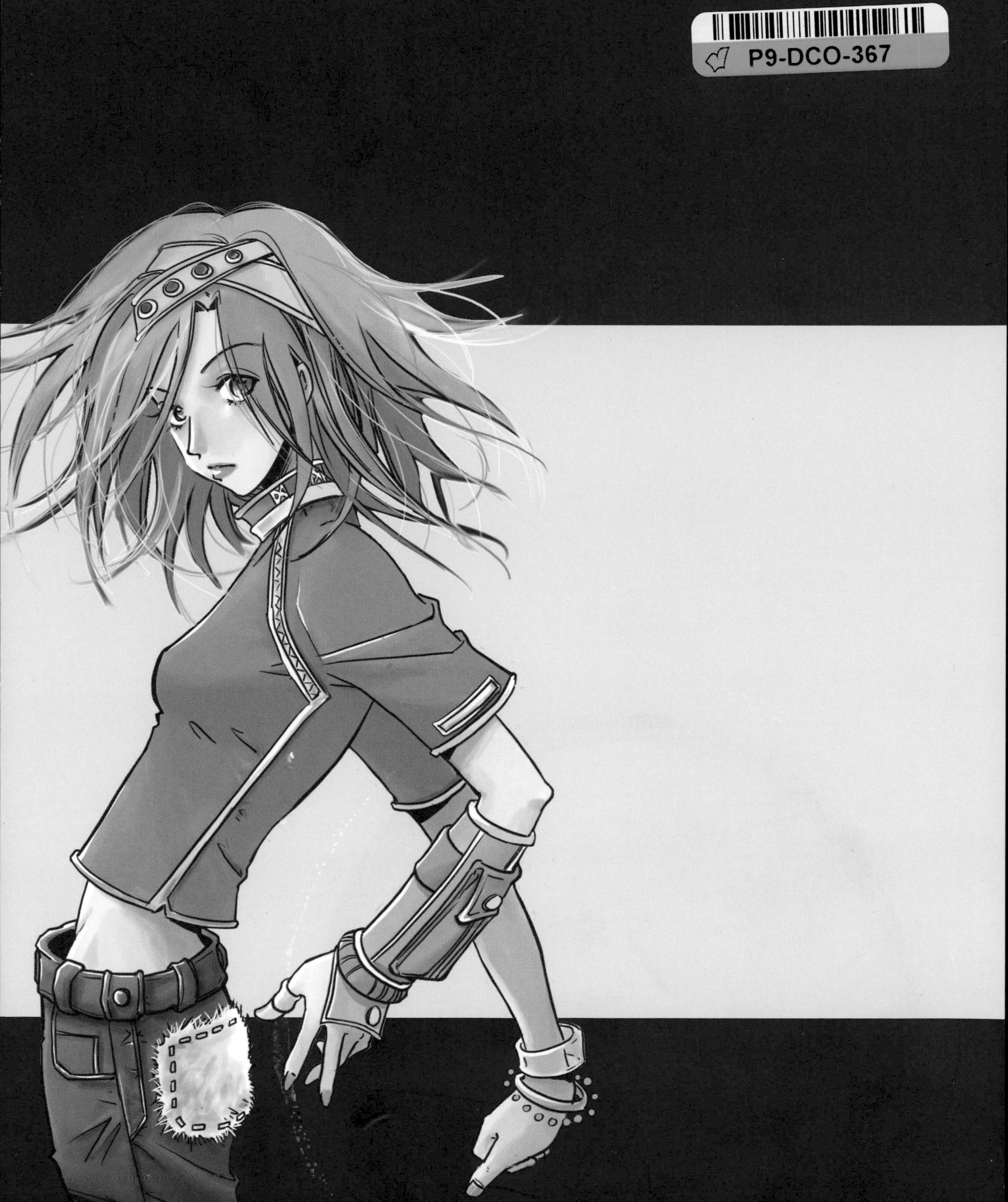

SHOUJO

ART STUDIO

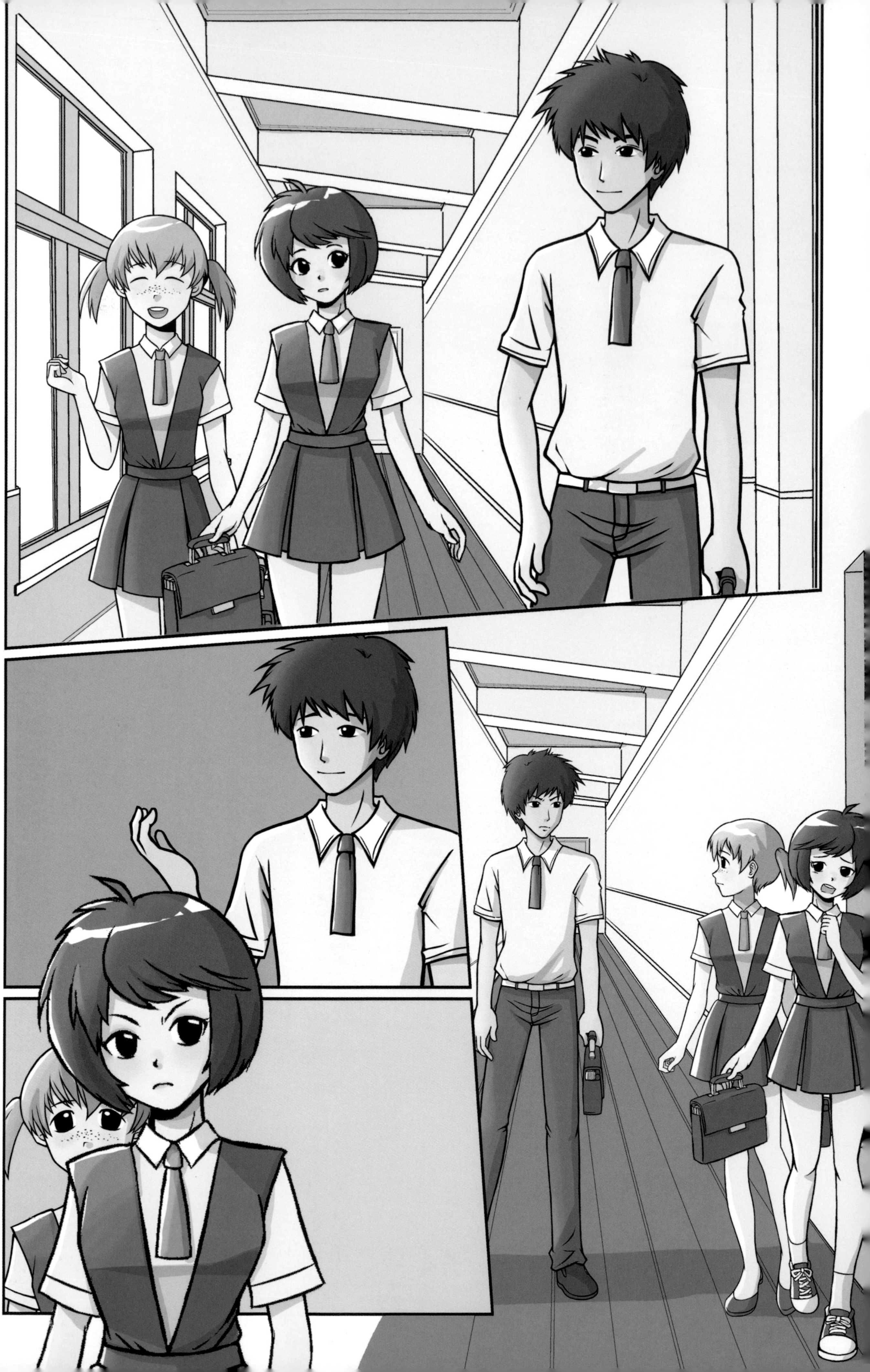

YISHAN LI WITH YISHAN STUDIO AND ANDREW JAMES

SHOUJO
ART STUDIO

EVERYTHING YOU NEED
TO CREATE YOUR OWN
SHOUJO MANGA COMICS

Watson-Guptill Publications / New York

SHOUJO ART STUDIO

Published in the United States by Watson-Guptill

Publications, an imprint of the Crown Publishing Group,

a division of Random House, Inc., New York.

www.crownpublishing.com

www.watsonguptill.com

This book was conceived, designed, and produced by

The ILEX Press, 210 High Street, Lewes, BN7 2NS, UK

Copyright © 2009 The Ilex Press Limited

FOR ILEX PRESS

Publisher: Alastair Campbell

Creative Director: Peter Bridgewater

Commissioning Editor: Tim Pilcher

Managing Editor: Nick Jones

Editor: Ellie Wilson

Art Director: Julie Weir

Designer: Jon Raimes

Design Assistant: Emily Harbison

Library of Congress Control Number: 2009920544

ISBN: 978-0-8230-9973-3

Manufactured in China

CONTENTS

SHOUJO

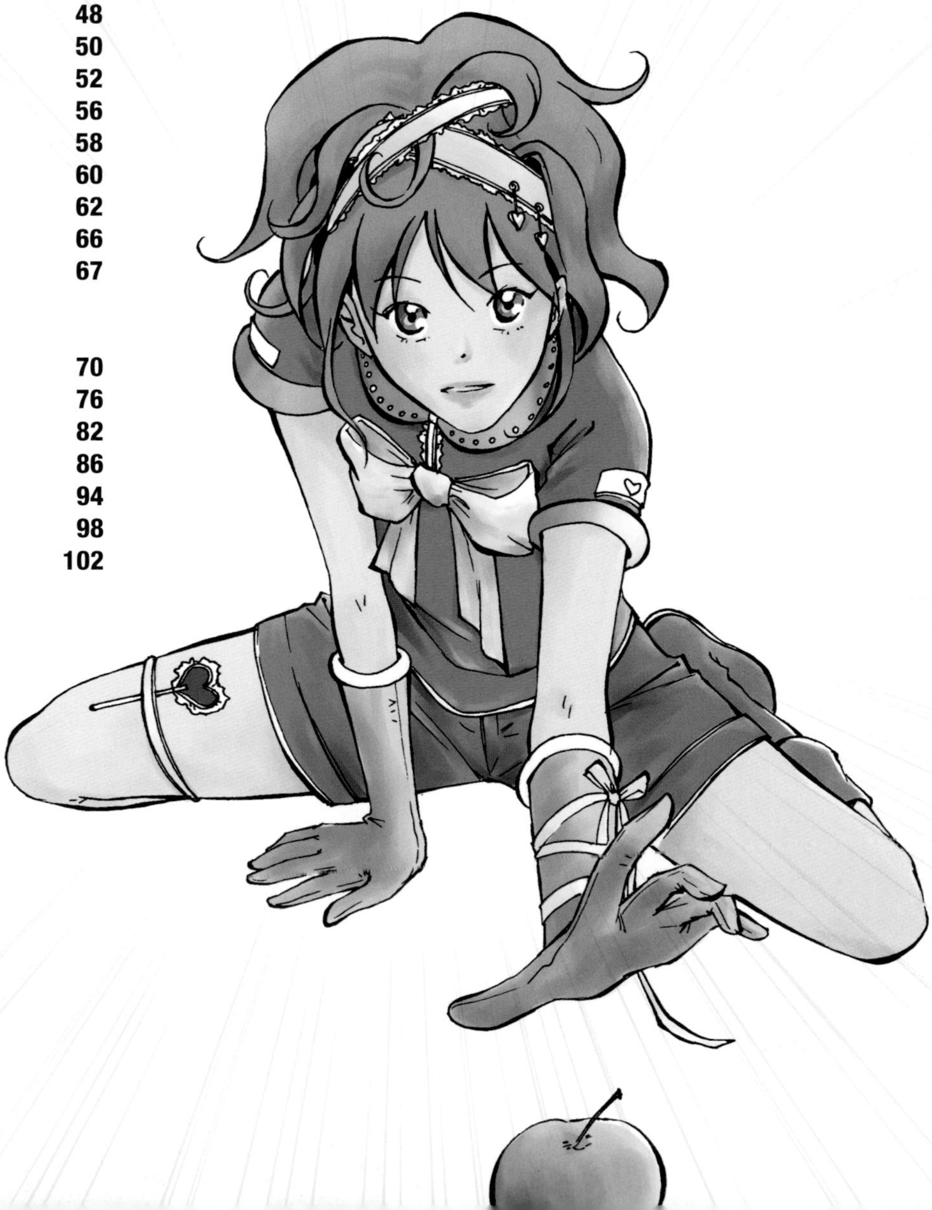

INTRODUCTION SHOUJO

IN THE WEST, WE'VE COME TO VIEW *SHOUJO* AS A WAY OF TALKING ABOUT CERTAIN STYLES OF MANGA AND ANIME—THOSE CONCERNED WITH RELATIONSHIPS AND CHARACTER DEVELOPMENT—BUT IN JAPAN, IT JUST MEANS AIMED AT GIRLS. THIS MEANS THERE ARE NO LIMITS TO WHAT IT CAN DEPICT, OR WHAT YOU CAN CHOOSE TO WRITE AND DRAW ABOUT. WHETHER YOU'RE TELLING A SERIALIZED SOAP OPERA ABOUT EVERYDAY TEENAGE GIRLS OR A HIGH-SCHOOL SWIM TEAM THAT TRANSFORM INTO MAGICAL WARRIORS FIGHTING FOR LOVE AND JUSTICE, SHOUJO CAN ENCOMPASS THESE EXTREMES—AND MORE!

Shoujo manga may seem like a relatively new art form, given that it has only existed in its present state for a mere fifty years. However, its roots—like those of all manga—stretch all the way back into the 19th century, when a form of Japanese printing called *ukiyo-e* was emerging. Chief among the artists of this period, and the unofficial founding father of manga, was a man called Hokusai. He carved stunning and iconic images of daily life— men, women, and animals translated beautifully onto the printed page. Hokusai was among the first to use the term manga, a word

which has been translated in dozens of ways from whimsical pictures, to involuntary sketches, and even irresponsible pictures. The natural evolution of the ukiyo-e art form, already spurred by the increased number of weekly and monthly magazines being printed in the early years of the 20th century, received an explosive boost after World War II. Under the influence of Western comic and animation styles, particularly Disney, manga took a quantum leap in both maturity and popularity, splintering into dozens of unique styles, genres, and target audiences.

Manga's massive appeal today is often credited to the sheer breadth of its content; there is literally something for everyone. Modern manga tell stories of the fantastical, the futuristic, the romantic, and the humdrum. Whatever your age or interest, there will be a series out there for you.

Moving from history to the present day, the book you now hold in your hands is an introduction to the exciting world of shoujo manga. Tutorials in the first half of the book will provide you with some quick and easy steps to launch you into the world of shoujo, from character design and illustration, to laying out your pages, and how to tone, color, and letter. Though manga is a fun and diverse form that relies largely on your own creativity, it never hurts to know a few basic rules before starting out. From simple structure—of narratives, characters, and pages—to color theory, this book will see you on your way. Whether you are a newcomer to the vast world of manga artwork, or an experienced artist looking to specialize in the rewarding field of shoujo, this book will provide you with the foundations that you need. And, of course, there's the accompanying CD. By using the line-art images included on the CD and following the simple step-by-step instructions, you will be able to create full-color manga illustrations and detailed shoujo story pages with ease.

ON THE DISC

On the CD you will find a wide variety of shoujo characters and accessories. Whether you are an experienced artist or a manga novice, there will be something here for you. We have done most of the hard work for you, so you will be able to create your own characters, settings, and page layouts in a matter of minutes. It's as simple as selecting the look you want, assembling the sections of line-art you like, and then transplanting your finished creations into one of the provided page layouts, where you can add colors, graytones, and speech balloons to give your project the professional touch!

You can use the provided illustrations as building blocks to create your own characters and then add color or tones digitally via your computer. Or you can print off your linework and use inks, pencils, or paints to bring your pictures to vibrant life. The CD enables you to create an assortment of shoujo heroines and heroes, with a variety of faces, hairstyles, and fashions—not to mention the latest must-have accessories! A vast array of possibilities lie ahead of you—the only limit is your imagination!

Shoujo Art
9 items, Zero KB available
1 Characters
2 Page Layouts
3 Word Balloons
4 Speedlines
5 Focus lines
6 Tones
7 Backgrounds
8 Accessories
RTF
License Agreement.rtf

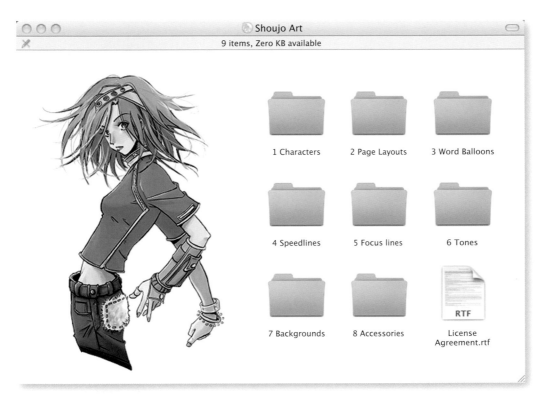

ON THE DISC

1. Characters
2. Page layouts
3. Word balloons
4. Speedlines
5. Focus lines
6. Tones
7. Backgrounds
8. Accessories

License agreement

TAKING IT FURTHER

There's no need to feel constrained to using the line-art provided on the disc. In time, you will hopefully find you have your own ideas for characters, or perhaps you have an item of clothing in mind that is not on the CD. You can use your experience with this package as a guide to creating your own designs. Incorporate your own scanned line-art with the images provided on the CD to give you even more variety. When you feel confident enough, you may even want to create an entire cast of characters, and a stunning shoujo comic, from scratch. Either way, you will be able to use this package to gain experience and insight into how shoujo characters and pages are put together. Enjoy yourself, apply your creativity to what has been provided, and you're on your way!

SHOUJO

HISTORY AND RULES
OF SHOUJO MANGA

SHOUJO IS THE ENGLISH WAY OF WRITING THE JAPANESE CHARACTERS 少女, WHICH LITERALLY MEAN YOUNG GIRL. SHOUJO USUALLY REFERS TO MANGA MARKETED TO A FEMALE AUDIENCE BETWEEN THE AGES OF 10 AND 18 (THOUGH READERS CAN, OF COURSE, BE OLDER!), AND IT MARKS THE FLIPSIDE TO MANGA TARGETED AT YOUNG BOYS, CALLED SHONEN.

Although there are many similarities between different shoujo stories, you will find that there are really no limits on what can be shown in a shoujo manga. From historical drama and fantasy adventure to teen high school comedies and science fiction, shoujo tales can be grounded in any time and place. What ties all these stories together is a strong emphasis on emotions and romantic relationships. Whatever the time or place, a shoujo story will delve into your characters' inner lives and turbulent loves!

Simple manga first appeared in Japanese magazines for girls as early as 1910, with sophisticated humor strips edging out text pieces to become the essential features in the 1930s. But it wasn't until the postwar revolution across all of manga led by famed *manga-ka* Osamu Tezuka that longer, more dramatic and character-based stories began to appear; the first attempts at the shoujo we know and love today. In the late 1960s, another, even more important, revolution overtook shoujo manga. Up until that point, all of the creators had been men, but between 1969 and 1971, a flood of female creators burst into the industry and transformed the shoujo landscape, creating a wide range of sub-genres, and garnering critical praise and popular acclaim for their novel and experimental tales. Since then, the majority of shoujo stories have been written and illustrated by women.

Shoujo magazines and book collections continue to sell hundreds of thousands of copies every week; in Japan, America, and all over the world. It remains a thrilling, fresh, and exciting art form—and now you can be a part of it!

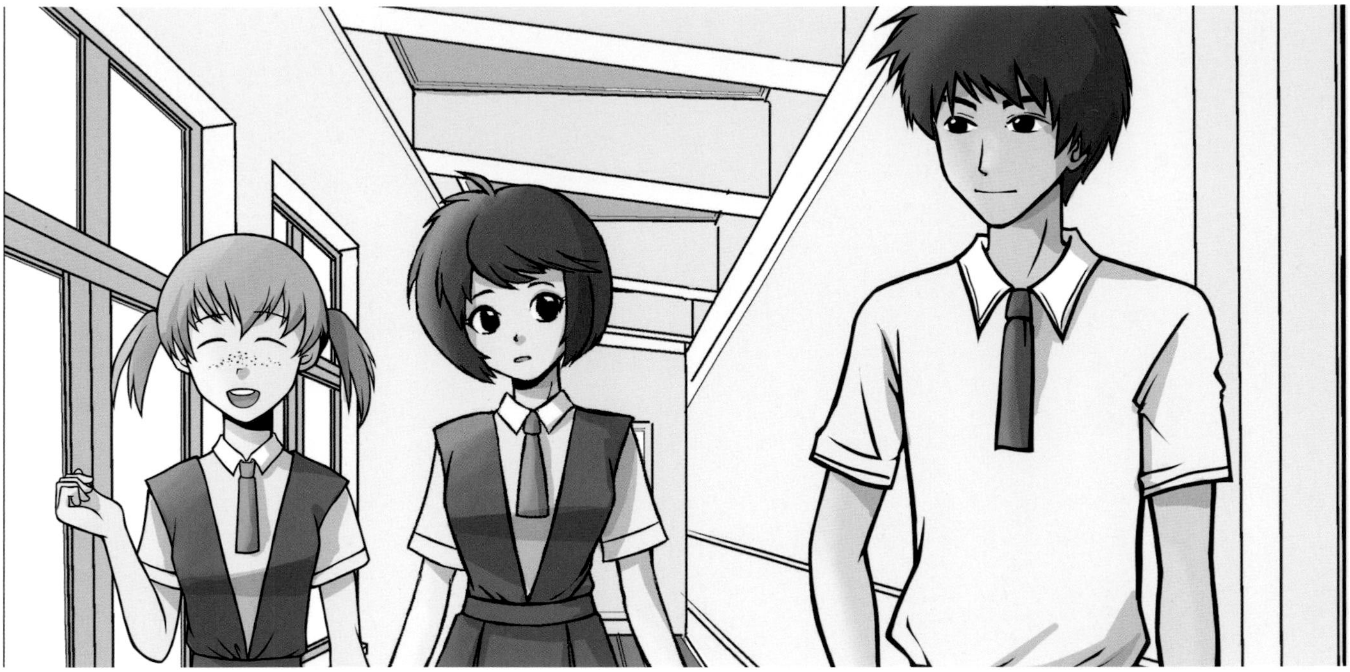

THE "RULES" OF SHOUJO

Girl meets boy is the quintessential shoujo story, and though every one is different, some plot devices recur.

Some heroines are still damsels in distress, but most are independent and successful in their own right. However, supremacy in school or magical combat rarely translates to confidence around boys! Shoujo characters won't quickly admit to being in love. The men and boys are either heroic and romantic, or shy and easily embarrassed. They display their emotions openly. Men in shoujo stories often look quite feminine!

Casts vary wildly, but you may see: the heroine, her best friend (a potential love rival), the athletic and handsome male love interest, the geeky "boy next door" who holds a torch for the heroine, and a funny animal. On top of this core cast, you'll find all sorts of secondary characters, from crushed-on schoolteachers to irritating younger siblings!

Many shoujo stories feature characters who "just happen" to be famous—an idol singer attending high school, for example. Cross-dressing turns up regularly! A girl may dress as a guy to make herself popular or play sports; a humorous mix-up may force a boy to dress as a girl. Complications ensue as the "undercover" character tries to hide his/her secret!

In terms of art, grace of composition is paramount. Backgrounds can often be replaced by a swash of color or a pattern such as cherry blossoms or flowers. Eyes are large and full of character. Fashion and hairstyles range from the everyday to the fantastical, though you may often find the heroines dressed in school uniforms, such as the famous sailor outfit—a pleated skirt with a white shirt, and a large colored bow. Shoujo characters are always well-dressed—especially when cross-dressing!

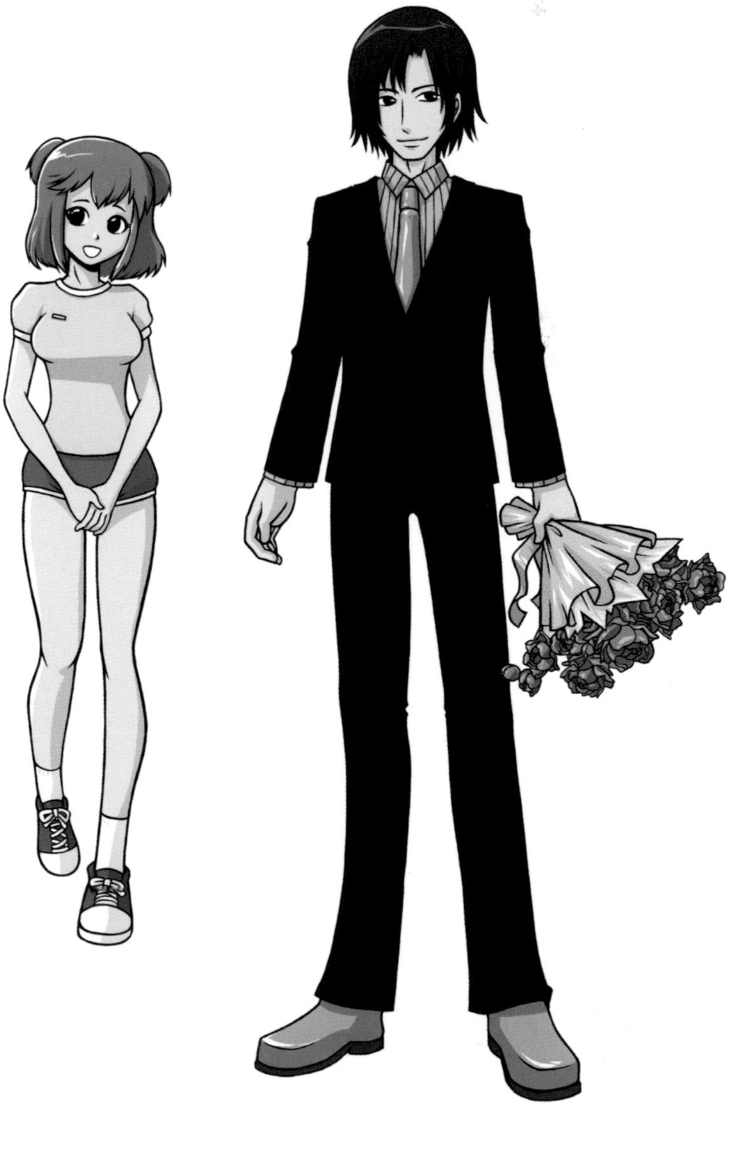

SHOJO

01 //
DIGITAL MANGA

THE DIGITAL WORLD HAS OPENED UP NEW AVENUES FOR MANGA ARTISTS, WHO CAN NOW CREATE SHOUJO USING JUST A COMPUTER, AND PUBLISH ON THE INTERNET. THIS CHAPTER COVERS FROM START TO FINISH, HOW TO CREATE A GOOD SHOUJO STORY, AND THE DIGITAL PROCESS BEHIND PROFESSIONAL MANGA—FROM THE BASICS OF USING PHOTOSHOP'S CREATIVE SOFTWARE TO THE DIGITAL TECHNIQUES OF THE PROS.

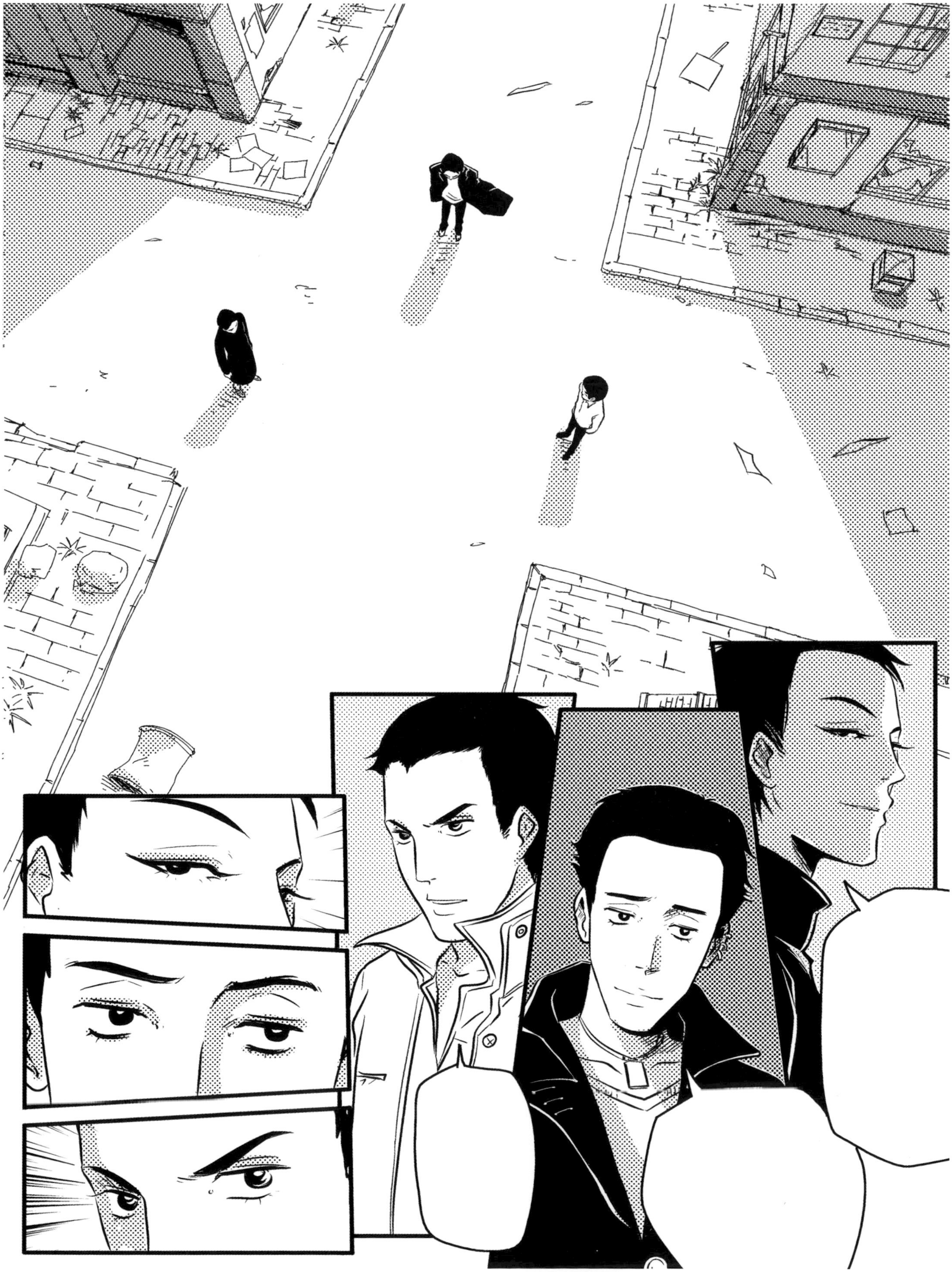

SHOUJO

INTRODUCTION TO DIGITAL ART

THE USE OF COMPUTERS IN THE PRODUCTION OF ART HAS REVOLUTIONIZED THE WAY ARTISTS WORK AND HAS MADE IT VERY EASY TO CREATE PROFESSIONAL-QUALITY IMAGES. FAST AND POWERFUL COMPUTERS ARE ALREADY A FIXTURE IN MANY HOUSEHOLDS, AND ART-FOCUSED PERIPHERALS HAVE BECOME INCREDIBLY POPULAR. COMBINED WITH THE IMPROVEMENTS IN SOFTWARE, THIS HAS MADE IT EASIER THAN EVER BEFORE TO CREATE FANTASTIC MANGA ARTWORK.

COMPUTERS LIKE THE ONE SHOWN ARE CAPABLE OF MANY THINGS—STORING YOUR MUSIC, EDITING YOUR VIDEOS, AND, MOST SIGNIFICANTLY FROM OUR PERSPECTIVE, EDITING IMAGES. THERE HAS BEEN A GREAT DEAL OF DEVELOPMENT IN THAT FIELD RECENTLY, AND WE CAN USE POWERFUL APPLICATIONS LIKE PHOTOSHOP TO OUR ADVANTAGE. YOU MAY ALREADY HAVE ACCESS TO MOST, IF NOT ALL, OF THE EQUIPMENT SHOWN. IF NOT, IT CAN ALL BE ACQUIRED RELATIVELY CHEAPLY. EVEN PHOTOSHOP ITSELF IS NOW AVAILABLE IN A CUT-DOWN FORM CALLED PHOTOSHOP ELEMENTS. FOR THE PURPOSES OF THIS BOOK, EVERYTHING CAN BE ACHIEVED WITH THIS SIGNIFICANTLY LESS-EXPENSIVE PROGRAM. ELEMENTS WILL ALSO SHOW YOU THE COLOR-CODED LAYERS WE'VE USED TO MAKE THE CREATION OF MANGA CHARACTERS AS EASY AS POSSIBLE, THOUGH IT WON'T LET YOU CHANGE THE CODES. FROM A PROFESSIONAL PERSPECTIVE, THE FULL VERSION'S CMYK FACILITIES AND MASKING TOOLS ARE INVALUABLE, BUT AT HOME YOU'LL BE ABLE TO DRAW, COLOR, AND HAVE FUN WITH EITHER.

INTERNET

The Internet has made it much easier for artists to share their work, and by publishing your artwork online you can get immediate feedback and impressions from other shoujo enthusiasts. It's also possible to get advice and support when trying to improve your skills. Looking at other people's work can be both inspiring and informative when learning skills like computer coloring, and it's often possible to ask artists questions about how specific illustrations were made. Make the most of this great resource and allow the whole world to see your shoujo creations.

MOUSE

Every computer has a pointing device, but it is well worth making sure you have a good one if you intend to use it for artwork. Ideally, you should use a laser- or LED-based mouse. These are much more precise than traditional ball-based mice, and won't jam or become slow. Their other advantage is that they don't require such frequent cleaning to operate reliably. The only drawback is that they can be a bit picky about the surface they operate on.

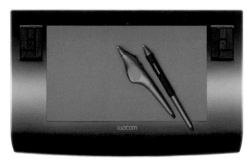

GRAPHICS TABLET

Although it takes a little practice, it's much easier to draw and color on a computer if you're using a graphics tablet. Many different brands and types of tablet are available. When buying a tablet, consider the software that is bundled with it, and whether or not the pen requires batteries. Although some popular brands can be more expensive, their quality and reliability can more than justify the cost.

INKJET PRINTER

Color printing now offers a higher quality, and it's certainly worth buying a color inkjet to see your creations on paper. Even relatively low-cost printers are able to create good-quality prints, and quality can be improved considerably with the use of photographic paper (so long as you set the appropriate options in your printer's software).

It's worth knowing that certain colors will look different when printed than on a monitor. Many shades of purple will look different in print, as well as bright shades of blue and yellow, but your pictures will look great regardless of this small inaccuracy.

LASER PRINTER

Although laser printers—particularly the more affordable ones—usually only print in black and white, they do have some advantages over inkjets. The lines are often crisper and the printing speed is significantly faster. Importantly, the ink from a laser printer is waterproof and alcohol resistant. This means that printed pages can be handled without risk of being smudged by fingers, which is great for comic pages. It also means that it is possible to use markers to color in your characters, without risk of the ink smudging. Inkjet inks would mix with the pens and run (one way around this is to use a photocopy).

FLATBED SCANNER

If you get the itch to draw your own shoujo manga Illustrations, a flatbed scanner is essential to import your black and white linework into the computer for subsequent toning and coloring. A scanner that can take letter-sized (or A4) pages is relatively inexpensive, and all you need at this stage.

PHOTOSHOP AND
PHOTOSHOP ELEMENTS

PHOTOSHOP HAS BECOME THE STANDARD FOR DIGITAL
ART AMONG BOTH HOME USERS AND INDUSTRY
PROFESSIONALS. ALTHOUGH ORIGINALLY DESIGNED
FOR PHOTO MANIPULATION, THE VARIETY OF TOOLS
THE SOFTWARE OFFERS MAKES IT THE PERFECT CHOICE
FOR ILLUSTRATION TOO. FROM AN ILLUSTRATOR'S
PERSPECTIVE, AND THEREFORE THAT OF A SHOUJO ARTIST,
PHOTOSHOP OFFERS FLEXIBILITY COMBINED WITH THE
ABILITY TO HANDLE VERY HIGH-RESOLUTION IMAGES.

PHOTOSHOP COMES IN TWO VERSIONS: THE CLASSIC
IMAGE EDITOR, NOW PART OF THE POWERFUL ADOBE
CREATIVE SUITE AND PHOTOSHOP ELEMENTS, A CUT-
DOWN VERSION FOR HOME USE. BOTH ARE IDEAL FOR
OUR PURPOSES. LET'S SEE WHY.

PALETTES

Both versions of Photoshop equip you with a number of floating
windows, known as palettes. In Photoshop CS3, these are held in a
Toolbox on the right side of the screen. Perhaps the most useful is
the Layers palette, where you can switch the alternative elements
in the files supplied in this book on and off. This is done by clicking
on the box to the left of the layer. An eye logo indicates that the
layer is visible, or on, while the colored bar shows which layer is
currently active and being edited.

PIXELS

(Below) Adobe Photoshop CS3 shown running on an Apple iMac.
If your computer has a large monitor, you'll find yourself with
more room for your palettes. You can also zoom in and out of your
image, but you should always check your artwork at 100%. That's
because only at that size are the pixels in the file seen 1:1 with the
pixels on your monitor. At other sizes, false pixels can create a less
pleasing, and less accurate, simulation of the final printout.

File Edit Image Enhance Layer Select Filter View Window Help
Undo
Redo
Organizer
EDIT
CREATE
SHARE
Full
Quick
Guided
Navigator
Effects
Layers
Line-art
Color

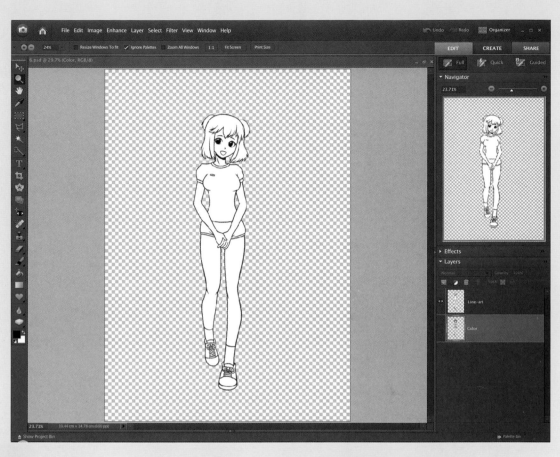

TOOLBOX

Although they differ slightly, both versions of Photoshop have a Toolbox, which, by default, appears on the left of the window. In Photoshop Elements, it might also be docked at the side of the window as a long single column, as shown.

TOOL OPTIONS BAR

While the Toolbox provides access to many different functions, the Tool Options bar allows you to refine the selected tool. If you're using the Brush tool, for example, you can pick different sizes and textures here.

Layers
Multiply
Opacity: 100%
Lock:
Line-art
Color

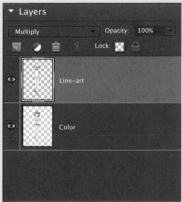

LAYERS

Layers are one of the most useful features of digital imaging. Imagine each layer is a clear piece of acetate plastic with only one part of a picture drawn on it, creating the complete image only when the layers are stacked together on top of one another. Because each layer can be edited and manipulated independently, it is possible to work much more freely, without the risk of spoiling your underlying artwork. You can use layers to experiment with positioning, colors, and filters, simply turning them off if you don't like the results, and also dedicate layers to specific areas of your image, like shadows and highlights. Using layers is essential to building your shoujo characters.

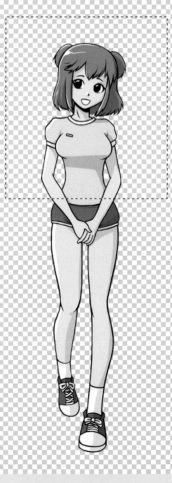

SELECTION AREAS

When working in Photoshop, selections are an important way to control which part of the picture is affected by your painting. A selection is outlined by "marching ants," and any changes you make will only affect the part of the image bounded by that selection. In this way you can isolate and work on specific parts of the image—or specific areas of color—without overlapping the rest of your picture. You can define a selection using tools—for example, the Rectangular Marquee draws a simple box, while the Magic Wand selects areas of similar color, irrespective of shape. Switch the Contiguous option on to use the Magic Wand to select specific areas on your uncolored line-art, and turn it off to select all areas of a single color at once. Don't forget to switch off, or deselect your selection when you are finished with it—click outside the selection or choose Select > Deselect to do so.

SHOUJO

PHOTOSHOP TOOLS

THE PHOTOSHOP TOOLBOX IS THE CENTERPIECE OF YOUR DIGITAL SHOUJO WORLD. WITHOUT IT YOU COULDN'T ZOOM IN AND OUT OF YOUR CREATIONS, MOVE YOUR CHARACTERS' ACCESSORIES AROUND, OR COMBINE THEM IN ANY FASHION YOU WISH. HERE, WE'LL HAVE A QUICK LOOK AT THE MAIN TOOLS IN THE PHOTOSHOP ELEMENTS TOOLBOX. PHOTOSHOP ITSELF HAS VERY SIMILAR TOOLS, AND THE ONLY ONES WE NEED TO USE APPEAR IN BOTH VERSIONS OF THE PROGRAM.

NAVIGATION

The ability to move around a document easily is an important part of working digitally. Whether it's to focus on a different part of the body, to zoom out and see the big picture, or simply to check the color of a different part, being able to get around the image quickly will help you to work more efficiently.

NAVIGATOR WINDOW

This window will enable you to move around your document quickly without using the Toolbox or keyboard. This is especially useful if you're using a graphics tablet and prefer to avoid using the keyboard.

TERMINOLOGY

Occasionally this book will mention keyboard shortcuts that can save time. While the letter is usually the same, control keys vary between PCs and Macs, so Ctrl/Cmd + Alt + C means hold the keys marked Ctrl and Alt and tap C on a PC, but on a Mac use the keys marked Cmd + Alt + C.

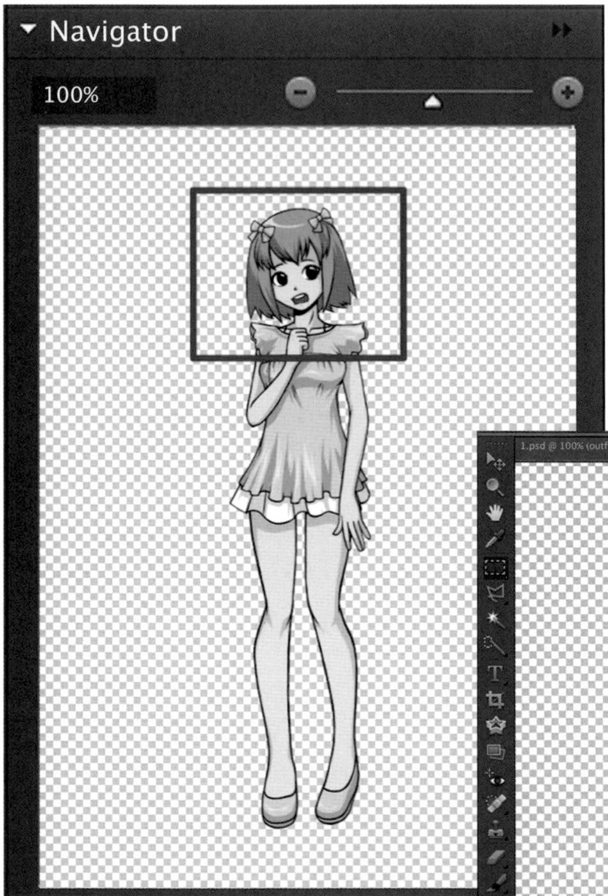
Navigator
100%

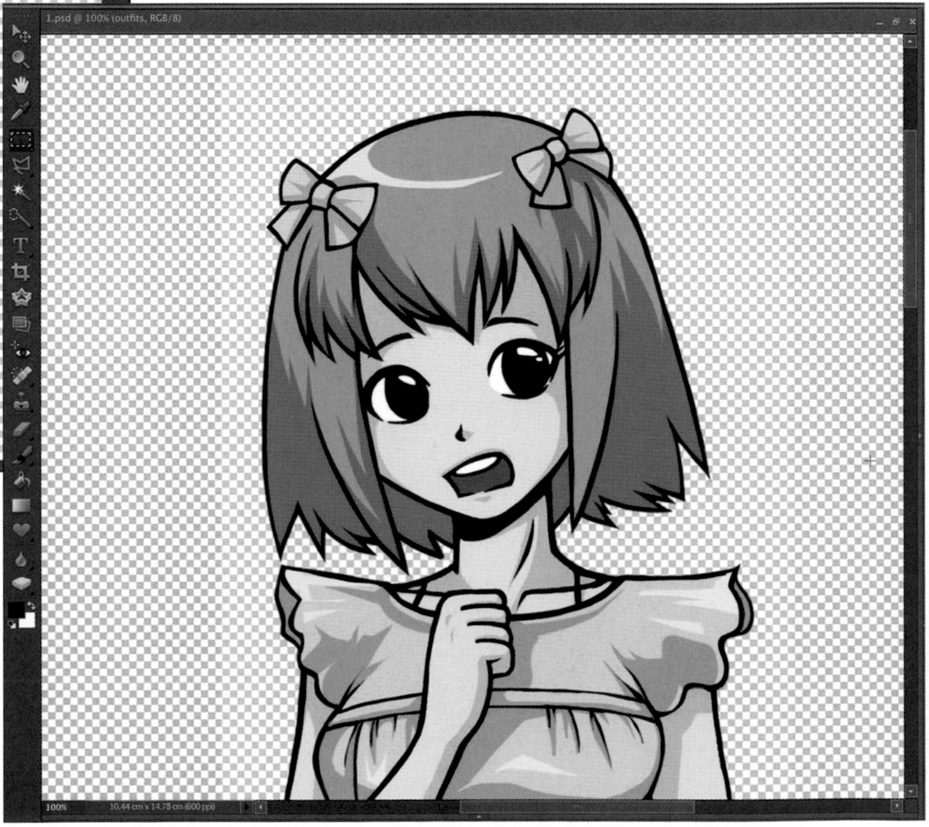
1.psd @ 100% (outfits, RGB/8)
100%

Tip Holding the Shift key when using a selection tool will add your selection to an existing selection. Holding Alt will allow you to delete from the existing selection area. Look out for the + and – signs next to the mouse cursor. They'll indicate whether you'll be adding or subtracting.

MOVE
Click and drag to move the currently active layer or selection.

 HAND
The Hand tool lets you pan (or scroll) around the image, making it possible to see different sections.

 ZOOM
Using the Zoom control will let you enlarge and reduce the preview of your image. Holding Ctrl/Cmd and pressing the + and – keys will allow you to zoom in and out at any time. Similarly, holding Alt and moving the scroll wheel on your mouse will accomplish the same effect.

 EYEDROPPER
The Eyedropper tool selects any color you click on and makes it the foreground color (as shown at the foot of the Toolbox). Set the mode to "point sample" to ensure precise color picking. The Alt key has the same effect when you're using the Brush tool.

SELECTION

Accurate selections are vital for professional-looking artwork. Luckily, there's a tool for every situation.

 MARQUEE TOOLS
In both Rectangular and Elliptical form, these are the simplest selection tools, enabling you to highlight a simple rectangle or ellipse by clicking and dragging. Hold Shift while you click and drag for a perfect square or circle.

 LASSO TOOLS
These tools allow you to select any shape you wish. The Freehand Lasso allows you to quickly define a shape with the mouse, but it can be difficult to control precisely. The Polygonal Lasso creates a selection by drawing a series of lines between waypoints you define.

 SELECTION BRUSH
The Selection Brush allows you to "draw" the selection directly onto the page. The Selection Brush is exclusive to Photoshop Elements, but Photoshop has the Quick Mask feature as an alternative, which allows other tools to be used to "paint" the mask.

 MAGIC WAND
The Magic Wand tool allows you to select areas of a specific color in the image.

PAINT TOOLS

The paint tools are used to draw lines and add color to an image. Different shapes and sizes of brush will affect the way the lines appear on the image. See page 18 for more information on brushes.

 PENCIL
A special variation of the Brush tool for creating pixel-perfect (or "aliased") lines. This is very useful for cel-style coloring (see page 56), since by default the computer tends to soften edges. It is also perfect for touching up or altering line-art, whether it's images from the CD or creations of your own that you have scanned.

 PAINTBRUSH
The standard painting tool, useful for soft edges and smooth lines. This is a great coloring tool, and there are many stylistic options in the Tool Options bar.

 DODGE, BURN, AND SPONGE
These brush-like tools adjust the color in different ways. Dodge lightens the current color, while Burn makes the color darker and richer. These tools can offer easy ways to shade images, but most artists prefer to use layers and other methods of shading. The Sponge tool absorbs the color and turns the image gray.

 ERASER
The Eraser works in the same way as a conventional eraser, removing areas of the picture on the selected layer.

 PAINT BUCKET
This tool fills an area with a selected color or pattern, and is perfect for laying block colors on an illustration. Click on an area and it will be filled to its edges (the level of contrast required to define this edge is called Tolerance, and can be adjusted in the Tool Options bar). To make a selection in this way, without filling, use the Magic Wand tool set to Contiguous. This can be useful for selecting areas on a line-art layer, before filling the area with color on a separate layer underneath.

 SMUDGE, BLUR, AND SHARPEN
These tools have no color of their own. Instead, the Smudge tool will smudge the colors around it in the direction of the cursor. Blur and Sharpen will alter the contrast of neighboring pixels to soften the definition, or increase sharpness.

DODGE

BURN

SPONGE

SMUDGE

BLUR

SHARPEN

PHOTOSHOP BRUSHES

WHEN YOU START DRAWING YOUR OWN SHOUJO MANGA, OR EDITING SOME OF THE ARTWORK ON THE CD ACCOMPANYING THIS BOOK, THE BRUSH AND PENCIL TOOLS WILL BE YOUR MAIN ALLIES. THEY REPRESENT THE MOST BASIC METHOD OF ADDING LINES AND COLORS TO AN IMAGE. BY CHANGING THE BRUSH SHAPE AND OTHER SETTINGS, YOU CAN SET THE BRUSH TOOL TO BE OPAQUE LIKE PAINT, TRANSLUCENT LIKE A MARKER PEN, OR EVEN REMOVE AREAS LIKE AN ERASER. THE NIB CAN BE BLUNT LIKE A PIECE OF CHALK, SHARP LIKE A PENCIL, OR EVEN VARY IN WIDTH LIKE A PAINTBRUSH OR NIB PEN. LEARNING HOW TO EASILY CHANGE AND CONTROL THESE SETTINGS WILL GIVE YOU MUCH MORE FREEDOM WHEN WORKING IN PHOTOSHOP OR PHOTOSHOP ELEMENTS.

Brushes: Basic Brushes
1 2 3 4 5 6
7 9 12 13 16 18
19 24 28 32 36 38
48 60 1 2 3 4

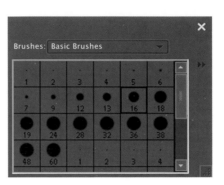

BRUSH

Choose the type of brush you want to use from this menu. Pressing < and > will cycle through the range of brushes.

Size: 90px
Normal
Strength: 50%
All Layers

Size: 33px

SIZE

This adjusts the size of the currently chosen brush. You can use the [and] (square bracket) keys to perform the same function.

Opacity: 100%

OPACITY

This changes how transparent the ink or paint will be; 0% would make the paint completely invisible, 50% is half-transparent, and 100% is completely solid.

AIRBRUSH

This changes the brush to Airbrush mode, which gives you a gradual flow of paint (depending on the Flow setting). Although this is useful, many people just use a soft brush instead.

1
2
3
4

BRUSH SHAPES

HARD BRUSH (1)

These brushes give you a solid shape and smooth outline. Although the edge is anti-aliased (softened), it is still sharp enough to give a convincingly hard line.

SOFT ROUND (2)

These brushes have a gradient of density, and their opacity is reduced toward the edge of the basic shape. They are perfect for soft, airbrush-style coloring.

NATURAL BRUSHES (3 + 4)

A selection of irregularly shaped brushes are available with the intention of emulating "natural media" such as paints, pastels, and charcoal. This style is covered later in the book (see page 62).

BRUSH SPACING

A simple setting in the Brushes palette, this can make a big difference in the quality of your lines, as well as the performance of your computer. By reducing the brush spacing, the dots will be drawn closer together, resulting in a smoother line (in most instances) and translucent areas of the brush will appear darker. However, as more dots will be drawn, it also means that your computer will have to work harder. When using a graphics tablet it is often crucial to increase the spacing in order to avoid the line breaking when the pen is moved very quickly.

Learn more about: Additional Brush Options
Fade:
0
Hue Jitter:
0%
Scatter:
0%
Keep These Settings For All Brushes
Spacing:
100%
Hardness:
0%
Angle: 0°
Roundness: 100%

GRAPHICS TABLET PRESSURE SETTINGS

One of the biggest advantages of using a graphics tablet over using a mouse is that the pen is pressure-sensitive. This allows you to change the way a Photoshop tool behaves, depending on how firmly you press the tip of the pen against the tablet.

Usually you'll want to set the pressure control to Size when drawing inks and block colors, and to Opacity when shading or adding color.

Some more expensive tablets (such as the Wacom Intuos series) also allow for pen tilt recognition, which allows for additional settings to be adjusted depending on how close the pen is to being held vertical. This is a handy feature, but not as useful as the pressure control.

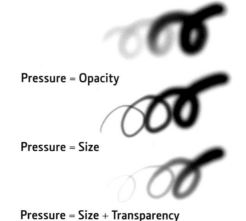

Pressure = Opacity

Pressure = Size

Pressure = Size + Transparency

KEYBOARD SHORTCUTS

QUICK BRUSH RESIZING

The [and] keys allow you to quickly resize your brush (holding down the Shift key at the same time also alters the hardness). By making the most of this you can quickly adjust the level of detail you're working with, without having to switch focus from the portion of the illustration you are working on. This is especially useful when using soft brushes to color your images.

QUICK COLOR CHANGES

When working with the Brush or Pencil tools, you'll often want to change color quickly. By holding the Alt key and clicking over a pixel of the color you want, you pick up that color from the canvas. (You might even want to keep a palette area of dabs of color on your image until you're finished.) Also worth noting is the X button, which quickly alternates between your foreground and background color.

PAINTING WITH OPACITY CONTROLS

The number keys along the top of the keyboard act as handy shortcuts for adjusting the opacity of your brush. Press 1 for 10% opacity, 2 for 20% opacity, etc. If you press 2 and 5 quickly, you will get 25% opacity. This is useful if you want to introduce subtlety to your coloring, but don't want to change color. These shortcuts, combined with the X button, can allow for very fast monochrome illustrating.

SHOUJO

CREATING CHARACTERS

BUILDING A SHOUJO CHARACTER FROM THE FILES SUPPLIED ON THE CD IS SIMPLE. HAVE FUN WITH THE DIFFERENT COMBINATIONS AND LOOKS YOU CAN CREATE FOR EACH CHARACTER. THE FILES HAVE BEEN DESIGNED TO BE AS EASY TO USE AS POSSIBLE, SO IT IS REALLY JUST A MATTER OF PLAYING AROUND WITH THE LAYERS.

Layers
Normal
Opacity: 100%
Lock:
accessory1
accessory2
accessory3
accessory4
hair1
hair2
hair3
eyes1
eyes2
eyes3
eyes4
mouth1
mouth2
mouth3
mouth4
mouth5
head
right arm1
right arm2
right arm3
left arm1
left arm2
left arm3
arms4
bicycle
outfit1
outfit2
outfit3

1 Insert the CD-ROM supplied with this book. It doesn't matter whether you're using a Mac or PC. Find the folder labeled Characters. Inside this folder, you'll find a layered .PSD (Photoshop) file for each character in this book. Go to File > Open in Photoshop or Photoshop Elements, or drag the .PSD file onto the Photoshop icon, then choose the character you want. The layers within the files act like a traditional animator's acetate film—all you need to do now is put the elements together to form a character. Simply turn the visibility of various layers on and off, by clicking in the colored box to the left of the layer's name. A visible layer shows the image of an eye.

2 Turn to the corresponding pages of this book to see the options for your character, including a full listing of the layers available (in the form of a Layers palette). To help you, the layers have been color coded for ease of use. Generally, you will not want to turn on more than one head, legs, or torso at once.

3 For many projects, you'll be finished at this point. Simply click Layers > Flatten, then save the image onto your computer using File > Save As from the menu. You will not be able to save over the original file since it is on the CD. If you are creating different angles, expressions, and poses of the same character, for use on a shoujo page or story, you may want to create a folder on your computer for each character you create, for future ease of use, or save an unflattened .PSD file with the name of your character, so you can quickly change expressions and import the relevant layers into your shoujo story.

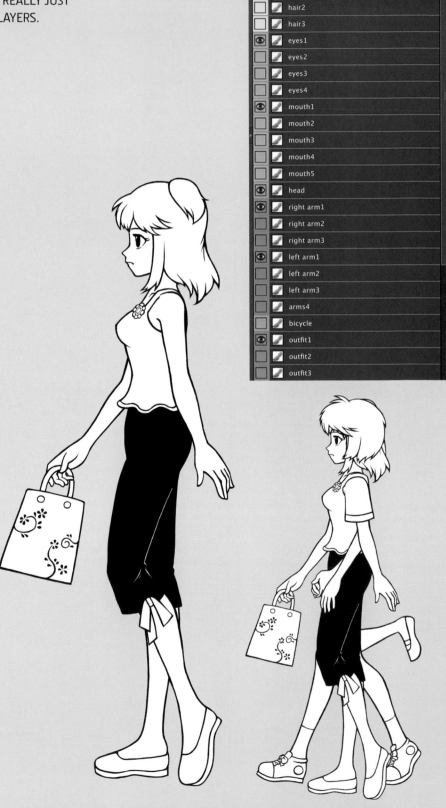

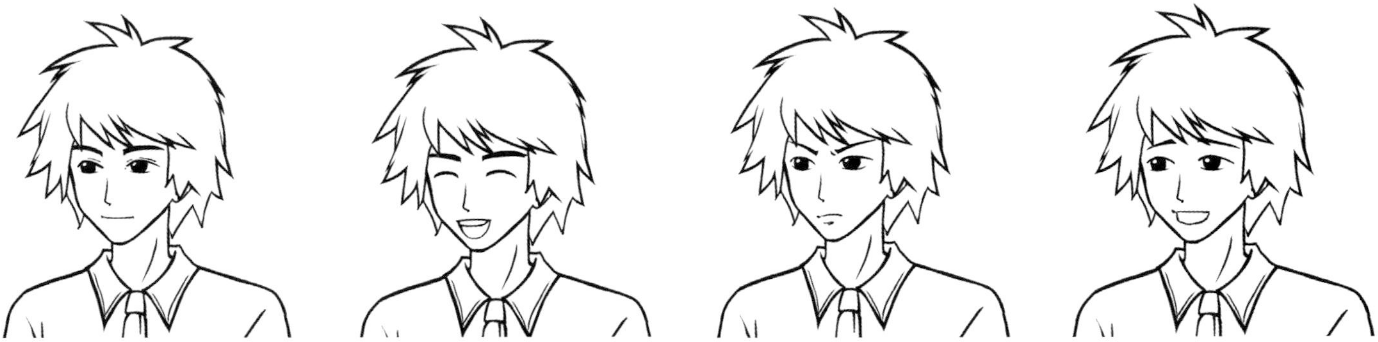

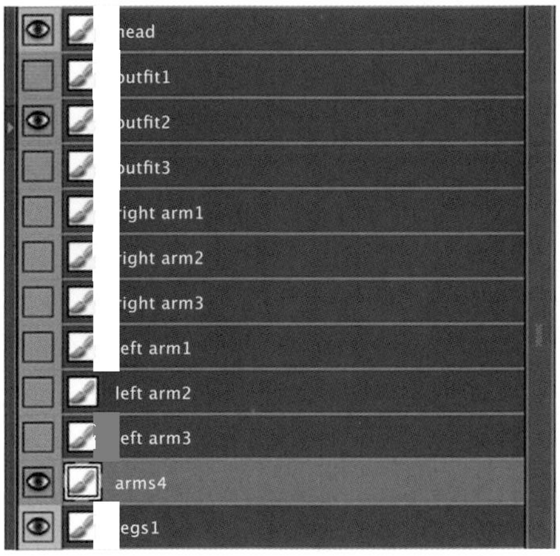
head
outfit1
outfit2
outfit3
right arm1
right arm2
right arm3
left arm1
left arm2
left arm3
arms4
legs1

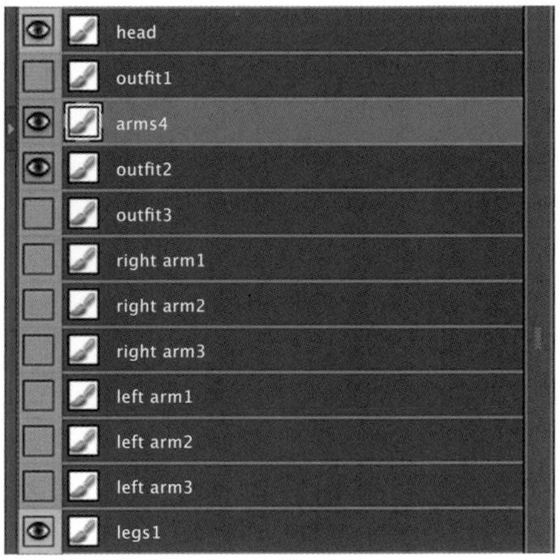
head
outfit1
arms4
outfit2
outfit3
right arm1
right arm2
right arm3
left arm1
left arm2
left arm3
legs1

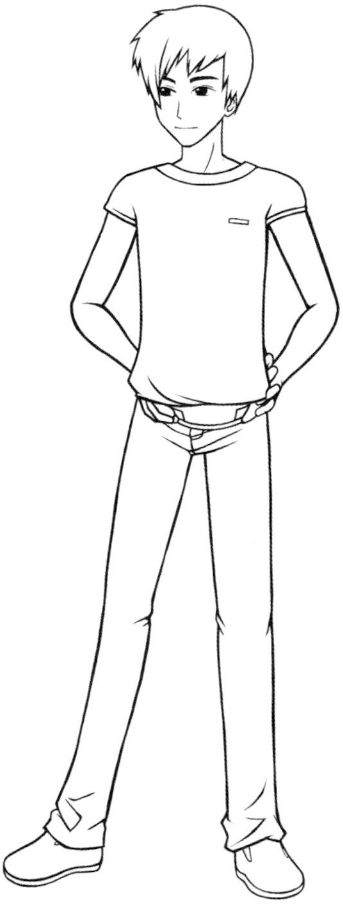

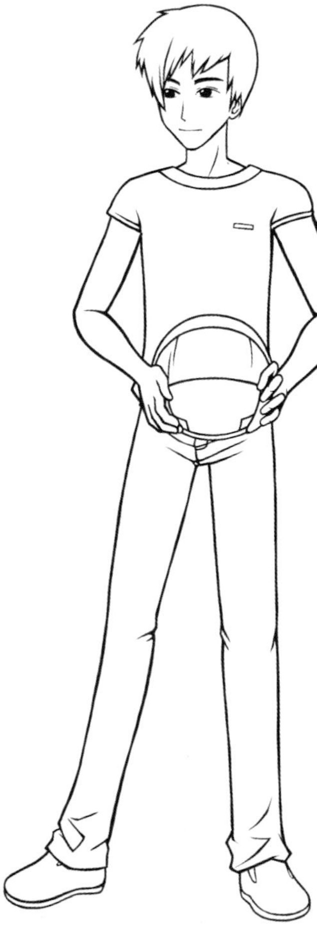

4 The characters' facial expressions can also be adjusted by turning the relevant layers on and off. Simply choose a mouth and a set of eyes to suggest different emotions.

5 Some combinations of clothing or accessories may require you to adjust the order of the layers. Alternatively, you may want to adapt the look of your character by changing the layer order. For example, a T-shirt can be tucked into trousers by moving it behind the legs layer. Simply drag the layers up and down on the Layers palette to change the order.

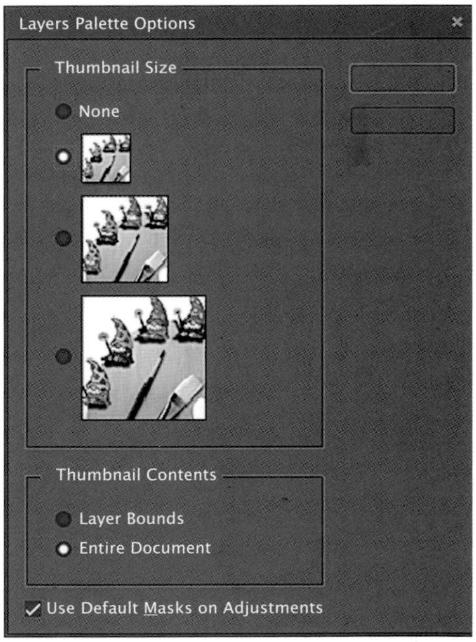
Layers Palette Options
Thumbnail Size
None
Thumbnail Contents
Layer Bounds
Entire Document
Use Default Masks on Adjustments

Tip SEE MORE OR LESS LAYERS

To change the number of layers you can see in the Layers palette, you can change the size of (or add/remove) the image preview. Simply click on the More arrow at the top left of the palette and choose Palette options. The larger the preview, the fewer layers will be visible at once.

SHOUJO

ADDITIONAL CLOTHING

The suggestion of additional clothing can be introduced to the characters with simple lines drawn onto the character after construction. Think about how the final image will be toned or colored, and about areas that could suggest extra clothing or layering with an additional line. You could also create new looks by erasing lines of existing artwork with the Eraser tool, or using the Brush tool to color over lines with white.

TRY SOME OF THESE:
* Stockings
* Long socks
* Arm warmers
* Gloves
* Vests and tight clothing
* Collars and chokers

Make sure that if you are going to be showing the same character from a lot of different angles you make the same additions and customizations to each version, or your panel-to-panel continuity will be very confusing for your readers!

USING ACCESSORIES

A large number of accessories are included to add detail to your shoujo story scenes.

1 Open up the accessory and your target image alongside each other.

2 Simply drag the accessory layer onto your target image. Alternatively copy the accessory and paste it onto your target image.

3 Using the Move tool, drag the shape into position.

4 Use the Rotate and Resize functions (explained on the next page) to adjust the shape of the accessory.

RESIZING, ROTATING, AND FLIPPING

You can use the Free Transform tool (Edit > Free Transform, or keyboard shortcut Ctrl/Cmd + T) to make your characters even more dynamic, by changing the size and direction of accessories. The only disadvantage of doing so is that by transforming the image like this you will cause portions of the image to become anti-aliased, which will cause problems at the coloring and toning stage. Remember to remove anti-aliasing before you continue with your coloring.

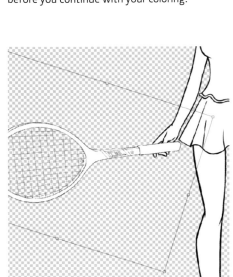

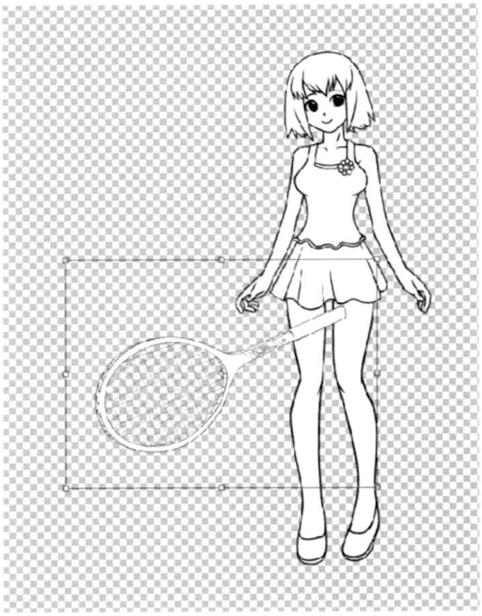

1 Select the portion of your image you want to rotate or change in size (scale) by making it the active layer, and choose Free Transform.

2 Use the white squares at the corners of the image to drag it larger or smaller (holding down Shift as you do so keeps the image in proportion), or enter a particular percentage in the Tool Options bar.

3 To rotate the selection, hover the mouse just outside the bounding box until the cursor turns into a curved, two-ended arrow. Dragging to the left or right will rotate the selection—though you can enter precise degrees in the Tool Options bar, as before. This is especially useful if you want to alter the position of arms and legs from panel to panel, to create the illusion of movement in your shoujo strips.

4 When you have finished adjusting the image, press the Enter key or the "tick check" on the right side of the Toolbar.

5 Flipping (or mirroring) your image, is also an ideal way to express movement or introduce variety. This can be done at any point by selecting Image > Rotate > Flip Horizontal.

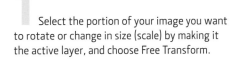

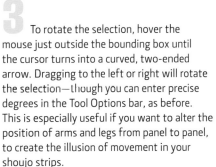

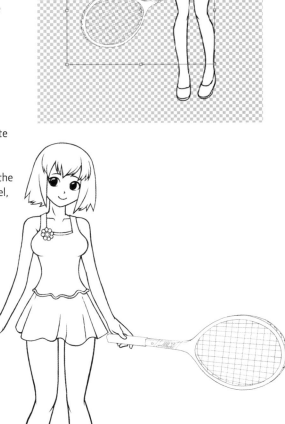

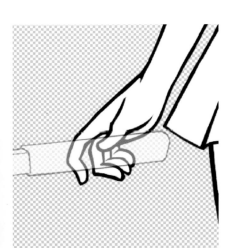

Tip Reducing the Opacity of the accessory layer can help you to position your object. Here, for example, by reducing the Opacity of the tennis racket you can place the handle in the character's hand, and erase areas of the handle so you can see the thumb.

CREATING CLOSE-UPS AND POSES

As we have seen on the previous pages, creating a character is simply just a matter of turning the characters' layers on and off in Photoshop. Adding accessories is equally straightforward, using the Free Transform tool to resize and rotate objects into place.

Using the same methods already described, you can also create close-ups and alternative poses for your main characters. As your shoujo strip will mainly feature your leading girl and guy, it's a good idea to alternate between their poses to make the panels more interesting. The main female and main male have special Head layers that can be manipulated using the Free Transform tool, to help you create alternative poses. Here's how to do it.

Layers
Normal
Opacity: 100%
Lock:
accessory1
accessory2
accessory3
accessory4
hair1
hair2
hair3
eyes1
eyes2
eyes3
eyes4
mouth1
mouth2
mouth3
mouth4
mouth5
head
outfit sleeve1
outfit sleeve2
accessory4
head
outfit sleeve1

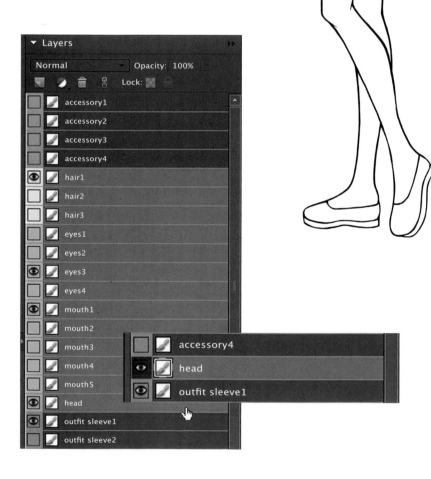

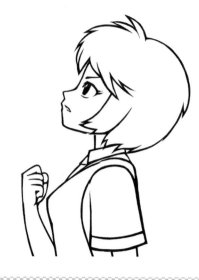

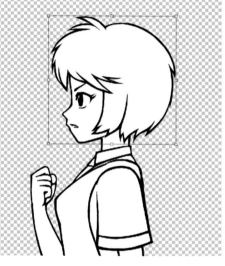

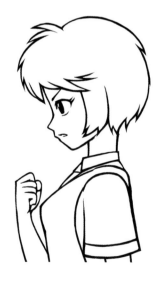

1 Open your main character in Photoshop and turn on the layers you want to use for the hair, eyes, and mouth, as well as the head layer.

2 Merge the Hair, Eyes, Mouth, and Head layers (Ctrl/Cmd + E) so they are all on one layer.

3 Using the Free Transform tool, rotate your character's head to create different poses, and suggest different states of emotion.

Tip This is an especially handy technique for when you come to adding your main characters to panels for close-ups.

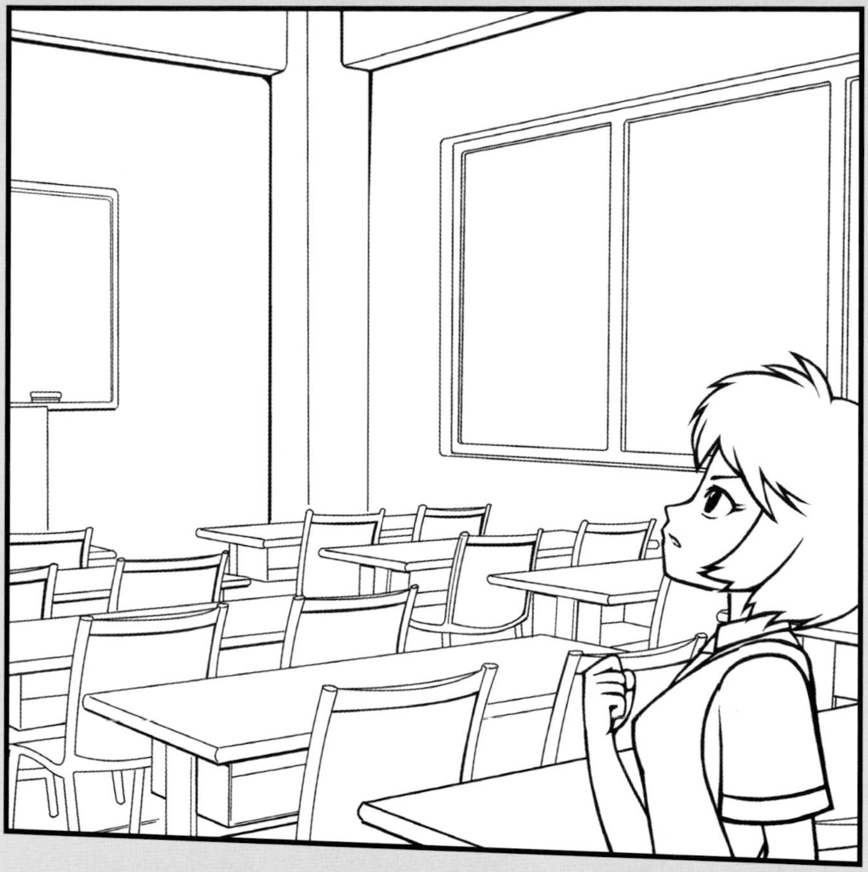

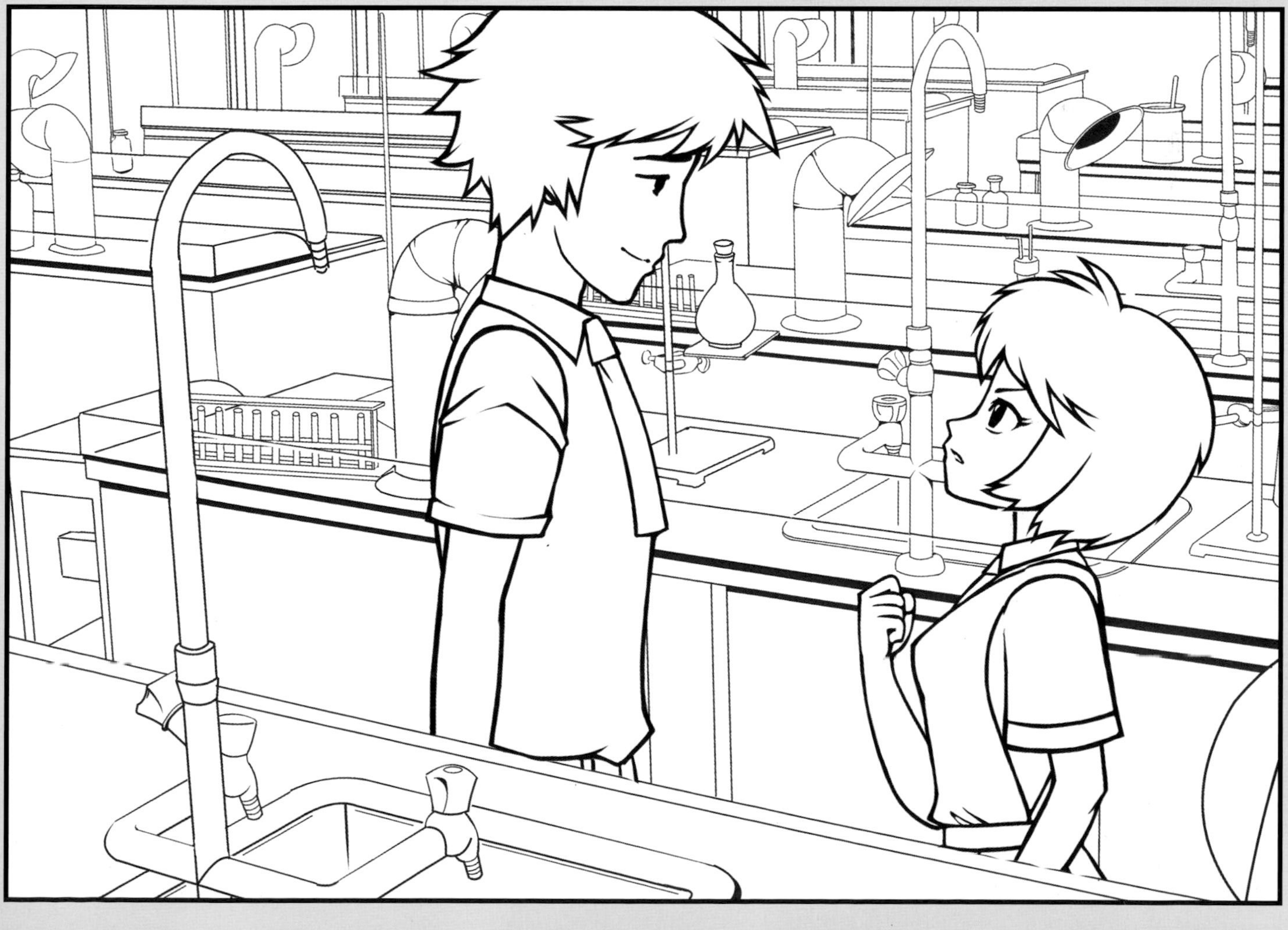

SHOUJO

PACING YOUR STORY TELLING

THE GOAL OF CREATING A MANGA IS TO TELL A STORY CLEARLY, USING A MIXTURE OF WORDS AND PICTURES. WHILE SKILLFUL AND ATTRACTIVE DRAWINGS ARE IMPORTANT, THE SKILL OF TELLING A STORY CLEARLY IS EVEN MORE SO. IMAGINE YOURSELF AS A FILM DIRECTOR, RESPONSIBLE FOR EVERY ASPECT OF YOUR CREATION: THE SUCCESSFUL MARKETING OF YOUR MOVIE MAY DEPEND ON THE ATTRACTIVENESS OF YOUR STARS, BUT WHAT WINS CRITICAL PRAISE AND THE LOVE OF YOUR AUDIENCE IS HOW WELL YOU TELL YOUR STORY, AND HOW CONVINCING YOU ARE IN PERSUADING THEM TO FEEL FOR YOUR CHARACTERS.

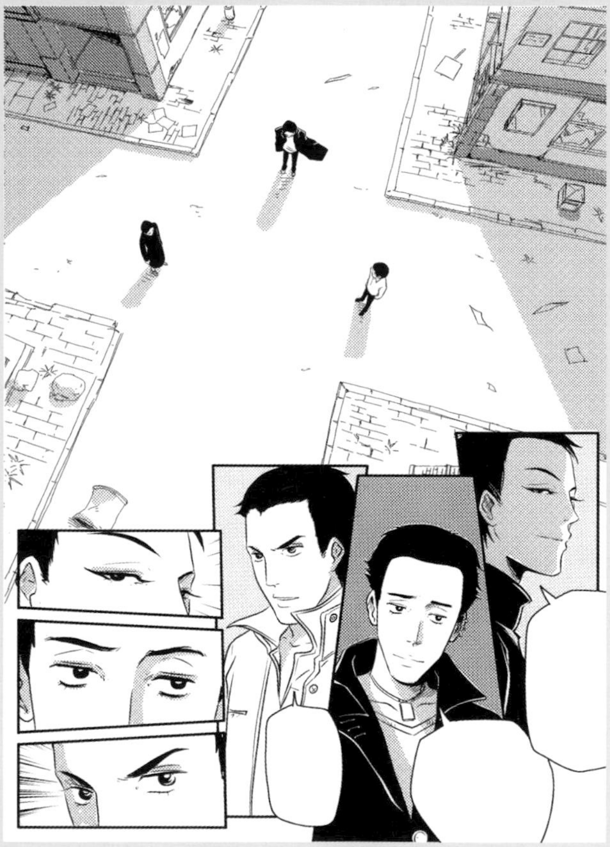

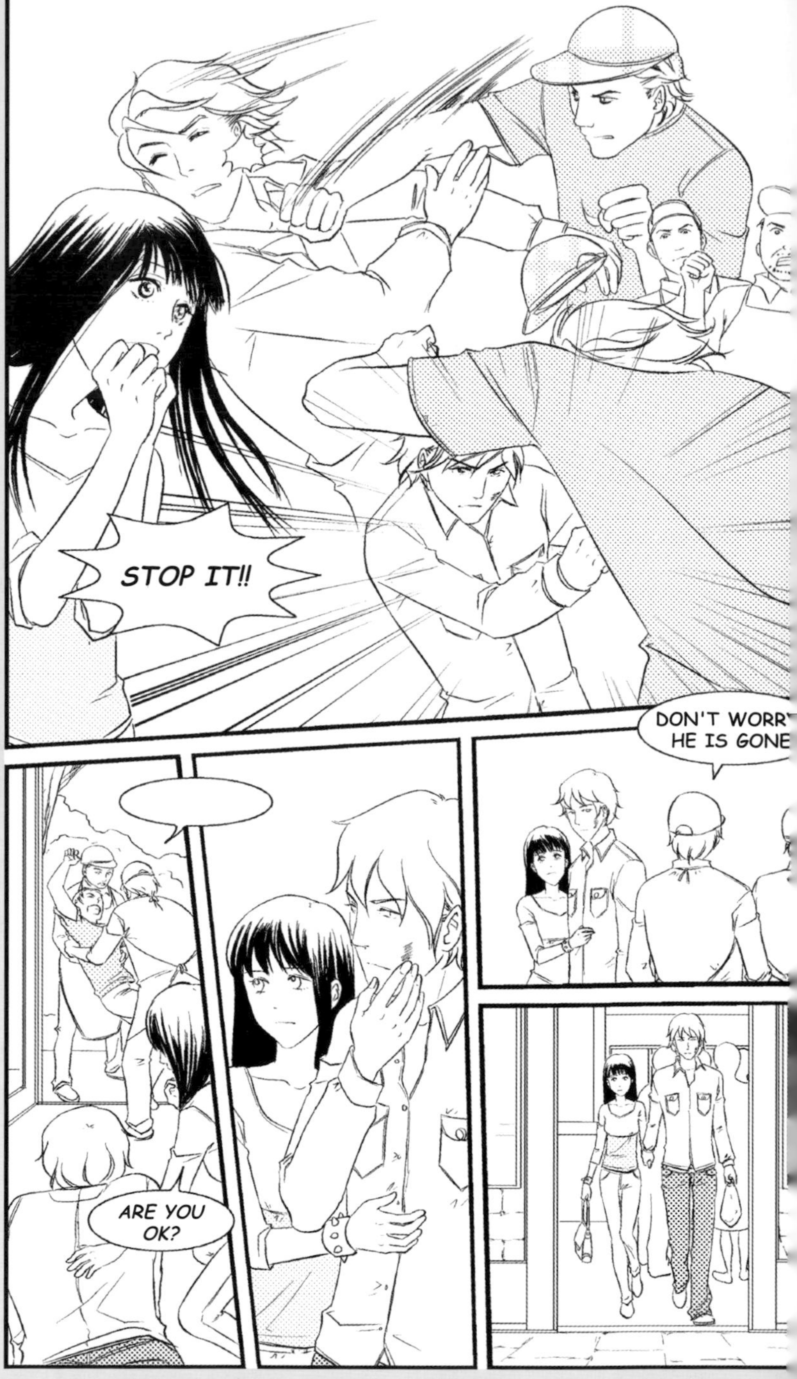
STOP IT!!
ARE YOU OK?
DON'T WORR
HE IS GONE

1 Before you can begin to pace out your shoujo story, you need to start with the basics. Find a concept for your story (a setting, some characters, the conflict that will get them to interact), and a rough idea of how long it will be. Don't be too ambitious and plan a manga in ten volumes; start with something small and achievable to build up your confidence. If you're stuck, why not look over your favorite works of shoujo manga for inspiration? Where is your story set? Who are your characters, and what are the tangled relationships between them?

2 Once you've found a concept for your story, try to write the first few pages as a script, paying attention to the action that will take place, and the dialogue—or conversations—that your characters will have. It is best to keep this dialogue as concise and interesting as possible: manga thrives on the interaction between the pictures and words on the page. The pictures in each panel do the hard work of telling the story, while the dialogue is there to clarify and entertain—you don't want to cover up the pages you create with word balloons!

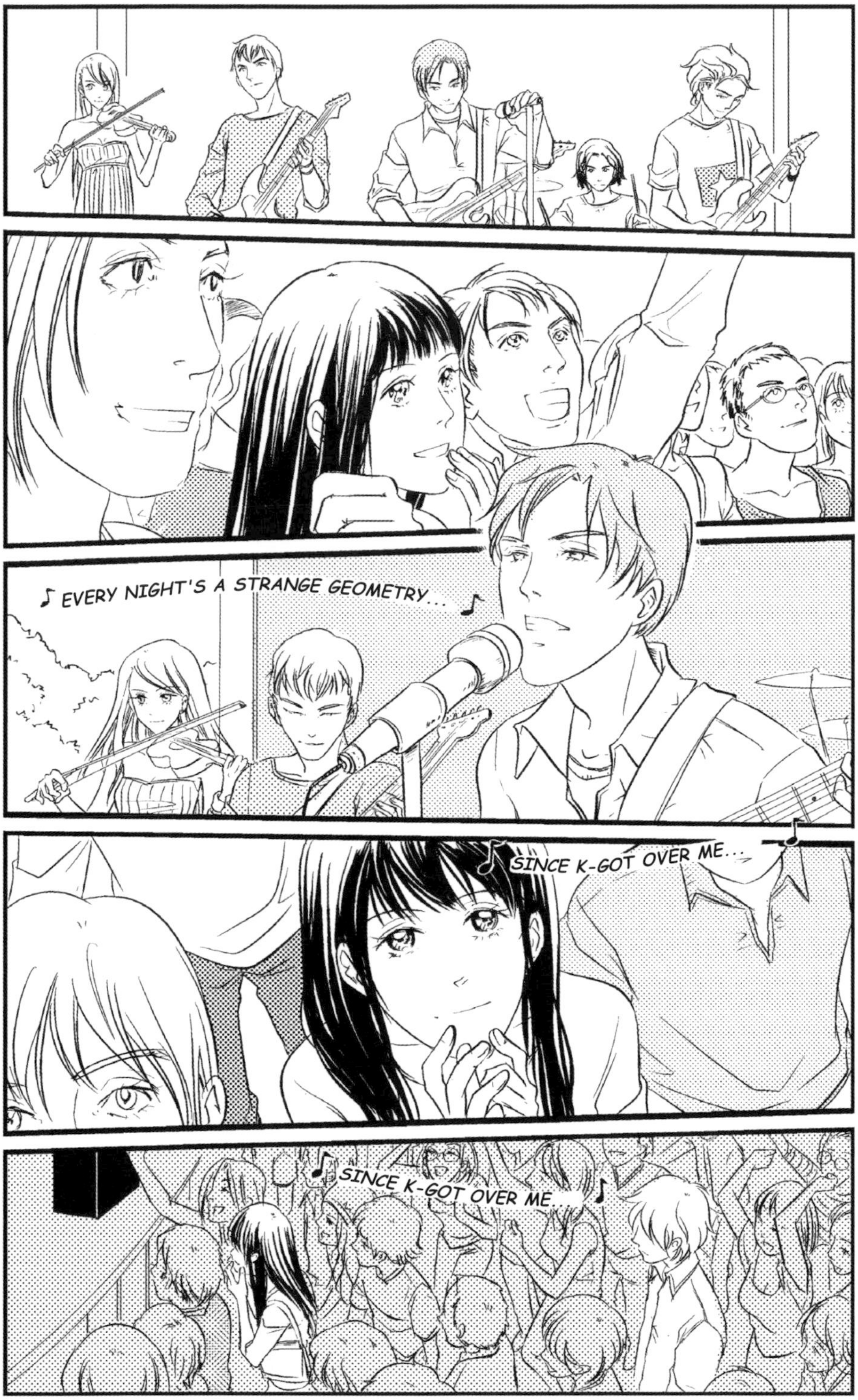
EVERY NIGHT'S A STRANGE GEOMETRY...
SINCE K-GOT OVER ME...
SINCE K-GOT OVER ME...

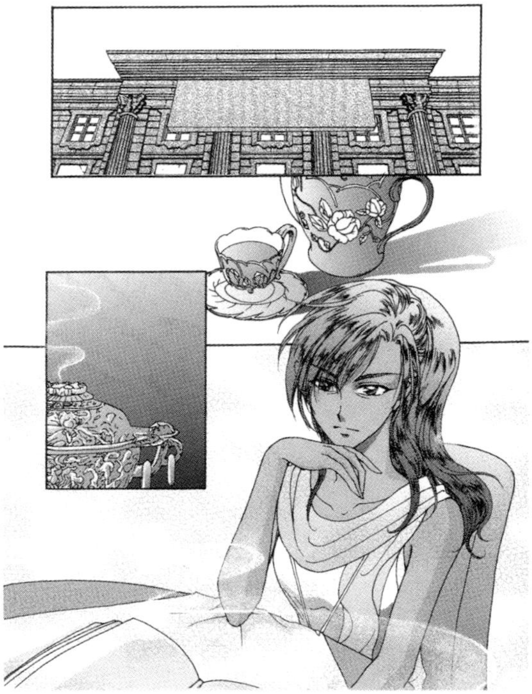

3 Look over the script for the episode you've just written. How many pages will it cover, and how many panels will be on each page? Shoujo manga is all about the expression of deep emotions, and tends to have a slower, more lingering pace than a frenetic action title. In a standard manga book, you will find most pages have between four and six panels—any more and the detailed artwork will become hard to follow at the small size, and your layouts will become confusing. Six to seven panels are possible, of course, but you will probably not want to go above that—with the exception of small panels for close-ups or *chibis* (exaggerated, miniature versions of your characters showing extremes of emotion). Give pages that establish new locations fewer panels, so that you can show the new environment (and the characters' relation to it) in all its glory. You may also wish to use bigger—or splash—panels to show the importance of other events in your story: the debut of a new character; the climax of an action scene; a stunning or unexpected development; or a longed-for kiss between your star couple!

CREATING MANGA PAGES

PREPARE THE PAGE LAYOUT

WHEN YOU HAVE EITHER CHOSEN YOUR CHARACTERS AND BACKGROUNDS FROM THE DISC AND SAVED THEM INTO AN APPROPRIATE FOLDER, OR HAVE DRAWN AND SCANNED IN YOUR IMAGES, THE NEXT STAGE IS TO ASSEMBLE THEM INTO AN ACTUAL MANGA PAGE.

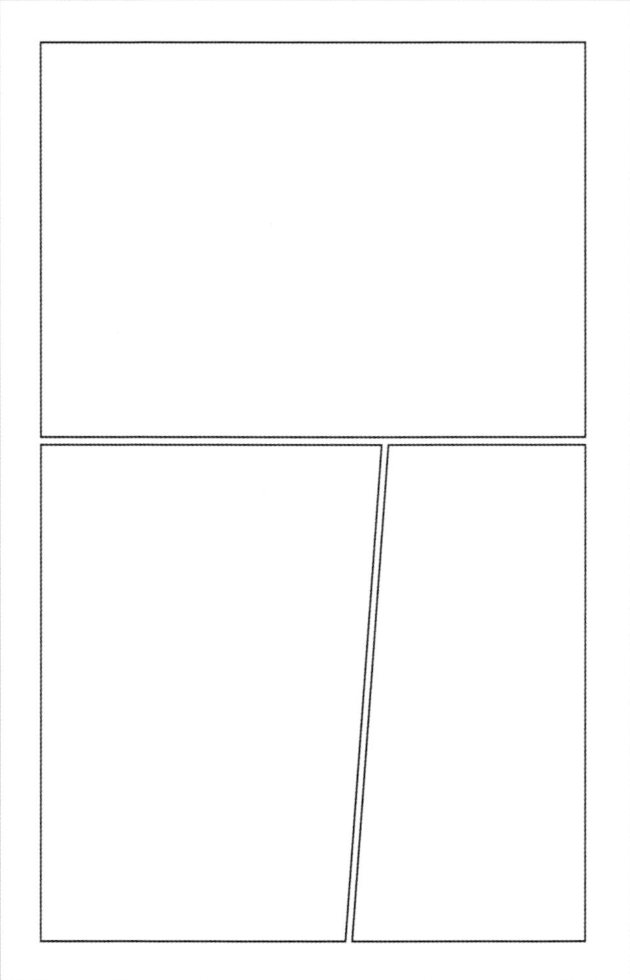

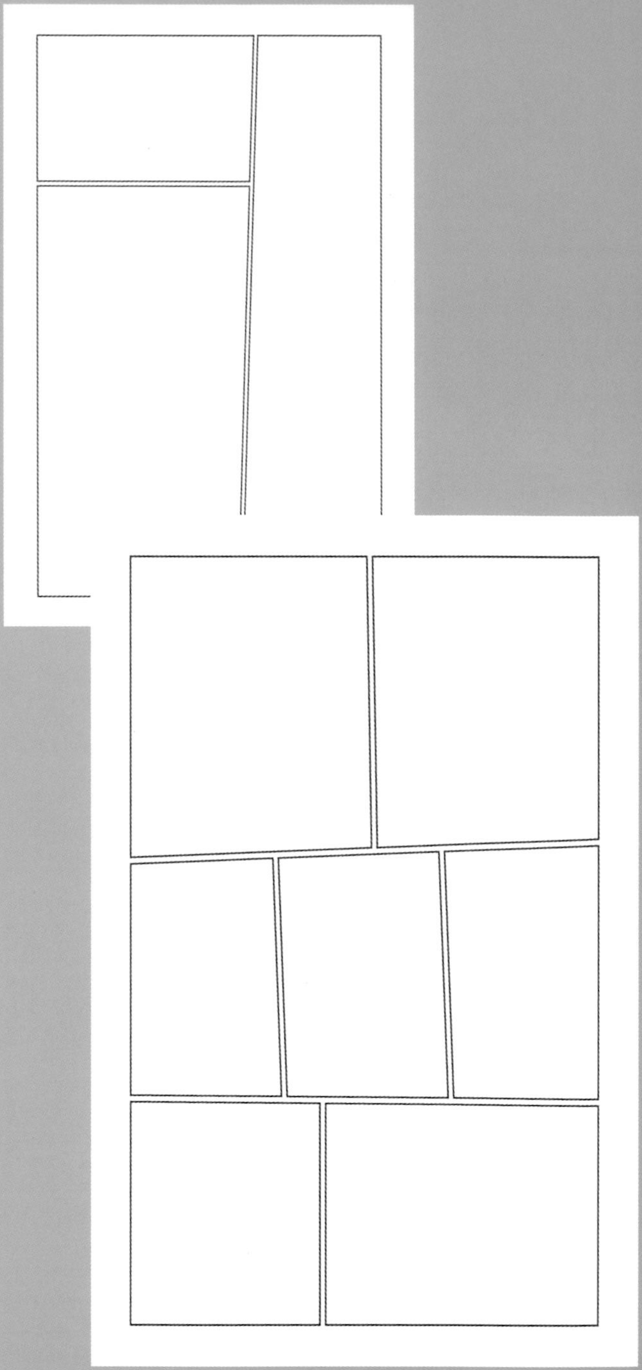

1 Decide what direction you will be telling the story in: left-to-right for a Western style, or right-to-left for a traditional manga feel. Most modern manga readers can handle both directions, but let them know which end of your book they should start from! Throughout this book we are using left-to-right.

2 There are numerous page layouts on the CD, ranging from three panels per page to seven panels per page, all with different combinations and sizes of panels. The page layouts are set at the dimensions of a standard manga book, or *tankubon*, such as those produced by TOKYOPOP. Of course, if your story requires a splash page, you can simply put your image on the blank page layout. Choose a panel layout for each page that best reflects the script you have written.

3 If you want to add variety to an existing panel layout, there are a number of techniques you can try. Erase panel lines to make a borderless panel, so that the art, or character, appears to float in space, or add a small panel within a bigger panel for a close-up of the events shown. You can also erase panels completely and replace them with shapes to your own liking by using the Pencil tool. You can draw straight lines with this tool by clicking a start point, then holding the Ctrl key and clicking the end point. Photoshop will draw a straight line between them. Don't forget, you can also flip the panel vertically or horizontally.

4 Feel free to experiment, but always remember that your new layouts must be as easy to read as the examples provided. A Western-style panel layout is designed to guide the eye of your reader from the top left of the page to the bottom right, reading all the panels in the order you want them to be read. Always double-check to make sure that your "panel flow" is clear.

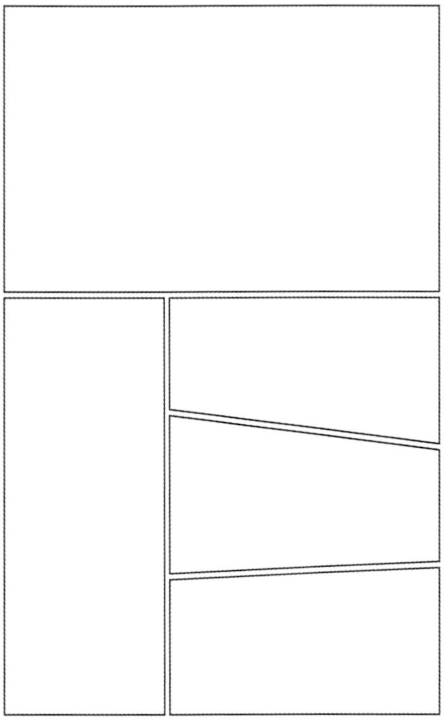

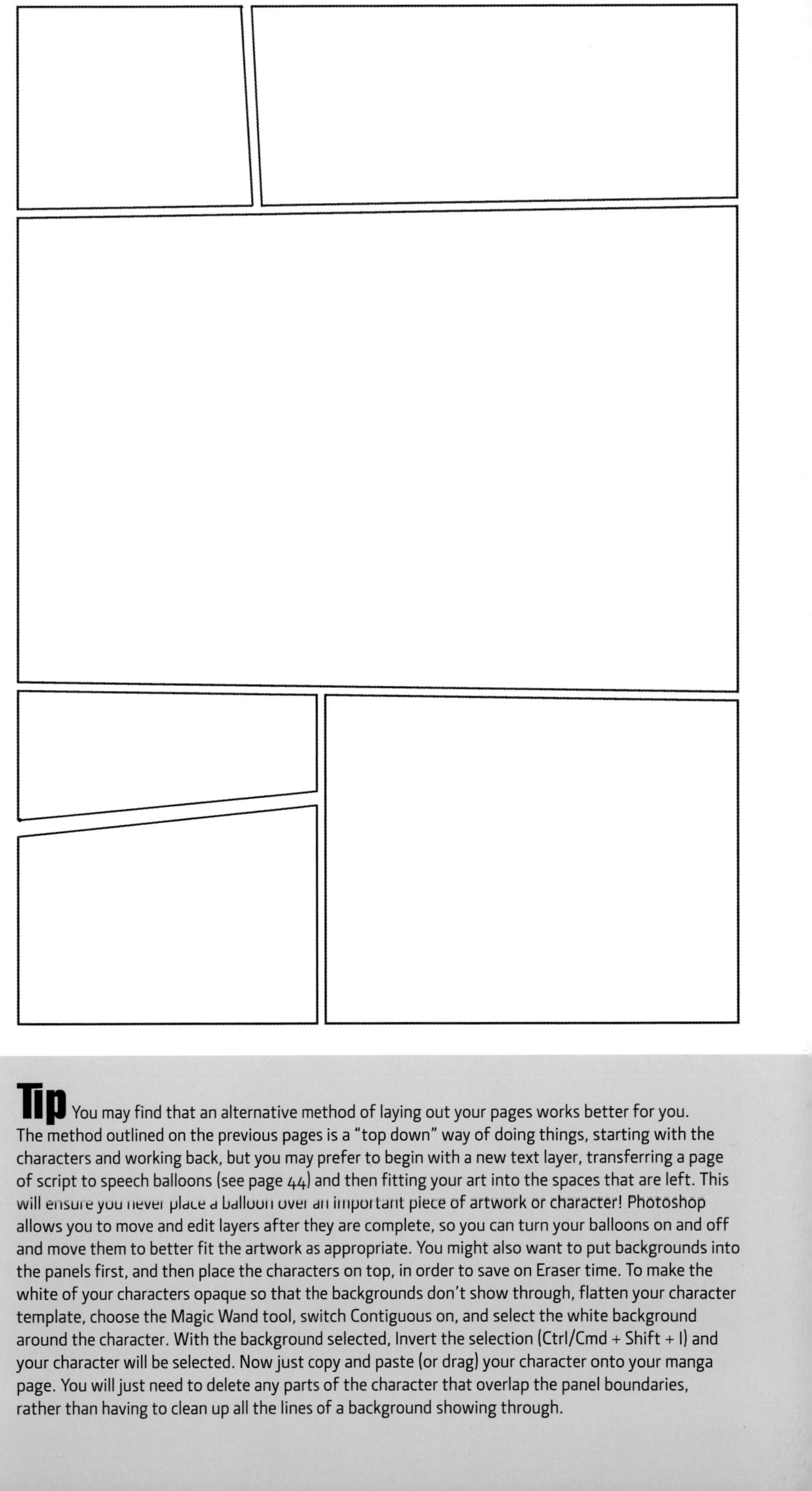

Tip You may find that an alternative method of laying out your pages works better for you. The method outlined on the previous pages is a "top down" way of doing things, starting with the characters and working back, but you may prefer to begin with a new text layer, transferring a page of script to speech balloons (see page 44) and then fitting your art into the spaces that are left. This will ensure you never place a balloon over an important piece of artwork or character! Photoshop allows you to move and edit layers after they are complete, so you can turn your balloons on and off and move them to better fit the artwork as appropriate. You might also want to put backgrounds into the panels first, and then place the characters on top, in order to save on Eraser time. To make the white of your characters opaque so that the backgrounds don't show through, flatten your character template, choose the Magic Wand tool, switch Contiguous on, and select the white background around the character. With the background selected, Invert the selection (Ctrl/Cmd + Shift + I) and your character will be selected. Now just copy and paste (or drag) your character onto your manga page. You will just need to delete any parts of the character that overlap the panel boundaries, rather than having to clean up all the lines of a background showing through.

PUTTING THE IMAGES ONTO THE PAGE

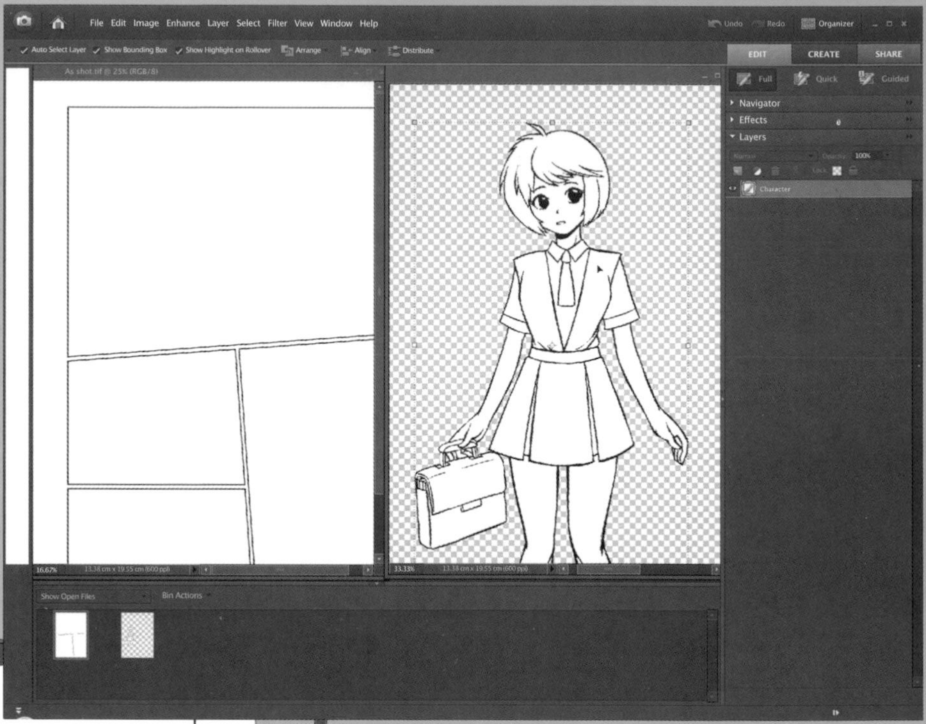
File Edit Image Enhance Layer Select Filter View Window Help
Undo Redo Organizer
Auto Select Layer Show Bounding Box Show Highlight on Rollover Arrange Align Distribute
EDIT CREATE SHARE
Full Quick Guided
Navigator
Effects
Layers
Character
Show Open Files
Bin Actions

1 The next step is to start inserting your characters. Open the first file you have saved containing the character you have made. You can simply drag this image from the Layers palette onto your manga page layout. You may only wish to drag across a hand or a face if the panel is an extreme close-up. If your character is still saved as separate layers, this can be done by just selecting the layers you want to use and dragging them across, as before.

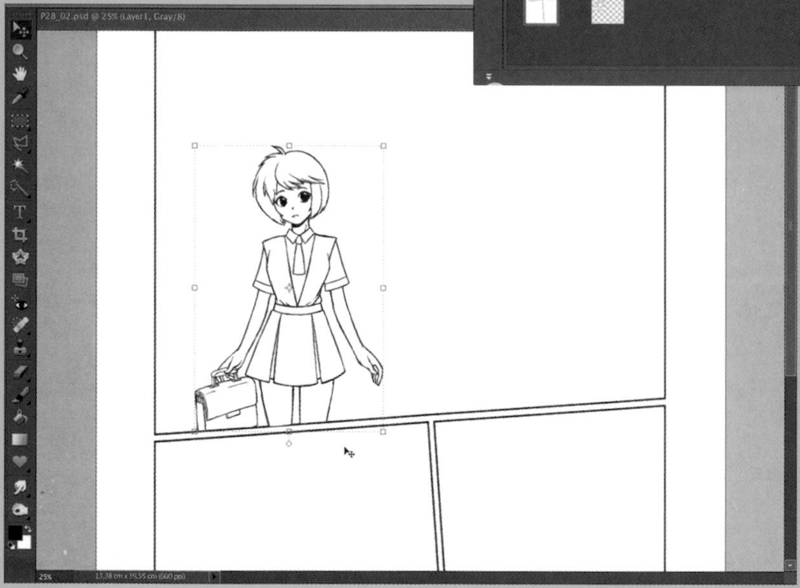

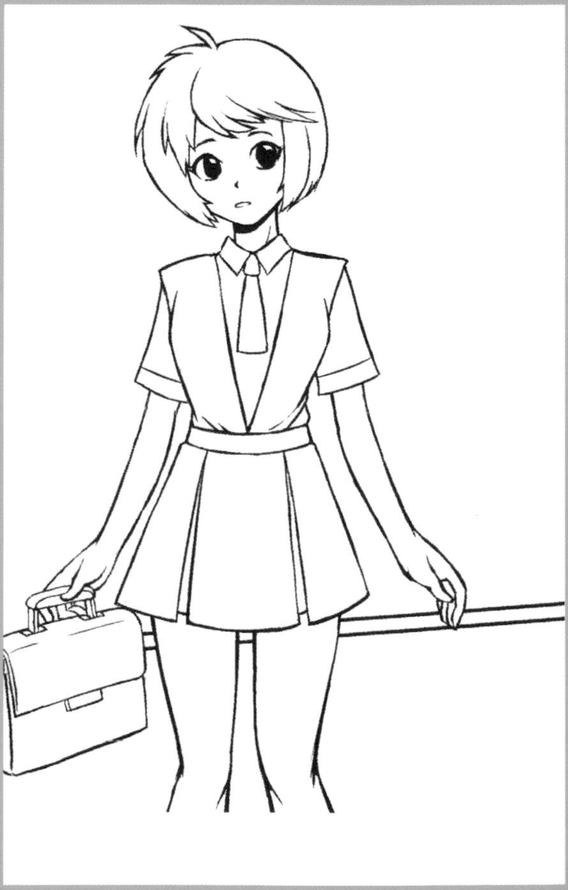

2 Use the Move tool to position the character where you want it, then use the Eraser tool to clean up any parts that fall outside of the chosen panel. If the panel is a regular shape you can speed up this process by using one of the selection tools to select anything outside of the panel, and then deleting it.

3 Follow the above steps to bring all of your figures onto the page.

4 Having all of the panels looking the same, whether they are at the same angle or the characters remain at the same size throughout, will quickly become boring for a reader. Make sure you flip, scale, and rotate your characters from panel to panel to keep things interesting. Always remember that you can edit the images from the CD with the Pencil tool if you want a unique expression or movement. Don't forget to leave some "dead space" in every panel for your word balloons!

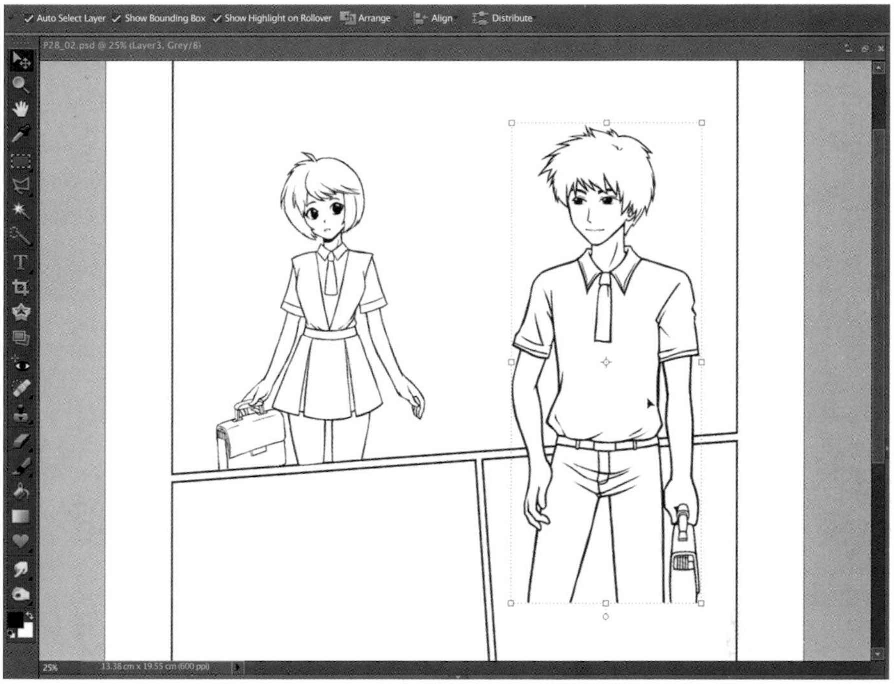
Auto Select Layer
Show Bounding Box
Show Highlight on Rollover
Arrange
Align
Distribute
25%

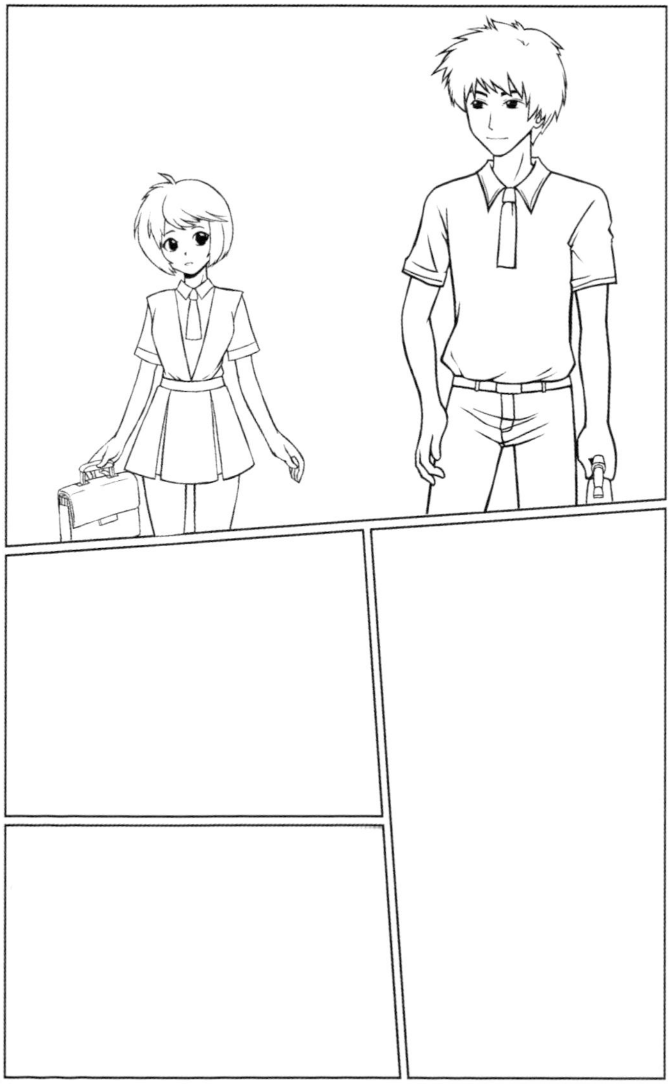

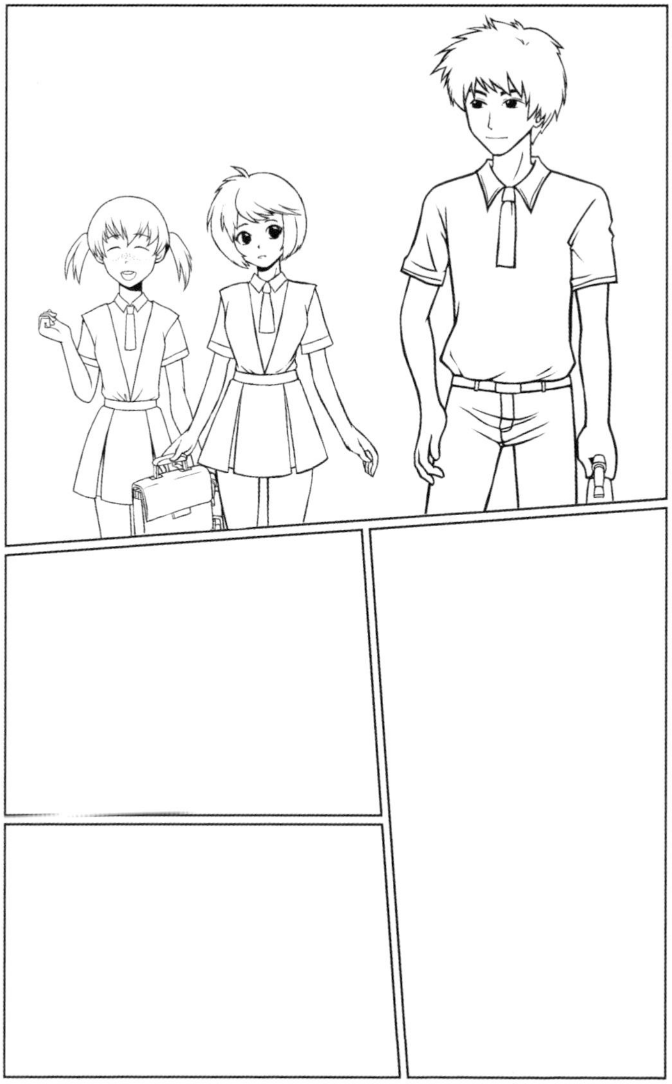

SHOUJO

5 Once your characters are in place, it's time to paste in the backgrounds. Those new to manga often find it boring or difficult to draw backgrounds, so they avoid doing so—but it is well worth rising to the challenge, as pages without backgrounds quickly leave readers confused! The readers need a cue to the setting in order to understand the story, and your characters need backgrounds to interact with to give them weight and realism. If you have an "establishing" panel (the first time a new location is shown), then it will normally be relatively big with a wide shot of the scene, and you will be able to paste in one of the provided backgrounds directly. For the other panels, you will need to chop, flip, and scale the background images in order to make them fit.

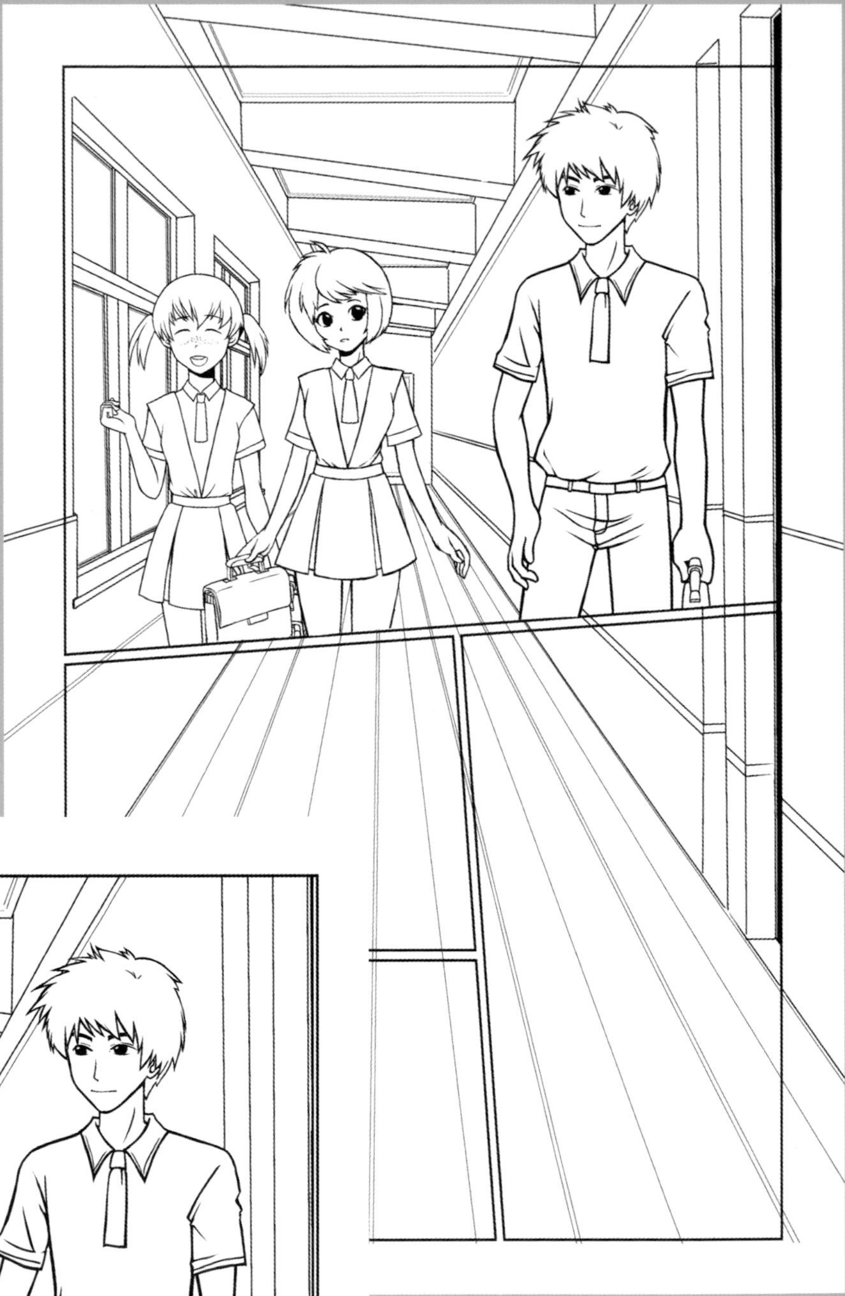

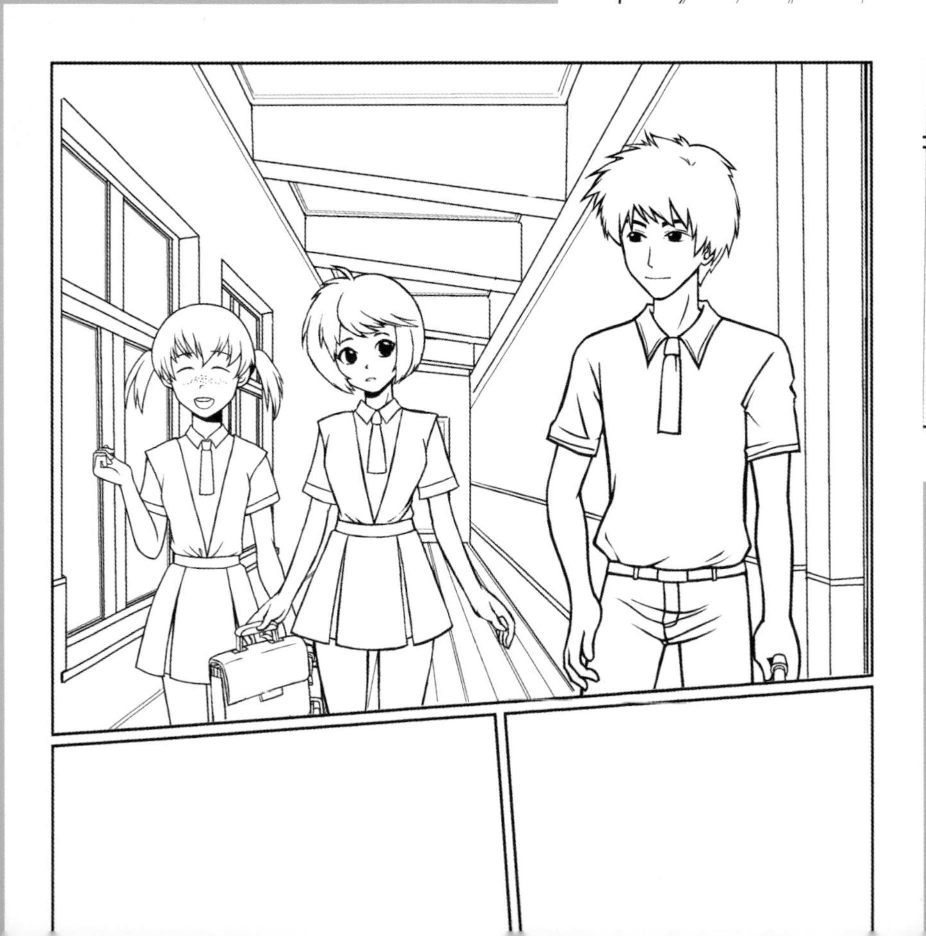

6 Once again, use the Eraser or selection tools to clear any areas that overlap.

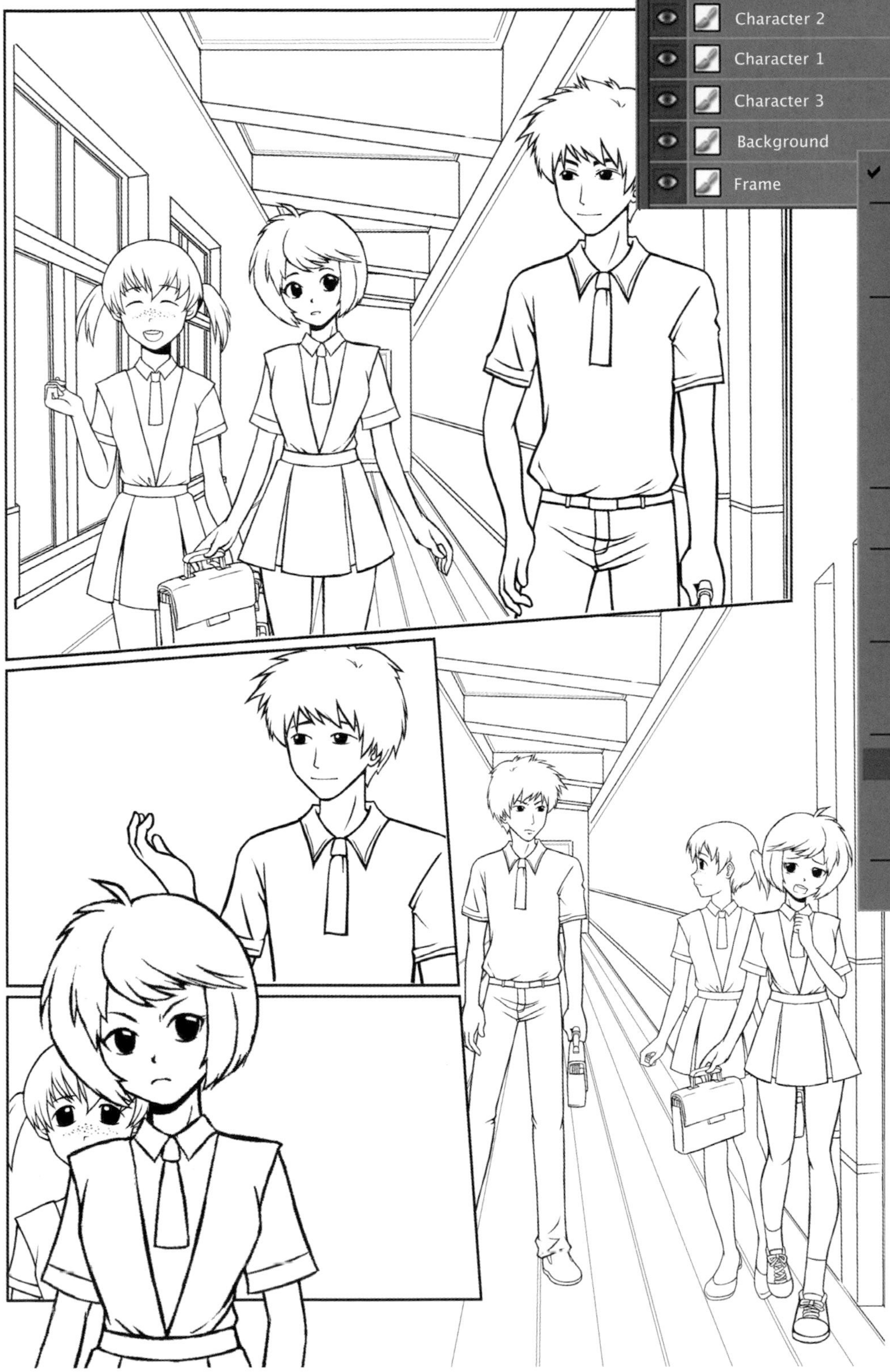

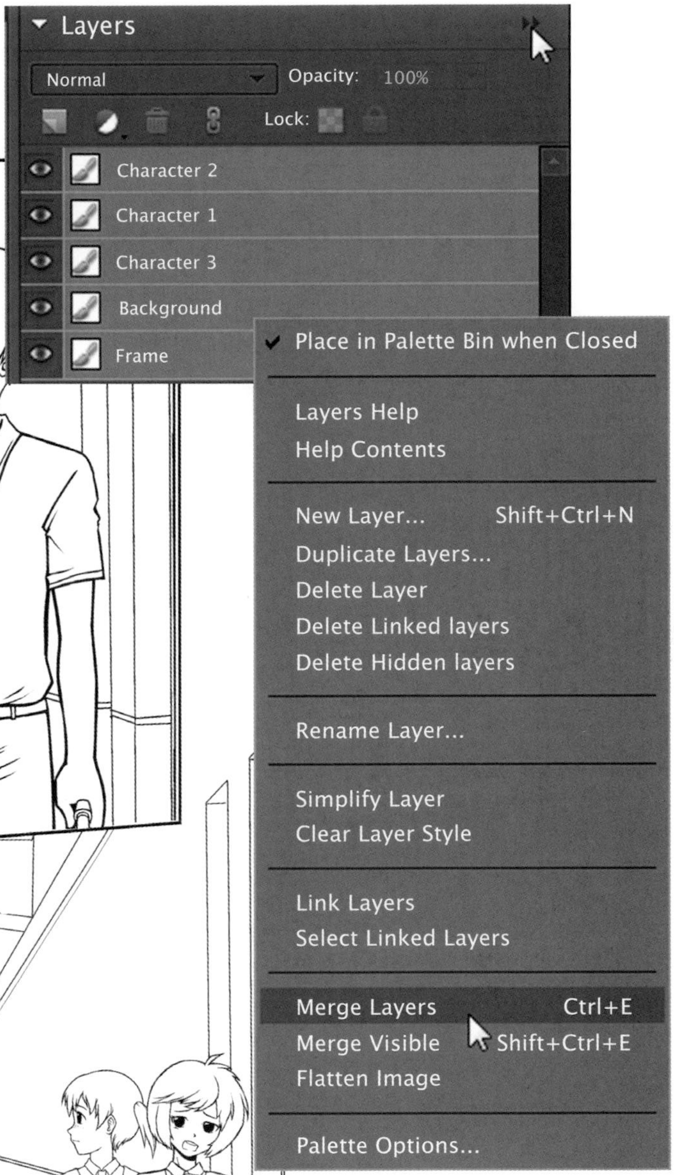
Layers
Normal
Opacity: 100%
Lock:
Character 2
Character 1
Character 3
Background
Frame
Place in Palette Bin when Closed
Layers Help
Help Contents
New Layer... Shift+Ctrl+N
Duplicate Layers...
Delete Layer
Delete Linked layers
Delete Hidden layers
Rename Layer...
Simplify Layer
Clear Layer Style
Link Layers
Select Linked Layers
Merge Layers Ctrl+E
Merge Visible Shift+Ctrl+E
Flatten Image
Palette Options...

7 Repeat these steps for each panel. When that is done, merge the background layer with the character layers, leaving the page layout layer intact, and name it linework. You will probably want to save this as the first page of your story in a new folder.

HOW TO CONVERT A PHOTO INTO A BACKGROUND

THERE ARE TEN GREAT BACKGROUNDS INCLUDED ON THE CD, BUT YOU WILL CERTAINLY WANT MANY MORE TO KEEP YOUR STORIES LOOKING AND FEELING FRESH. WHILE CONJURING YOUR OWN MAGNIFICENT ARCHITECTURE FROM SCRATCH IS DEMANDING AND TIME-CONSUMING, THERE IS A MUCH SIMPLER WAY THAT WILL MAKE THE MOST OF YOUR PHOTO COLLECTION! HERE ARE TWO EASY METHODS TO SHOW YOU HOW IT'S DONE.

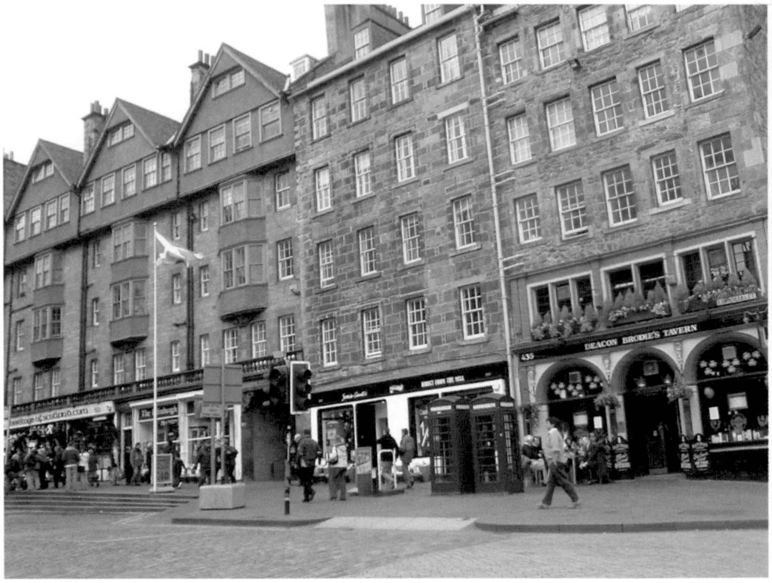

METHOD ONE:

1 Scan a photo, or import one from a digital camera, and open it in Photoshop. For our purposes, the bigger the photo is, and the higher the resolution, the better.

2 Change the photo into grayscale (Image > Mode > Grayscale).

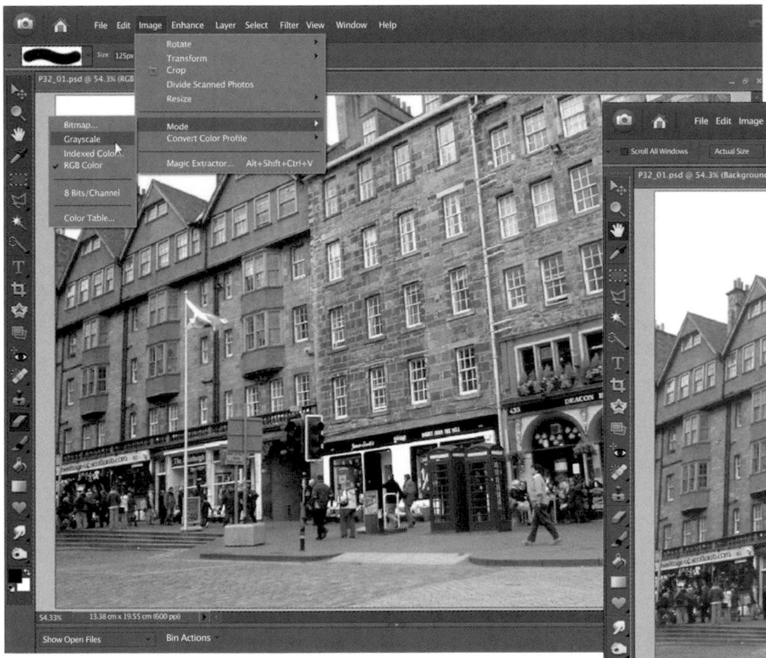

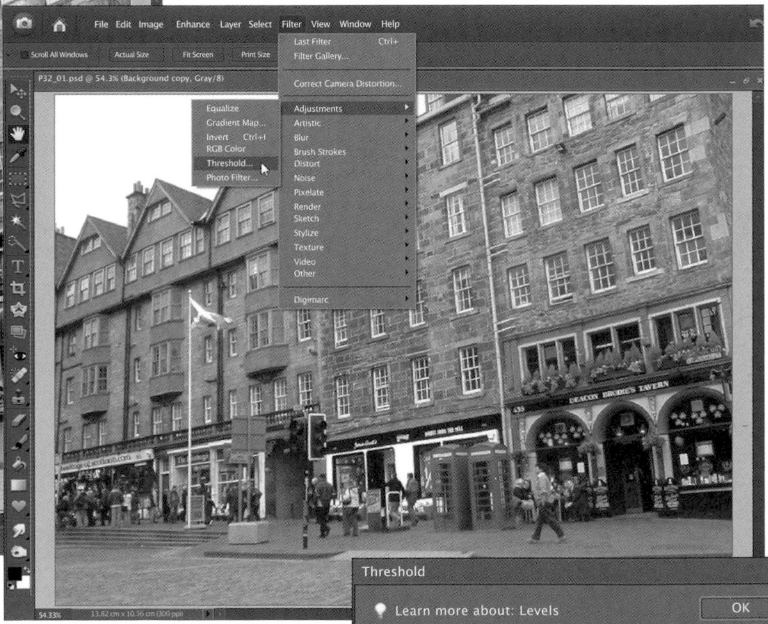

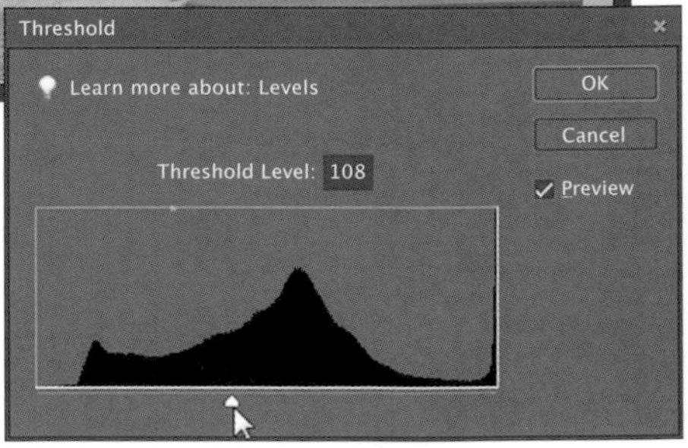
Threshold
Learn more about: Levels
OK
Cancel
Threshold Level: 108
Preview

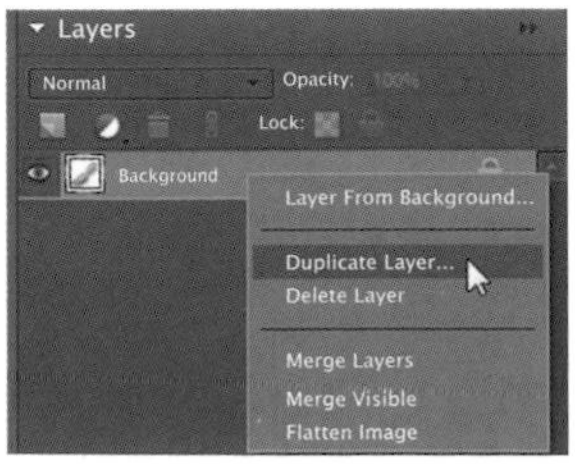
Layers
Normal
Opacity:
Lock:
Background
Layer From Background...
Duplicate Layer...
Delete Layer
Merge Layers
Merge Visible
Flatten Image

3 Duplicate the layer, keeping your original file for reference and in case you need to start the process again.

4 Click Filter > Adjustments > Threshold (or Image > Adjustments > Threshold in Photoshop). An option window will appear. Slide the bar inside it and try to find the position on the slider that best approximates line-art. For this particular photograph, a Threshold of 108 produces a good result.

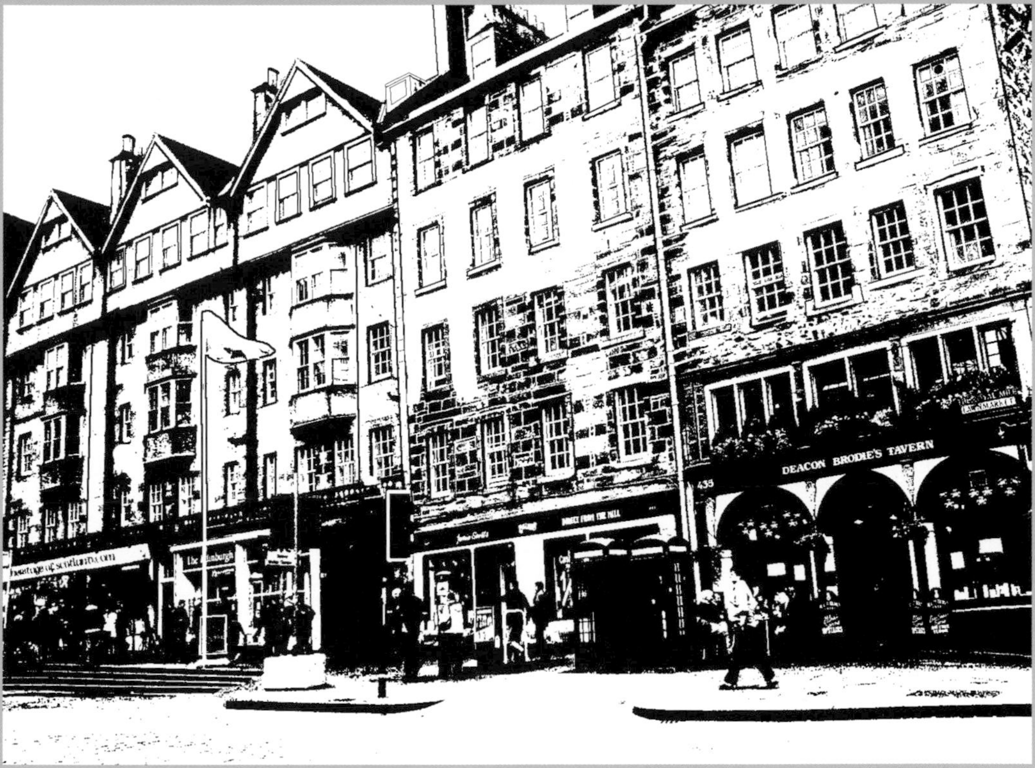
DEACON BRODIE'S TAVERN

5 Set the layer's Blending mode to Multiply to reveal the original photo underneath. Compared to the original, a lot of detail has been lost in the converted image. Use the Pencil tool to add back any pertinent details and clean up any areas that look too messy.

6 Turn Multiply off, merge the layers, and your background is ready to use!

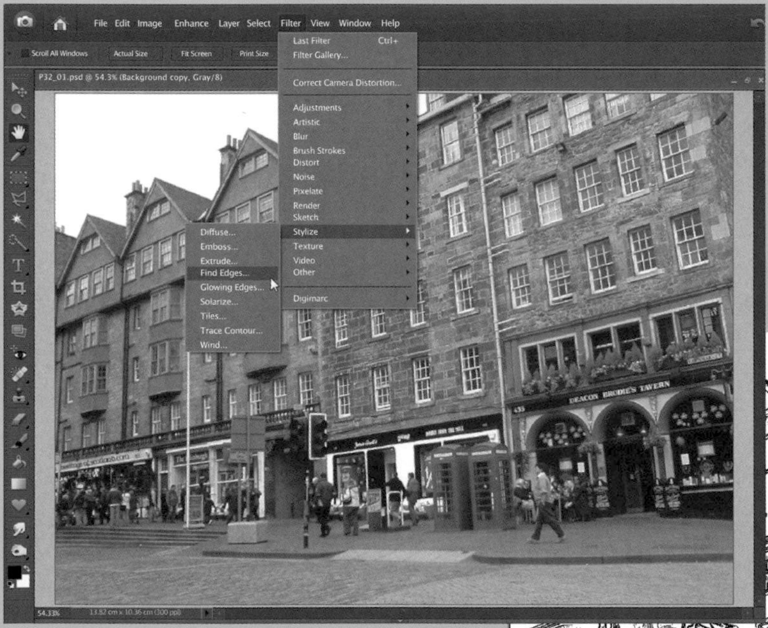
File Edit Image Enhance Layer Select Filter View Window Help
Last Filter Ctrl+
Filter Gallery...
Correct Camera Distortion...
Adjustments
Artistic
Blur
Brush Strokes
Distort
Noise
Pixelate
Render
Sketch
Stylize
Texture
Video
Other
Digimarc
Diffuse...
Emboss...
Extrude...
Find Edges...
Glowing Edges...
Solarize...
Tiles...
Trace Contour...
Wind...
DEACON BRODIE'S TAVERN

METHOD TWO:

1 Follow steps 1–3, as above.

2 Click Filter > Stylize > Find Edges. The photo is converted into line-art.

3 This method keeps more detail than the first, but the finished result is messier. Use the Pencil tool to adjust the level of detail until you are happy with it, then merge the layers as before.

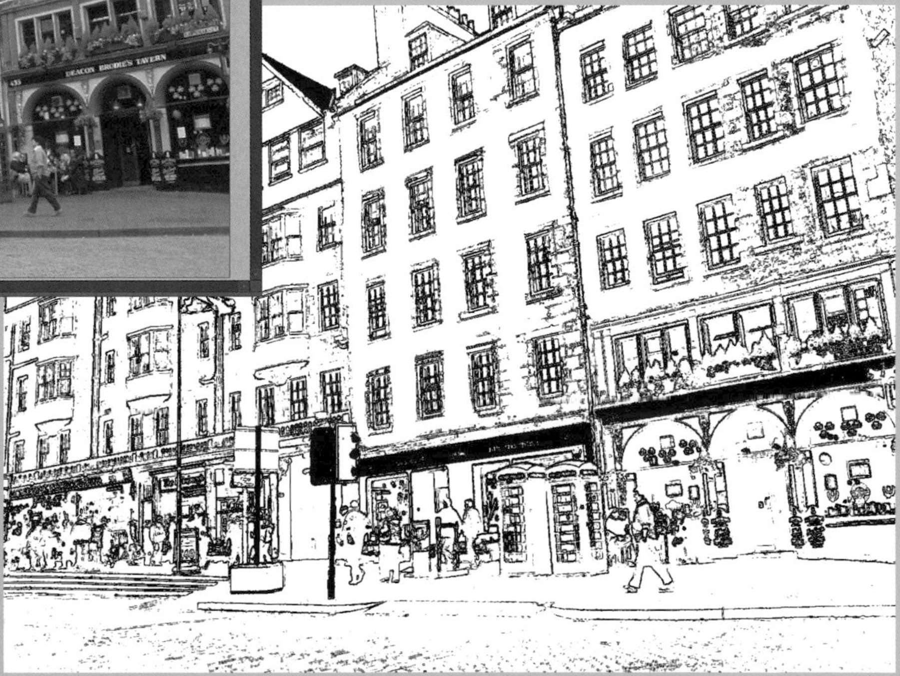

Tip There are many different filters in Photoshop, a great number of which can help you transform your photos into perfect background material. Don't be afraid to experiment, and be bold with your choices. You may find that adjusting the Levels (Image > Adjustments > Levels) of your raw grayscale photograph may give you cleaner results.

ADDING SPEEDLINES AND FOCUS LINES

AS A BARE DEFINITION, SPEEDLINES ARE A GROUP OF TIGHTLY PACKED, NEAR-PARALLEL LINES THAT SHOW DRAMATIC MOVEMENT, WHILE FOCUS LINES ARE A GROUP OF LINES THAT RADIATE OUT FROM—AND DRAW ATTENTION TO—A FOCAL POINT. THE EFFECTIVE USE OF THESE AS TECHNIQUES IN YOUR SHOUJO ARTWORK WILL ADD DEPTH AND VARIETY TO YOUR PANELS AND YOUR CHARACTERS' EMOTIONAL STATES.

SPEEDLINES AND FOCUS LINES CROP UP IN ALL KINDS OF PLACES, FROM ACTION SCENES, WHERE THEY ADD IMPACT AND VISUAL PUNCH, TO QUIETER SCENES, WHERE THEY EXPRESS STRONG FEELINGS, SUCH AS SURPRISE, ANGER, OR DEPRESSION. IN ACTION SCENES, JUST IMAGINE SPEEDLINES AS THE WIND THE MOVEMENT OF A CHARACTER HAS CREATED, OR AS LINES TRACKING THEIR PROGRESSION THROUGH SPACE. THESE LINES CAN BE EITHER STRAIGHT OR CURVED. FOCUS LINES, ON THE OTHER HAND, ARE MOST OFTEN USED TO HIGHLIGHT TENSION OR A SUDDEN SHOCK. THE MORE DENSE THE FOCUS LINES ARE, THE TENSER THE SITUATION.

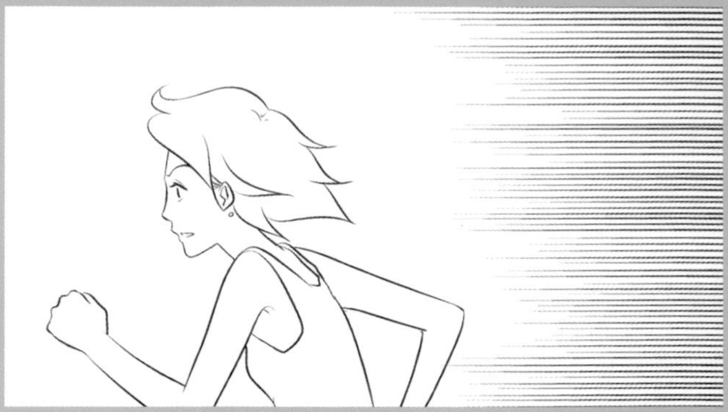

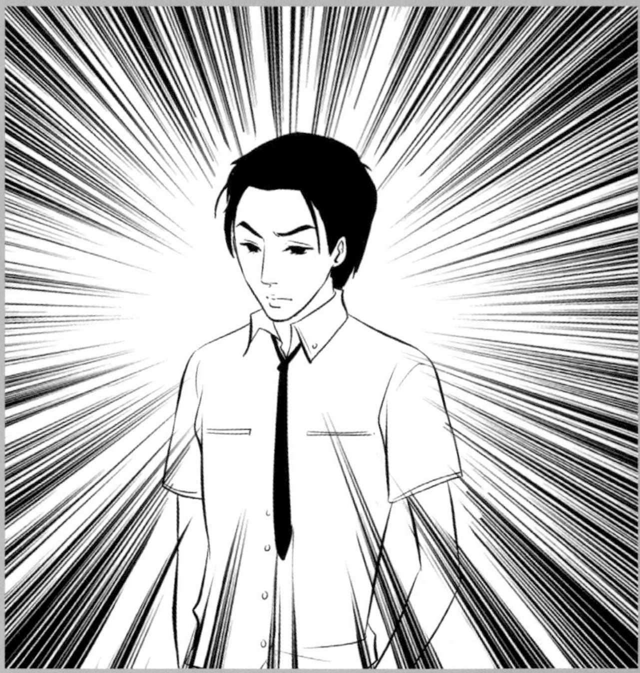

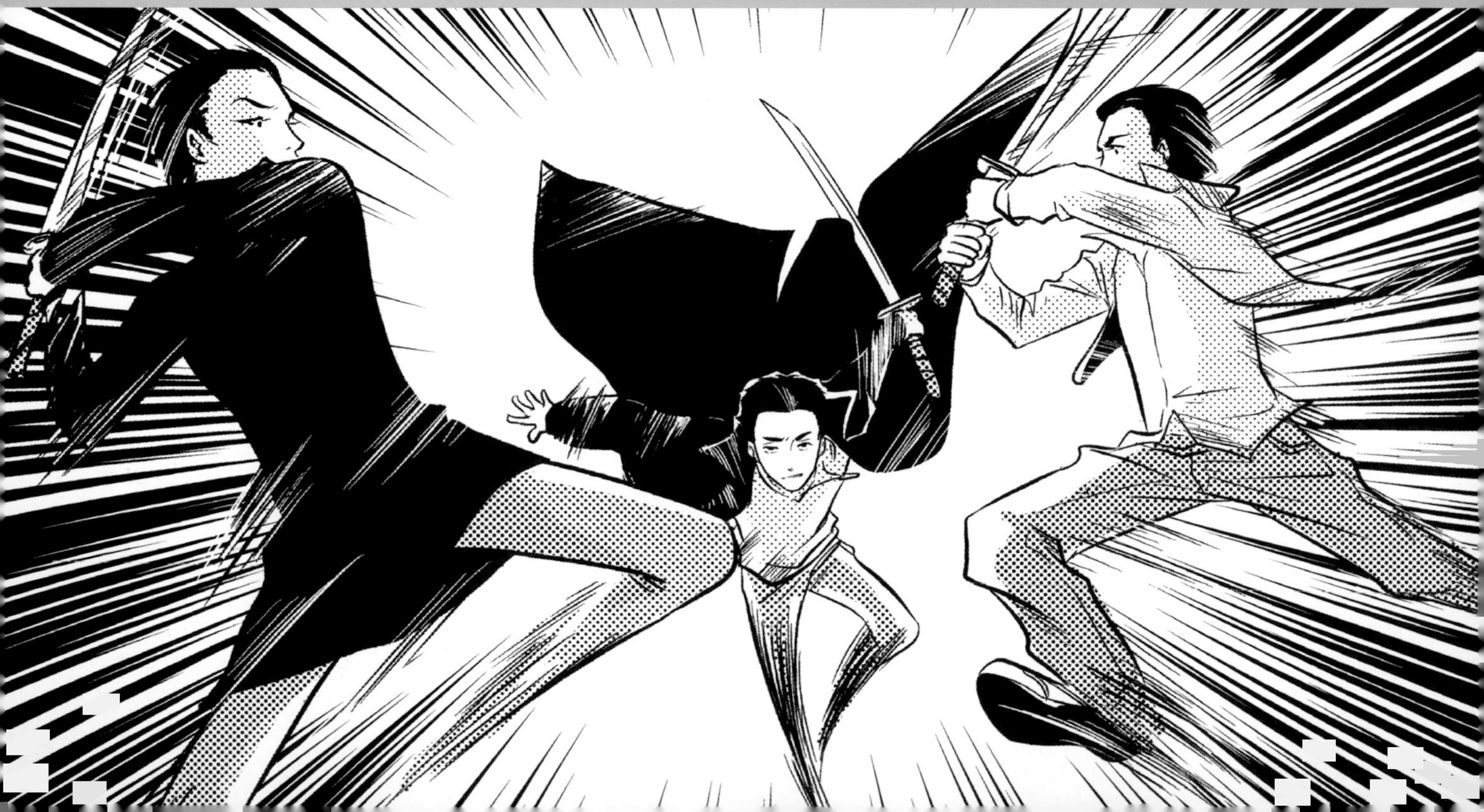

HOW TO ADD SPEED AND FOCUS LINES

1 Pick one speed or focus line image from the CD.

2 You probably don't need to paste the whole image into your panel. Instead, use the square selection tool to select part of the lines (most likely the central area) and paste it into the panel.

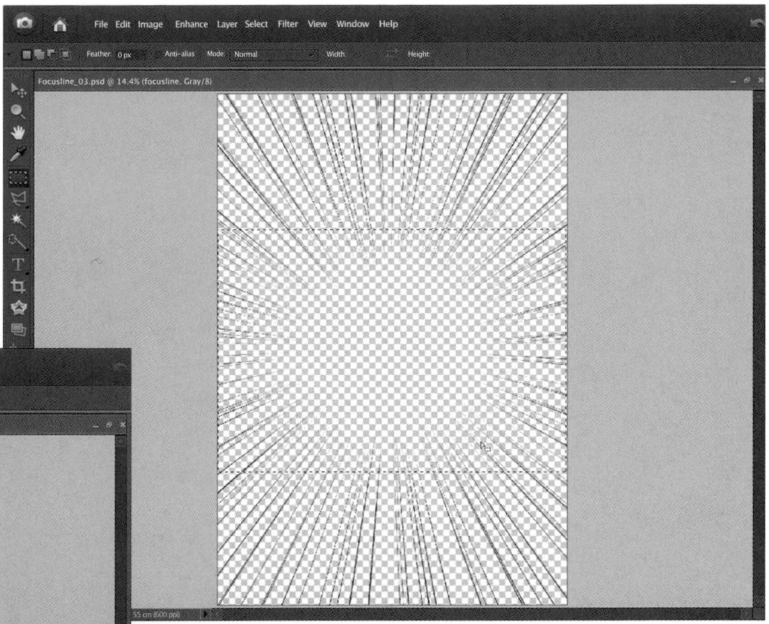
File Edit Image Enhance Layer Select Filter View Window Help
Focusline_03.psd @ 14.4% (focusline, Gray/8)

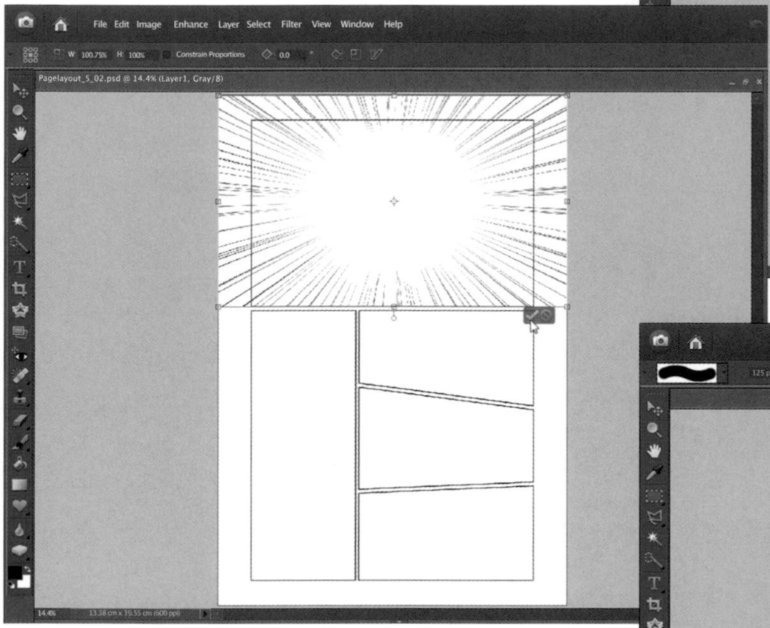
File Edit Image Enhance Layer Select Filter View Window Help
Constrain Proportions
Pagelayout_5_02.psd @ 14.4% (Layer1, Gray/8)

3 If needed, use Free Transform to adjust the shape to fit.

4 Using the Eraser tool on the line layer, clean away any parts you don't want. Speed and focus lines can overlap with backgrounds and background characters, so long as the character at their center remains unobscured.

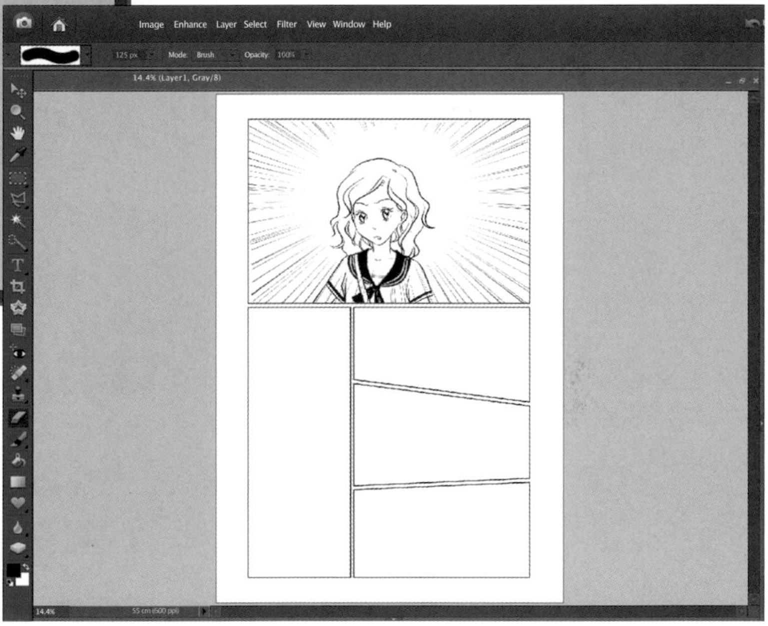
Image Enhance Layer Select Filter View Window Help
14.4% (Layer1, Gray/8)

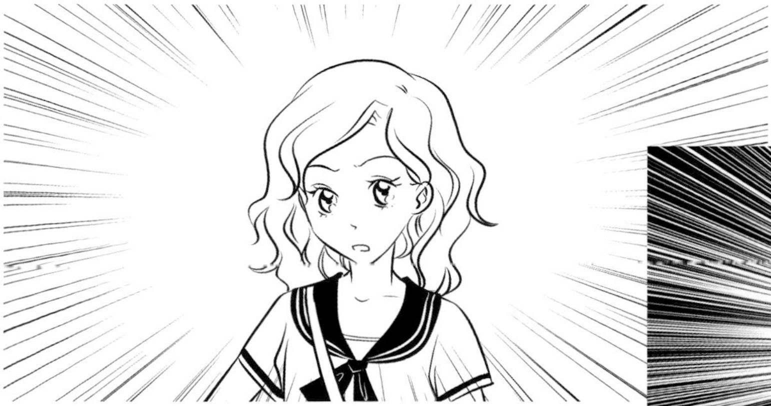

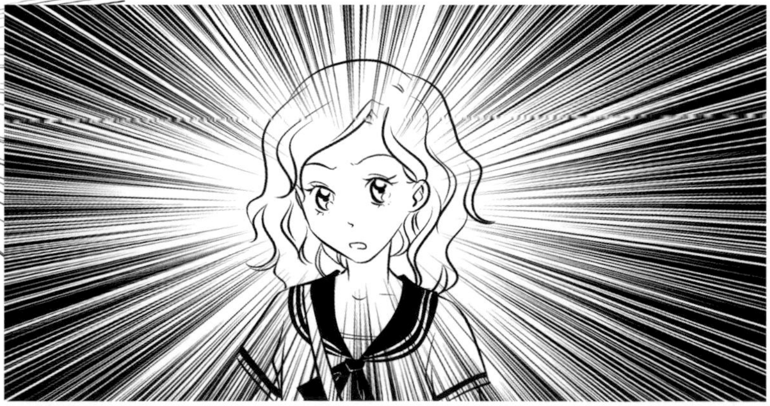

SHOUJO
ADDING TONE TO PAGES

WHILE WESTERN COMICS ARE NORMALLY COLORED, THE VAST MAJORITY OF MANGA ARE IN BLACK AND WHITE. THIS CREATES A PROBLEM WHEN CREATING SHADOWS, LIGHT, DEPTH, AND MOOD. THANKFULLY, TONING WAS INTRODUCED TO DEAL WITH THIS PROBLEM. THROUGH A SELECTION OF TINY, REPEATED DOT PATTERNS, TONING CAN QUICKLY ADD "COLOR," TEXTURE, AND DEPTH TO YOUR BLACK AND WHITE MANGA PAGE.

TRADITIONALLY, LETRATONE SHEETS WERE USED THAT ALLOWED AN INSTANT LAYER OF GRAY TONE TO BE ADDED TO THE ARTWORK, EFFICIENTLY CREATING SHADOWS AND TEXTURES. THESE SHEETS WERE EITHER RUBBED

DOWN AS TRANSFERS, OR CUT OUT AND STUCK ONTO ORIGINAL ARTWORK. THESE DAYS, MANGA ARTISTS IN THE WEST MOSTLY USE DIGITAL SCREEN TONES INSTEAD OF LETRATONE. IT IS CHEAPER, QUICKER, EASIER, HAS MORE VARIETIES, AND HAS THE ADDED BENEFIT OF BEING A LOT SIMPLER TO UNDO IF ANYTHING GOES WRONG.

TONING IS AN ART IN ITSELF. SOME MANGA ARTISTS USE A WIDE VARIETY OF DIFFERENT TONES, CREATING A LUXURIOUS FEEL THAT DRAWS ATTENTION TO THE QUALITY OF THE TONING, WHILE OTHERS STICK TO ONE OR TWO SIMPLE TONES TO KEEP THE PAGE NEAT AND THE STORYTELLING PARAMOUNT.

There are two methods of toning your page with the tones supplied on the CD.
METHOD ONE:

1 Select the tone you want to use and open it in Photoshop.

2 Estimate the size of the area you want to tone, then select an area of your tone that is slightly bigger than this. With the selection tool, drag your selection onto your manga page.

3 Using the Move tool, place the tone where you want it.

4 Tidy up the area using the Eraser tool.

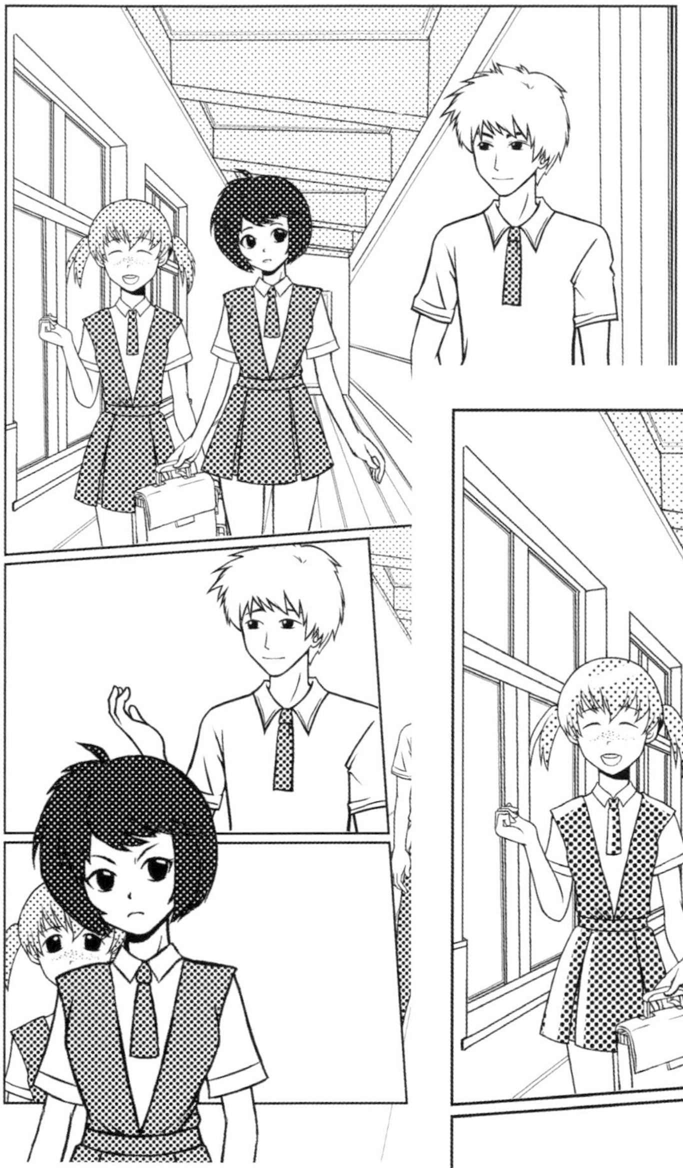

5 Repeat the above steps to add as many tones as you like to your page. Try not to overlap dotted tones if at all possible, because this is likely to create unintentional moiré patterns.

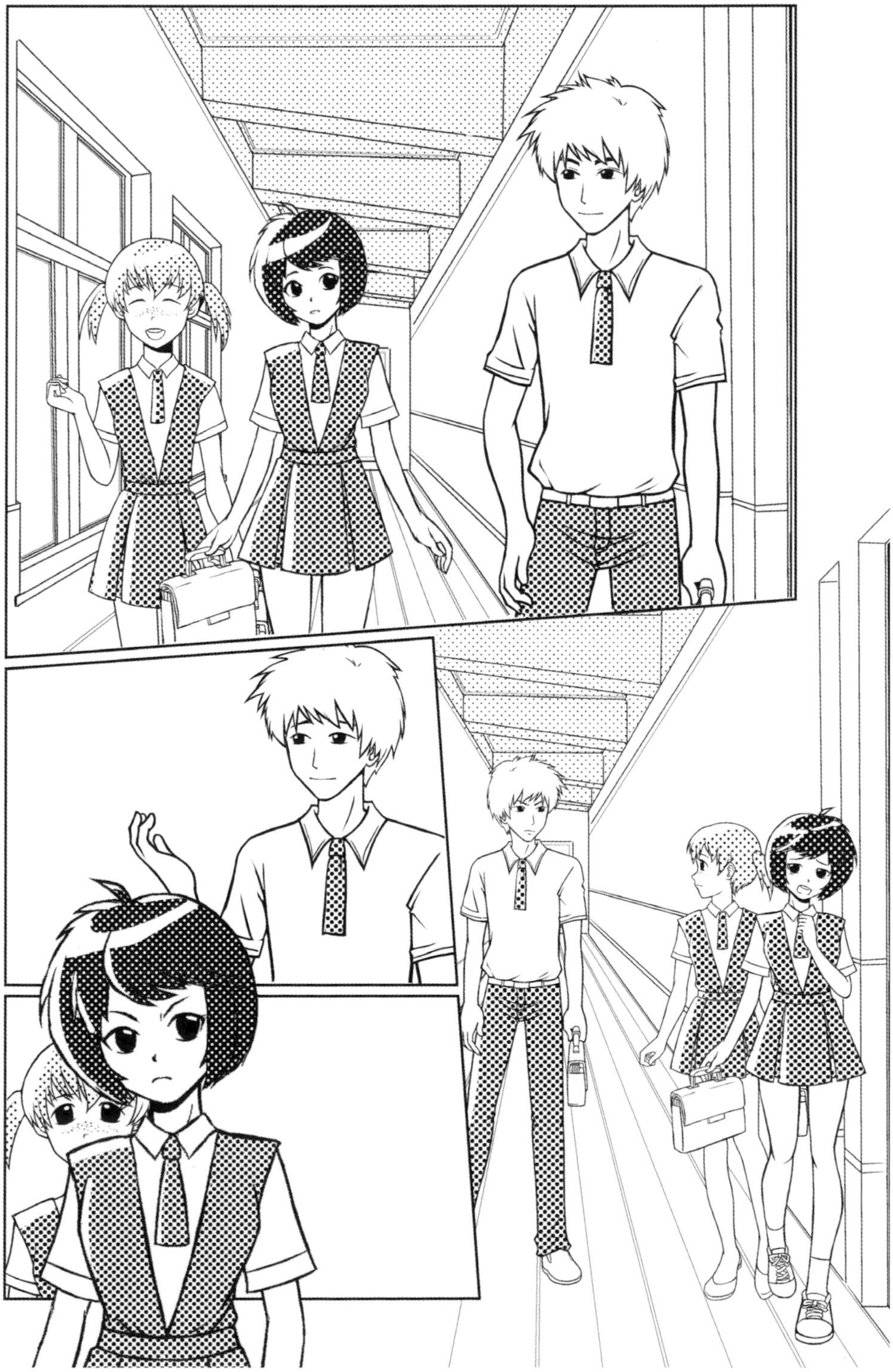

6 The Eraser tool is perfect for removing the areas of tone you don't want, but it is also perfect for adding highlights to areas of tone. Erase thin lines or circular points to give definition to hair and eyes, for example.

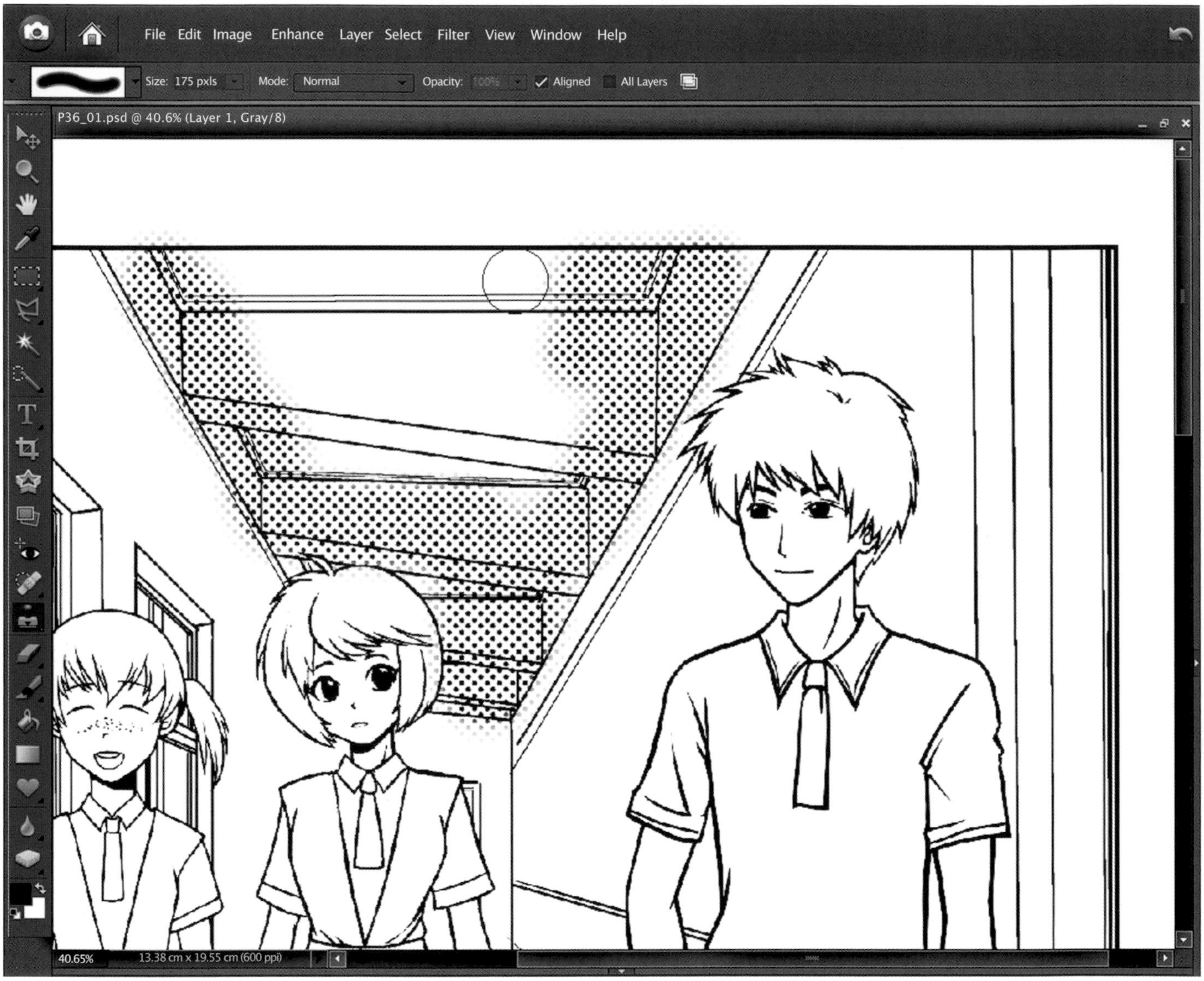
File Edit Image Enhance Layer Select Filter View Window Help
Size: 175 pxls Mode: Normal Opacity: 100% Aligned All Layers
P36_01.psd @ 40.6% (Layer 1, Gray/8)
40.65%
13.38 cm x 19.55 cm (600 ppi)

METHOD TWO:

1 Open the tone image you want to use, and select the Clone Stamp tool. Alt + click any area on the tone image. An area in the middle will give you the most flexibility when painting with the tone.

2 Use the Clone Stamp tool to draw directly onto the page. For best results, always do this on a new layer set to Multiply.

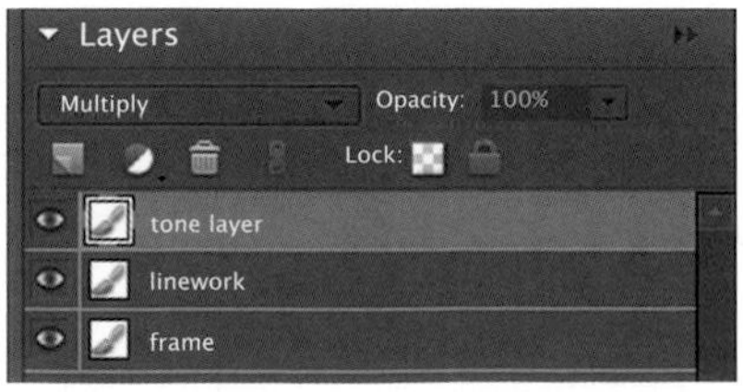
Layers
Multiply
Opacity: 100%
Lock:
tone layer
linework
frame

3 Use the Eraser to remove any areas of tone you don't want, and to add highlights where appropriate.

4 Repeat as required until your page is fully toned.

Tip If there are some tones you use a lot, you can set them as patterns in Photoshop. To do this, first select the area of the pattern you want on the tone image, then click Edit > Define Pattern, and name the pattern something memorable. When you need to use this tone again, just select the Pattern Stamp tool. A pattern box will appear in the Toolbar Options along the top of the screen with all the patterns you have defined. Select the pattern you want to tone with and paint directly onto the manga page.

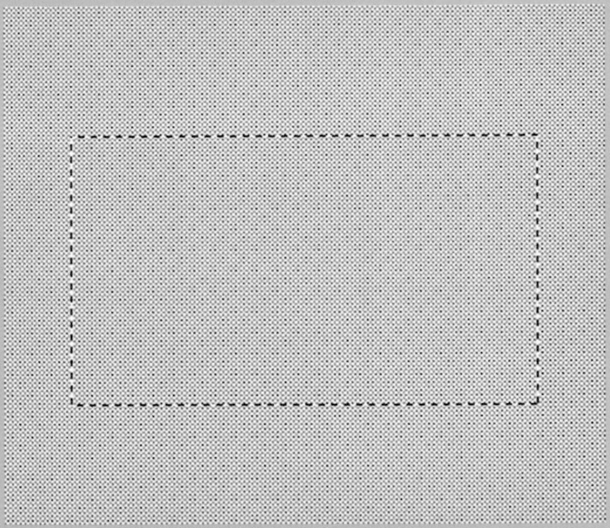

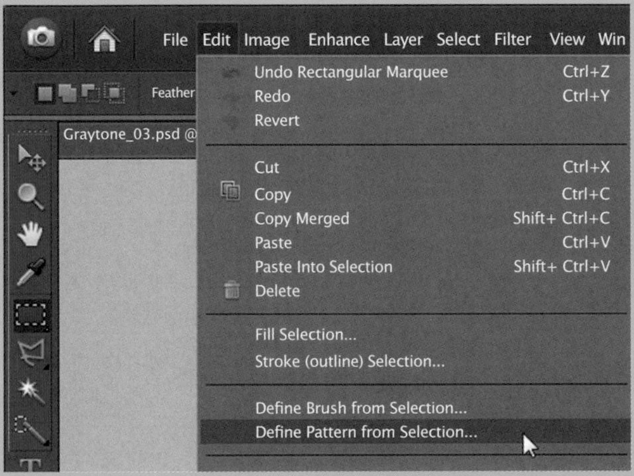
File
Edit
Image
Enhance
Layer
Select
Filter
View
Win
Feather
Graytone_03.psd @
Undo Rectangular Marquee Ctrl+Z
Redo Ctrl+Y
Revert
Cut Ctrl+X
Copy Ctrl+C
Copy Merged Shift+ Ctrl+C
Paste Ctrl+V
Paste Into Selection Shift+ Ctrl+V
Delete
Fill Selection...
Stroke (outline) Selection...
Define Brush from Selection...
Define Pattern from Selection...

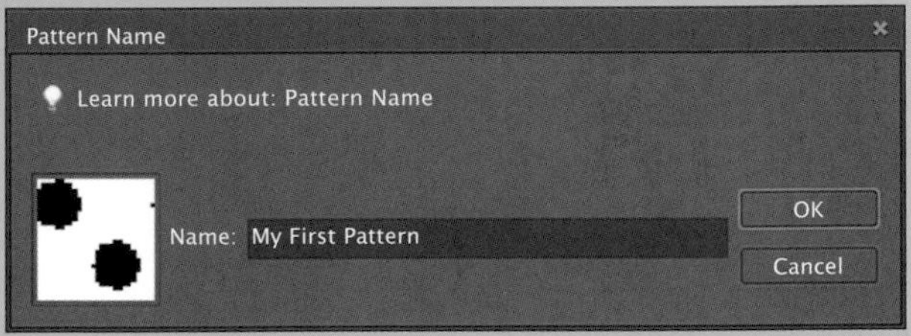
Pattern Name
Learn more about: Pattern Name
Name: My First Pattern
OK
Cancel

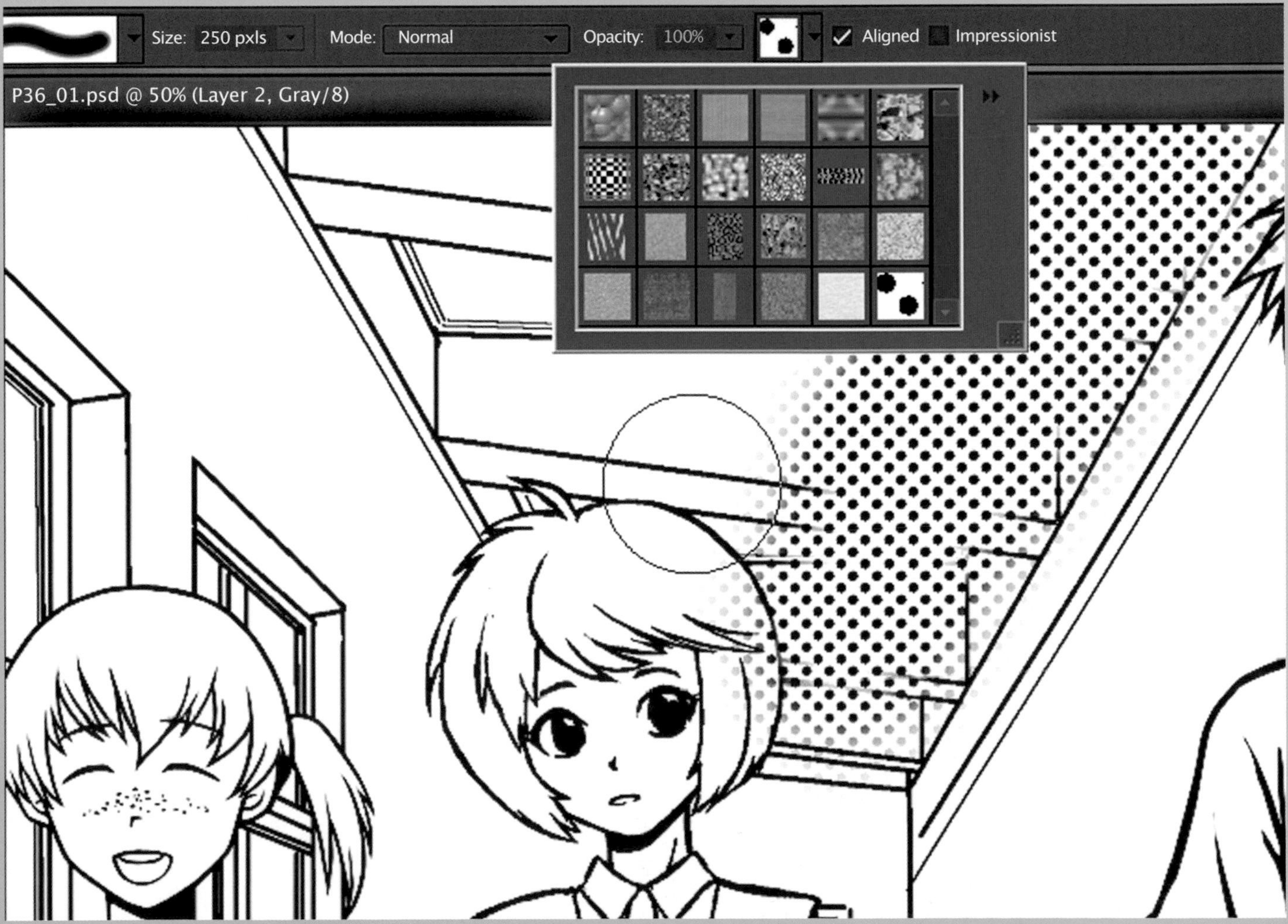
Size: 250 pxls
Mode: Normal
Opacity: 100%
Aligned
Impressionist
P36_01.psd @ 50% (Layer 2, Gray/8)

CREATING YOUR OWN TONES

THOUGH WE HAVE SUPPLIED A WIDE RANGE OF TONES, IT'S LIKELY—AND INDEED INEVITABLE—THAT YOU WILL WANT TO CREATE YOUR OWN AT SOME POINT. THE FOLLOWING STEPS WILL HELP YOU DO JUST THAT.

File Edit Image Enhance Layer Select Filter View Window Help
New
Open... Ctrl+O
Open As... Alt+Ctrl+O
Open Recently Edited File
Duplicate...
Close Ctrl+V
Close All Alt+Ctrl+V
Save Ctrl+S
Save As... Shift+
Save For Web... Alt+Shift+
Blank File... Ctrl+N
Image from Clipboard
Photomerge® Group Shot...
Photomerge® Faces...
Photomerge® Panorama...

New
Name: My Tone 1
Preset: Custom
Size: None
Width: 3160 pixels
Height: 4618 pixels
Resolution: 600 pixels/inch
Color Mode: RGB Color
Background Contents: White
OK
Cancel
Image Size:
41.8M

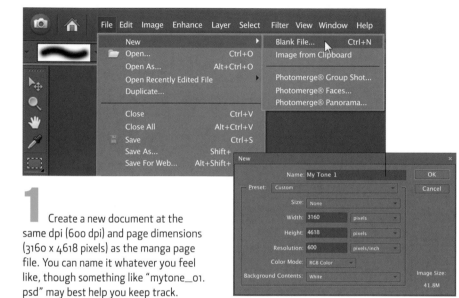

1 Create a new document at the same dpi (600 dpi) and page dimensions (3160 x 4618 pixels) as the manga page file. You can name it whatever you feel like, though something like "mytone_01.psd" may best help you keep track.

Select foreground color:
Learn more about: Choosing Colors
OK
Cancel
H: 0
S: 3 %
B: 75 %
R: 190
G: 185
B: 185
beb9b9
Only Web Colors

Enhance Layer Select Filter View Window Help
Color Halftone Ctrl+F
Filter Gallery...
Correct Camera Distortion...
Adjustments
Artistic
Blur
Brush Strokes
Distort
Noise
Pixelate
Render
Sketch
Stylize
Texture
Video
Other
Digimarc
Color Halftone...
Crystalize...
Facet...
Fragment
Mezzotint...
Mosaic...
pointillize...

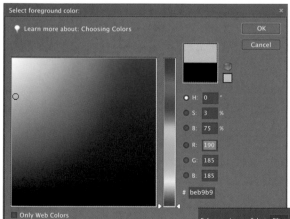

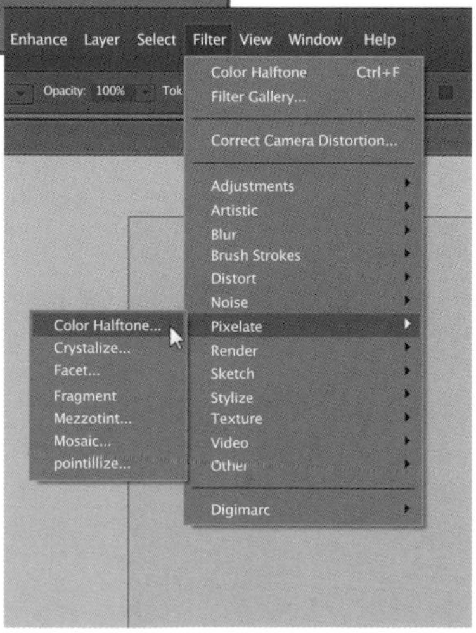

2 Fill the entire page with light gray.

a) If you are using Photoshop, go to Images > Mode > Bitmap. Bitmap is a file format that only supports black and white. By converting the light gray to a Bitmap, we can transform it into the familiar black dots used in manga books.

b) In Photoshop Elements you can achieve a similar effect using the filters. Go to Filter > Pixelate > Color Halftone.

3 a) After you select Bitmap mode, an option window will pop up. Change Method to "Halftone screen." In the next pop-up window, set Frequency at 32 lines/inch, the Angle to 45°, and select a shape. Round is the most common, but you can, of course, try the others. Create different tones by playing around with the various options in this menu.

b) Choose a Maximum Radius and experiment with the Channel settings to find a pattern you like.

Color Halftone
Max Radius 32 (Pixels)
Screen Angles (Degrees)
Channel 1: 45
Channel 2: 45
Channel 3: 45
Channel 4: 45
OK
Cancel
Default

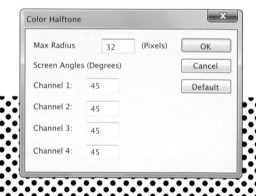

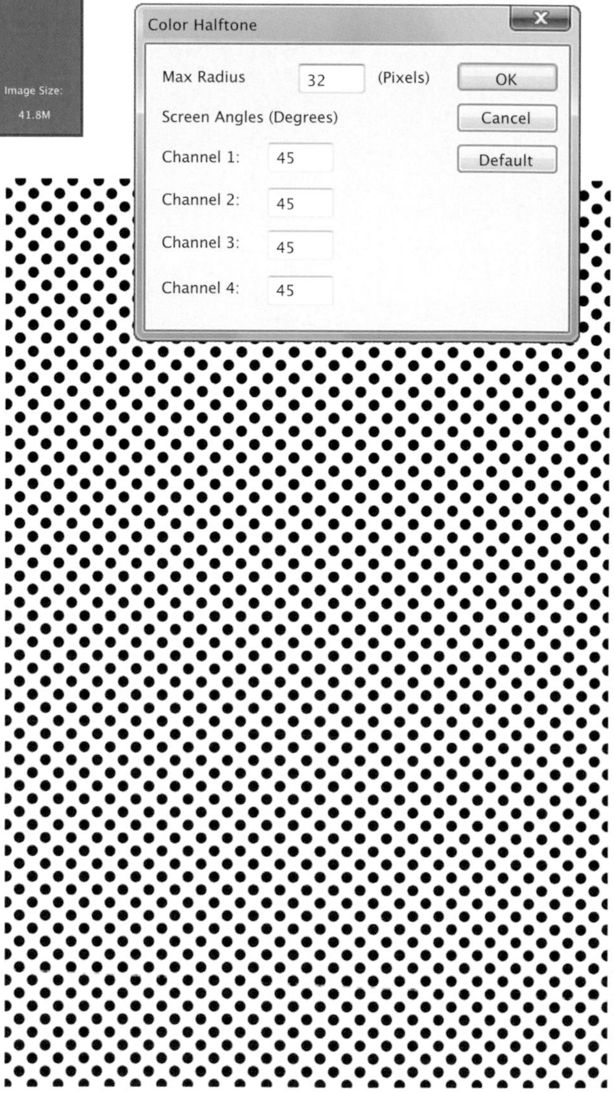

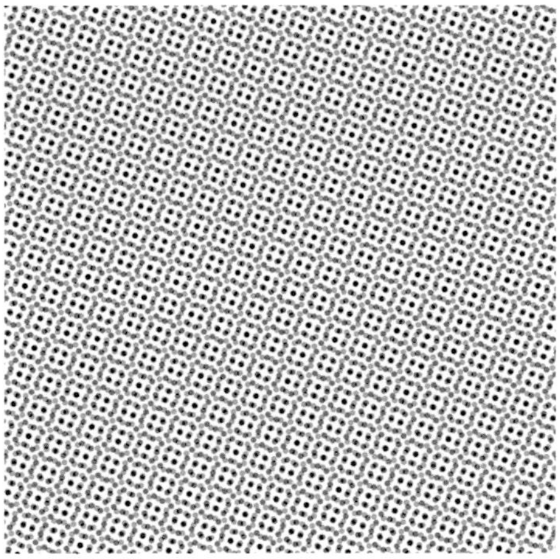

Color Halftone

Max Radius | 40 | (Pixels) | OK
Screen Angles (Degrees) | | | Cancel
Channel 1: | 100 | | Default
Channel 2: | 300 |
Channel 3: | 100 |
Channel 4: | 300 |

4 Convert the file back to Grayscale (Images > Mode > Grayscale), and in Photoshop, set the ratio to 1 in the pop-up option window. Your brand-new tone is ready to use.

Tip The toning fun doesn't stop there! You can create unique and personalized tones from things all around you, such as gift wrap, patterned bed sheets, or your favorite flowery dress. . . Anything and everything has the potential to be a great tone. Just scan your chosen texture, fabric, or image in at the same dpi as your manga page file, convert it to Grayscale, adjust the brightness/contrast settings so the pattern is clear, and then convert it to Bitmap as above, or use the Color Halftone filter in Elements. Be prepared to experiment with different settings before you stumble across one that gives you a great result, but just continue to adjust the brightness/contrast settings until you are happy. Don't forget to try out different filters before converting the image to Bitmap, as you can create some really interesting patterns this way.

SHOUJO

LETTERING: TEXT AND WORD BALLOONS

AT THIS STAGE, YOU CAN FINALLY TRANSFER YOUR WITTY AND AMUSING DIALOGUE FROM YOUR SCRIPT ONTO THE MANGA PAGE! LETTERING IS OFTEN AN OVERLOOKED ART IN THE CREATION OF MANGA, BUT AS YOUR READERS ARE RELYING ON THE DIALOGUE BALLOONS TO GUIDE THEM THROUGH EACH PAGE—AND TO TELL THEM THE STORY—IT IS ALSO ONE OF THE MOST IMPORTANT PARTS. THE FLOW OF YOUR WORD BALLOONS AFFECTS THE WAY PEOPLE READ THE STORY, WHILE THE FONTS YOU CHOOSE FOR YOUR CHARACTERS' SPEECH (AND THE SOUND EFFECTS AROUND THEM) AFFECT NOT ONLY THE LOOK OF YOUR PAGE, BUT ITS MOOD.

THERE ARE SAID TO BE 60,000 FONTS IN EXISTENCE, AND THAT MIGHT BE A CONSERVATIVE ESTIMATE—SO

YOU HAVE PLENTY TO CHOOSE FROM! MOST OF THESE ARE ONLY AVAILABLE FOR A FEE, AND SOME ARE QUITE EXPENSIVE, BUT YOU CAN FIND WEBSITES THAT ALLOW YOU TO DOWNLOAD GREAT FONTS FOR FREE. FOR A WIDE RANGE OF GENERAL FONTS, CHECK OUT 1001FONTS.COM, WHILE BLAMBOT.COM PROVIDES A NUMBER OF FONTS THAT ARE PERFECT FOR YOUR DIALOGUE BALLOONS, SUCH AS LETTER-O-MATIC, ANIME ACE, AND WEBLETTERERBB. MOST IMPORTANT OF ALL, MAKE SURE THAT ANY FONT YOU CHOOSE IS LEGIBLE, AND COMFORTABLE TO READ. CURSIVE, EXOTIC, AND HANDWRITING FONTS ARE A NO-NO, AS THERE'S NO BETTER WAY TO ANNOY A READER THAN TO MAKE THEM SPEND FIVE MINUTES DECIPHERING THE TEXT.

| ▼ | Comic Sans MS | ⌄ | Regular | ⌄ | 7.03 pt | ⌄ | A A | T T T T | ≡ | A | (Auto) | ⌄ | | Style: | ◨ | ⌄ | T | ↓T |

1 To get started on your lettering, choose a font from the drop-down list at the top left of the Tool Options bar that you think will be suitable for the story. For example, if your story is a scary one, use a gothic font that will assist the mood and help deliver the impact of your creepy punchline. Here, a free font that comes with most standard Windows systems called Comic Sans MS is used, and the size set to 7 pt (you can adjust the font size depending on the dialogue: if the character is shouting then set the pt size larger, it is flexible, as long as it is legible).

2 Select the Text tool (press T). Copy the dialogue for one balloon from your script and paste it (Ctrl /Cmd + V) on the page where you want it to go. Make sure your text is in capital letters. This is for legibility, as capital letters ensure there are no dangling "tails" from letters like "j" and "y" to get entangled with the lines of type below them. Next, center the text (Ctrl/Cmd + Shift + C) and use the Return key to arrange the text into a relatively round (or elliptical) shape so it can fit neatly into a word balloon.

3 Make sure the text is not too big or too small for the page. To adjust the size of the text, use the Character palette or the Free Transform tool (remember to hold down Shift to keep all the letters in proportion to one another). Don't forget that you can put words in bold and italics to add emphasis, such as when characters are drawing attention to something or when you want to add subtlety to your dialogue. Think about the tiny difference between "*Silly* boys," and "Silly *boys*," for example!

4 It's important to check that all of your lettering is inside the frame of the page, as if you were to print the page in a book, anything outside the frame may be cut, or "trimmed." This doesn't matter so much if you are looking to publish only on the web, but it's good to remember that even if your artwork overlaps the edges of the printed page (or bleeds), your lettering must always stay within it.

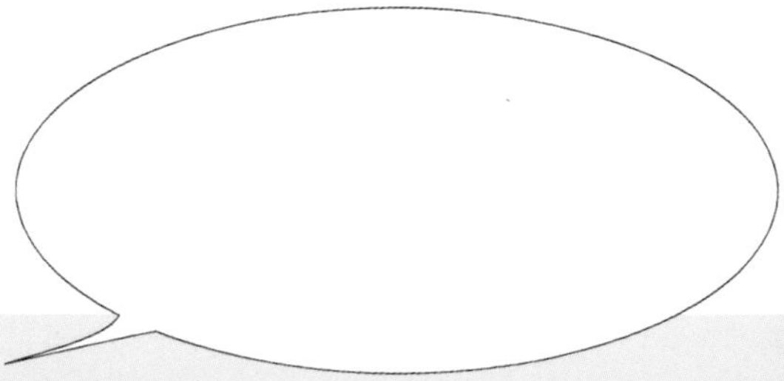

Tip In Photoshop, clicking Window > Character makes the character palette pop up. This allows you to edit your text more efficiently. By selecting the text and clicking on the small, inverted triangle at the top right of the Text palette (above the selections for Regular, Bold, etc.) you can change your caption into All Caps in the sub-menu, so you don't have to re-type your text in capitals.

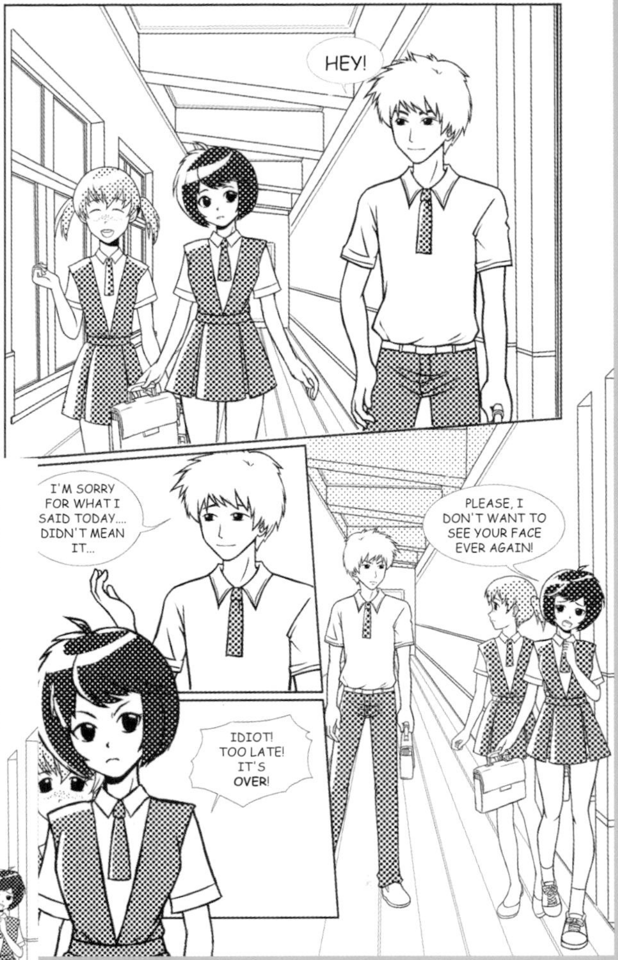
HEY!
I'M SORRY FOR WHAT I SAID TODAY.... DIDN'T MEAN IT...
PLEASE, I DON'T WANT TO SEE YOUR FACE EVER AGAIN!
IDIOT! TOO LATE! IT'S OVER!

5 Find a balloon shape you like on the CD. In manga, there are different types of balloons for normal dialogue, shouting, thinking, and captions (the boxes that introduce scene transitions and add commentary). Select one that is suitable for your text and drag it to the manga page, moving it onto the layer just beneath the text. Scale and flip the balloon to best fit, and make sure the tail of the balloon is pointing to the person talking.

6 Adjust the text and balloon to best show off the artwork and ensure that the panel and page flow correctly. Remember that if someone is the first to speak in a panel, they and their balloon should be at the left-hand side. If your artwork has placed them at the right, you can compensate by placing the balloon on the right higher than the one on the left, to underscore which should be read first. Make sure the balloons aren't covering up anything you are particularly proud of, or that's crucial to the plot.

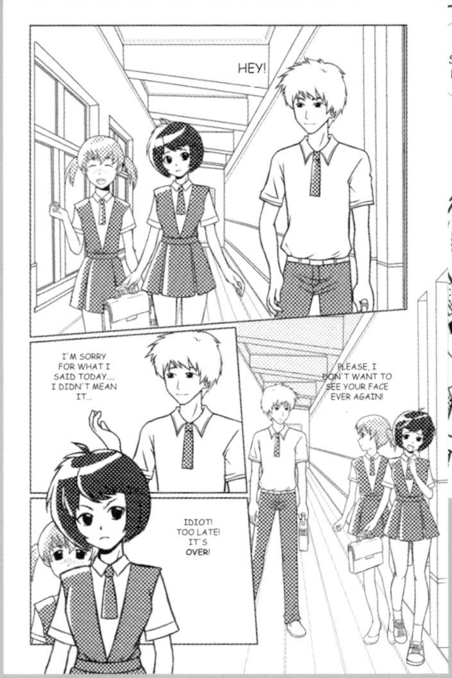
HEY!
I'M SORRY FOR WHAT I SAID TODAY.... I DIDN'T MEAN IT...
PLEASE, I DON'T WANT TO SEE YOUR FACE EVER AGAIN!
IDIOT! TOO LATE! IT'S OVER!

7 Repeat the above steps to transfer all your text into balloons on the page.

CREATING YOUR OWN BALLOONS

As with characters and tones, you may eventually want to experiment with your own balloons. Here is a quick and easy method.

1 Transfer or type your text onto a layer, as above, and create a new layer underneath your dialogue.

2 Using the elliptical selection tool, draw the balloon around the text, making sure you leave "breathing space" around the dialogue on all sides.

3 Holding down the Shift key to add to your selection, use the lasso tool to draw a tail pointing to the mouth of your character.

4 Use the Paint Bucket tool to fill the selection with black. Choose Select > Modify > Contract and set the contraction to between 2 and 6 pixels.

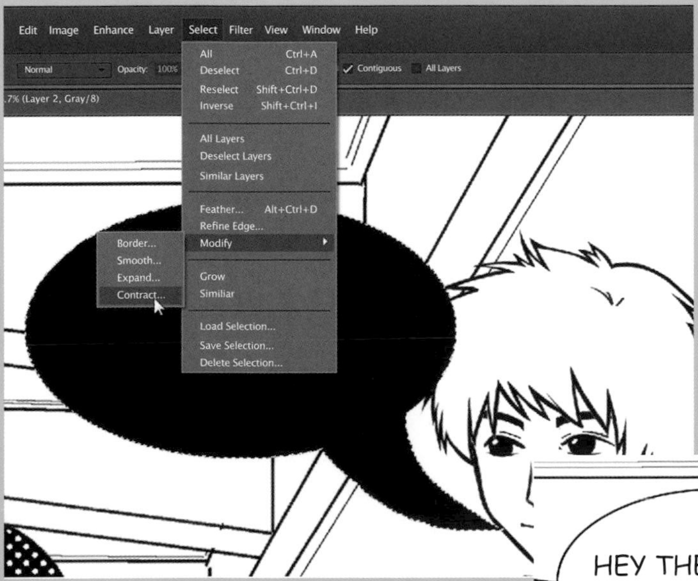
Edit Image Enhance Layer Select Filter View Window Help
Normal Opacity: 100%
Contiguous All Layers
All Ctrl+A
Deselect Ctrl+D
Reselect Shift+Ctrl+D
Inverse Shift+Ctrl+I
All Layers
Deselect Layers
Similar Layers
Feather... Alt+Ctrl+D
Refine Edge...
Modify
Grow
Similiar
Load Selection...
Save Selection...
Delete Selection...
Border...
Smooth...
Expand...
Contract...

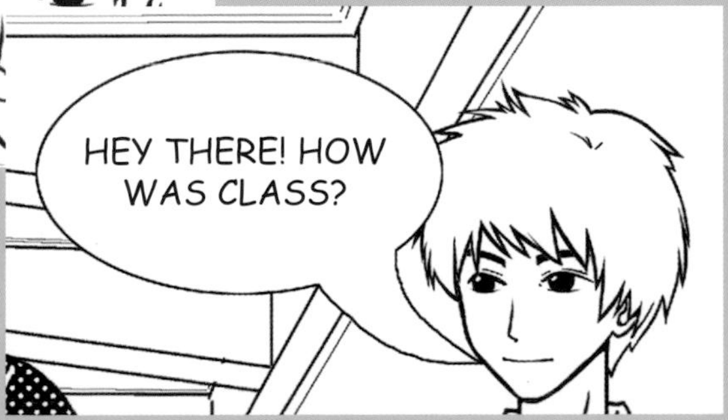
HEY THERE! HOW WAS CLASS?

5 Fill the selection with white. Congratulations, you've made a balloon! You can experiment with other shapes by drawing them freehand with the lasso—think of the outlandish effects you can create for shouting, screaming, and new ways of thinking.

SHOUJO

ADDING SOUND EFFECTS

SOUND EFFECTS ADD CHARACTER AND FLAVOR TO A MANGA PAGE, DRAWING YOUR READER DEEPER INTO THE ACTION. THEY CAN BE AS SMALL AS A SIGH OF EXHALED AIR, OR AS LARGE AS A THERMONUCLEAR EXPLOSION!

SOUND EFFECTS ARE NORMALLY APPLIED DIRECTLY ONTO THE PAGE, RATHER THAN PLACED IN BALLOONS, AND ARE A LOT MORE INDIVIDUAL THAN YOUR DIALOGUE, WITH EACH SOUND USUALLY HAVING ITS OWN FONT, SIZE, AND SHAPE. SOUND EFFECTS ARE SCALED IN RELATION TO THE LOUDNESS OF A SOUND, SO A LIGHT GUST OF WIND WOULD TRACE A TINY PATH ACROSS A PANEL, WHILE THE SLAM OF A DOOR CLOSING MIGHT BE SO LOUD AS TO BE WRITTEN ACROSS THE ARTWORK OF THE DOOR ITSELF, LEAVING THE INTERIORS OF THE LETTERS TRANSPARENT SO THAT THE ART COULD STILL BE SEEN. THE FONT SHOULD FIT THE SOUND, TOO—A ROUGH AND CHUNKY FONT WOULD BE APPROPRIATE FOR AN EXPLOSION, WHILE THE LETTERING FROM A RETRO CALCULATOR WOULD BE PERFECT FOR AN ELECTRONIC BEEP.

PHOTOSHOP AND PHOTOSHOP ELEMENTS BOTH ALLOW YOU TO WARP TEXT, USING THE CREATE WARPED TEXT OPTION IN THE TEXT OPTIONS TOOLBAR, WHICH IS PERFECT FOR CREATING ALL KINDS OF SOUND EFFECTS OR INNER DIALOGUES.

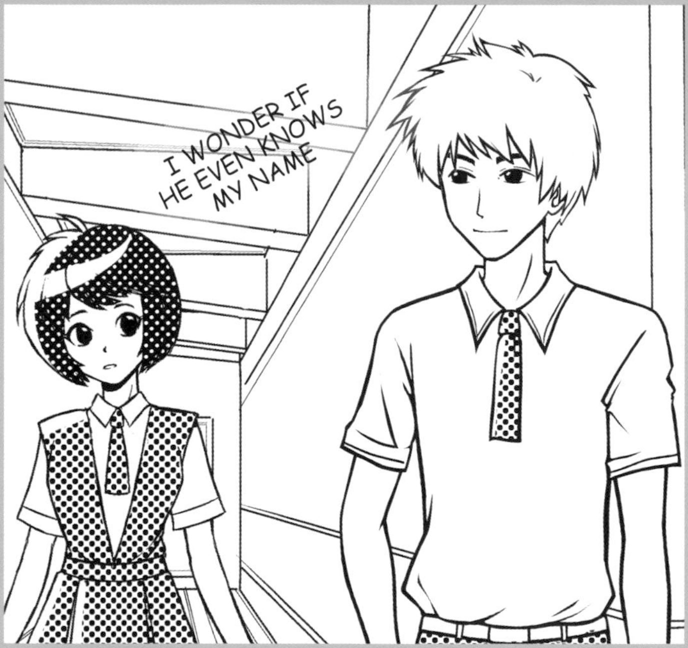
I WONDER IF HE EVEN KNOWS MY NAME

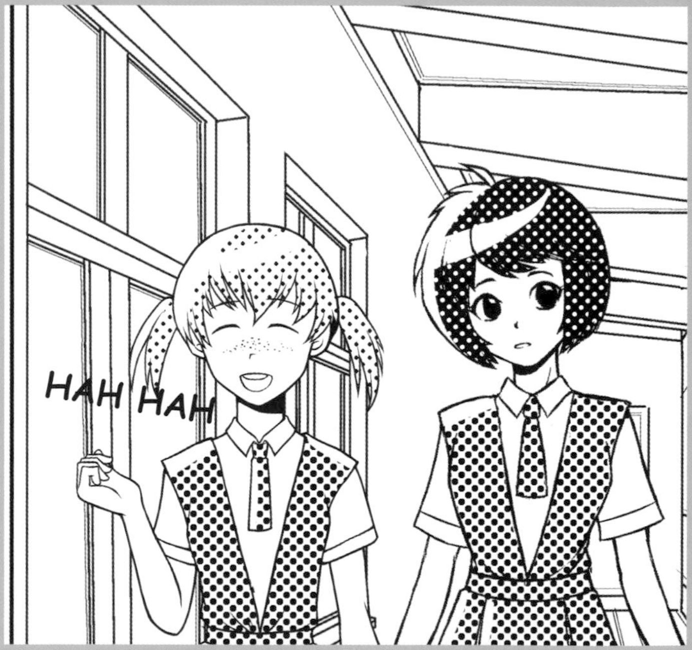
HAH HAH

Don't forget, too, that you can scale, rotate, and place your lettering. To do this you will first need to rasterize the lettering (Layer > Rasterize > Type) or simplify in Elements (Layer > Simplify Layer), which changes it from editable type into flat imagery. Make sure you have spelled everything correctly, and that the letters are in the color you want before doing so. Once rasterized, the text behaves like any other part of the image—you can alter it in any way you see fit using the Free Transform tools.

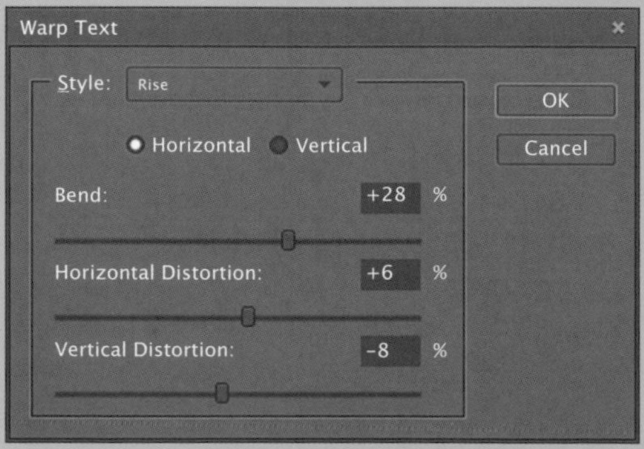
Warp Text
Style: Rise
Horizontal
Vertical
OK
Cancel
Bend: +28 %
Horizontal Distortion: +6 %
Vertical Distortion: -8 %

AH... SIGH

AH... SIGH

You may also wish to add a border around the letters in a complementary color to make them stand out from the background more. To do this, use a selection tool to select the sound effect, change to the Move tool, and hit any arrow key to make the selection tight around the letters. Now go to Select > Modify > Expand. The number of pixels to expand by will depend on the size of your sound effect—start with 10–15 and scale up accordingly. Once this is done, use the Paint Bucket tool (with Contiguous unchecked) to fill the expanded selection with another color. Then go to Select > Modify > Contract to create a smaller selection, and fill with white (as you did for steps 4 and 5 for Creating Your Own Balloons), giving your letters a punchy color border. It's best to do this stage before scaling or rotating your rasterized sound effect, as any Transformation of the image anti-aliases it and makes it difficult to fill.

Here are some examples of sound effects used in manga—creating new sound effects is endlessly rewarding and fun!

LAUGHS:
HAH HAH HAAA, HUH HUH HUH, HEEE HEE HEEE, HEH HEH HEEEH, HMM HMM HMM

SCREAMS:
AHHH, AYAAA, EEEYAA, EEEKKKK, GYEEE, HYAAA, UAAAA, YAAAH, YEEEE

GUSTS OF WIND:
HSSSHHH, HWOOO, HOWL, HURRRRR, OOOO, SHASHAA, SHHHHIIIIII, SHHHHSHH, WOOSH, WISSSHH

HITS:
BLAM, BANG, BOOM, BONG, BOFF, BOP, BLASH, CHOOM, CHAKKA, CRUNCH, CRASH, DOOM, FWAP, FAP, GLOMP, JACK, KRUNCH, KLONK, KONK, KANG, KRESH, KRUNCK, PAK, PLOK, PING, POW, PWOP, SPLACH, SLAM, SHOOM, SMACK, SMASH, THUD, TUK, THOMP, THOK, TUFF, TOK, WHUMP, WHOK, WHOMP, WONK, WHOOP

OTHER SOUNDS: (Can you work out what they may represent?)
BEEP, BZZBZZ, CLINK-CLANK, EHH, GRRR, GULP, GEEZ, HUFF HUFF, PSSTPSST, RING-RING, SIGH, TINK, TING, VAROOM, VOOSH, ZOAAM

SHOuJO

CHOOSING COLORS

NO MATTER HOW ATTRACTIVE YOUR LINE-ART, IF YOU CHOOSE THE WRONG COLORS TO GO INSIDE THOSE LINES, YOUR IMAGE CAN BE RUINED. YOUR CHOICE OF COLOR AND THE EFFECT IT CAN HAVE ON A PIECE IN TERMS OF COMPOSITION, DESIGN, AND MOOD IS KEY TO CREATING PROFESSIONAL-LOOKING MANGA ARTWORK.

ONE OF THE FIRST CHOICES YOU MAY COME ACROSS WHEN COLORING YOUR ARTWORK IS WHETHER YOU SHOULD CHOOSE COLORS THAT ARE REALISTIC AND BELIEVABLE, OR COLORS THAT SIMPLY LOOK THE PART. OF COURSE, IN THE WORLD OF MANGA, THESE LINES CAN OFTEN BECOME BLURRED. TAKE HAIR FOR EXAMPLE: IN THE CONTEXT OF MANGA, BRIGHT PINK HAIR DOESN'T SEEM ODD AT ALL!

HOWEVER, NO MATTER HOW RADICAL (OR HOW REALISTIC) YOUR TASTES, IT'S ALWAYS HELPFUL TO KNOW A LITTLE OF THE THEORY BEHIND THE COLOR PROCESS. CERTAIN COLORS WILL NATURALLY COMPLEMENT OTHERS, AND THESE WILL MAKE YOUR IMAGES MORE SUCCESSFUL.

The effect of a chosen color can range from evoking basic emotions to stimulating thought. For example, mixing red, white, and blue in a piece—even when not in the shape of a flag—subtly suggests American, British, or French nationality.

The colors in your piece can also speak volumes about the mood of the character captured within. Here are just a few examples of how colors can directly reflect or provoke a mood: Red, orange, and yellow are warm colors. They tend to suggest warmth, passion, or even danger. Our mind associates them instantly with fire or the sun. The color red, however, can suggest far more. It is the color of choice for warning signs, and neon lighting in certain morally dubious areas of town.

Blue, green, and purple are the cool colors. They can be soothing because of what they represent; green makes us think of nature, blue can denote the sky or the sea. However, blue can also show coldness, loneliness, and depression. It can sum up many negative emotions. Purple tends to represent something with more of an "edge" and is a relatively eccentric color. It can also be a symbol of wealth or nobility.

Finally, the neutral colors (gray, beige, and brown) can create a subtle and toned-down image. However, they are sometimes more effective when used to contrast with the more vibrant colors in an image.

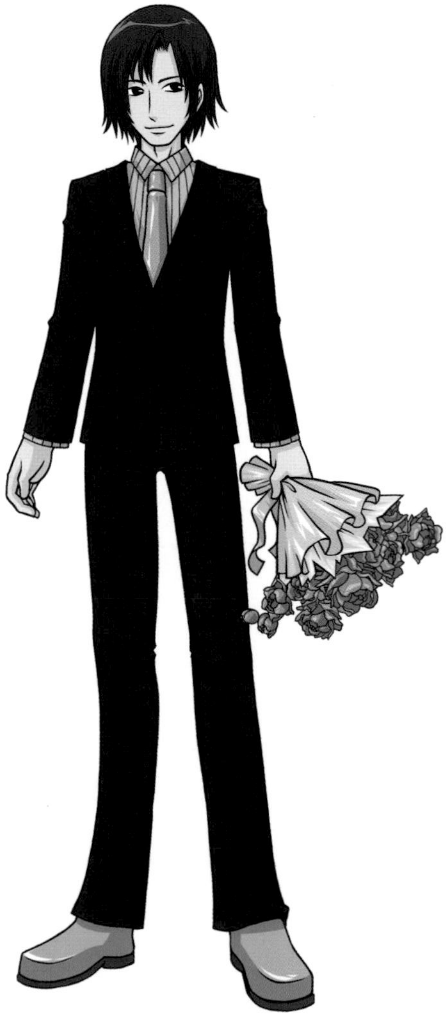

DESIGN

How you choose to combine colors is one of the main factors in giving your work a unique style. Sometimes you may simply want your character to wear a realistic, modern outfit. In that case, you are unlikely to want to use any color scheme that is too garish or clashing. Other times (and more frequently in manga) you may want to try something radical!

Don't feel that you should even be limited to conventional coloring styles. Try coloring an entire image in varying shades of just one color and see what kind of effects you can create.

THE THREE GOLDEN RULES OF COLORING

RESEARCH

If you are attempting to create a realistic piece, be sure that your colors suit the genre or timescale of your image. If your piece is a historical one, you will need to consider the common color schemes of the era.

DESIGN

When coloring an outfit, try to make sure that a design element is present. For example, if a character wears a red scarf, perhaps she would have matching red shoes or ribbons on her socks? A little consistency, even in the craziest color scheme, can add professionalism to an image.

HAVE FUN!

What you see here are the theories and starting points to help you choose which colors you want to use. Experiment and capture your own style and remember that coloring can be a long process, but very rewarding in the end.

PRIMARY

Most people think of the primary colors as red, blue, and yellow. More accurately, they are cyan, magenta, and yellow. These colors can be combined to create any single color of the spectrum.

SECONDARY

Fewer people may be aware of the secondary colors: orange, purple, and green. Each can be made by mixing two of the primary colors together.

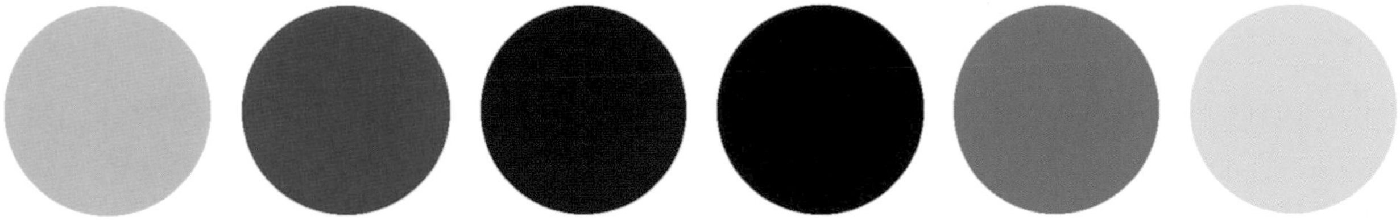

TERTIARY

Finally, we move on to the tertiary colors: yellow-orange, red-orange, red-purple, blue-purple, blue-green, and yellow-green. Each of these colors can be created using one primary and one secondary color.

BY PUTTING ALL OF THESE COLORS INTO A COLOR WHEEL, WE ARE GIVEN A SIMPLE OVERVIEW OF COLOR AND CAN QUICKLY SEE WHICH COLORS SHOULD BE USED IN CONJUNCTION WITH OTHERS.

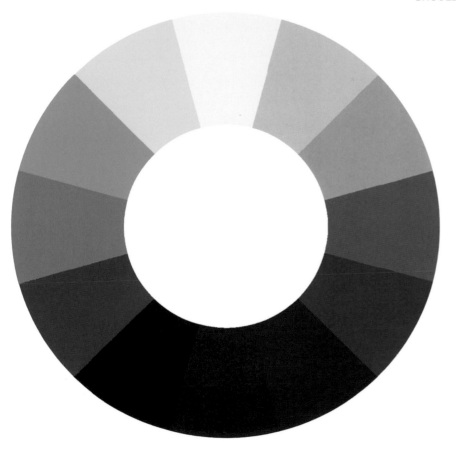

If you want colors that relate closely to each other, choose analogous colors—colors that are close together on the color wheel. By choosing several analogous shades, you can achieve a more subtle color scheme.

For something a little more daring, try complementary colors. By choosing two colors that are directly opposite each other on the color wheel, you can achieve some incredible contrast and vibrancy. However, be careful not to make your scheme too garish when trying this style.

Lastly, there is the triadic color scheme. As the name suggests, the idea here is to choose three colors that are evenly spaced on the wheel. One way to use this is to choose two colors to form the basic color scheme, and add a third as an occasional highlight for accent and depth. This works well because that third color will be equally different to each of the base colors.

SHOUJO

CHOOSING COLOR SCHEMES

WHILE TRADITIONALLY EXPENSIVE, IT IS GETTING INCREASINGLY CHEAPER TO PRODUCE MANGA IN COLOR THANKS TO ONLINE PUBLISHING SITES LIKE LULU.COM AND CAFEPRESS.COM, WHICH ALLOW YOU TO PRINT OUT YOUR MASTERPIECES IN VERY SMALL RUNS, OR SET UP A SHOP FROM WHICH FRIENDS, FAMILY, AND READERS FROM ALL OVER THE WORLD CAN PRINT OUT THEIR OWN COPIES. COLORING CAN ALSO BE COMBINED WITH TONING TO PRODUCE SOME STRIKING WORK—AND MAKE THE PROCESS MORE FUN!

To begin coloring, you'll need to convert your page to RGB mode first, if it is currently in Grayscale. If you are using Photoshop, rather than Photoshop Elements, and are aiming toward professional printing, you may want to use CMYK format. The latter format produces much bigger file sizes, and does not support the full range of Photoshop Filters (you have to flip between RGB and CMYK if you wish to use them), but the colors it uses are calibrated for the printed page. If you are going to publish your work online, RGB is the format to use, as it is designed for viewing on screens.

Coloring a manga page is slightly different from coloring a poster. Because a manga page contains several panels, it is very easy to end up with messy and conflicted colors if you don't plan your color schemes ahead of time. In order to harmonize your colors and make your pages work as a whole, a palette of custom swatches will be handy, featuring colors you have found work well together. Here's how to set one up.

1 Select a color in the color picker.

2 Open Window > Swatches and the swatches palette will appear. Click the small inverted triangle at the top right and select New Swatch.

3 Your cursor changes to a paint bucket when you move it over an empty place in the swatch palette. Click with the paint bucket to fill the empty spot with your chosen color.

4 To replace a color in the swatch, select the new color, move the cursor over the color you want to replace and hold down the Shift key. When the cursor changes to a paint bucket, click to replace the old color.

5 Once you are happy with your swatch, click the small inverted triangle, and in the drop down menu, select Save Swatch. Remember: you can always change or add more colors to your custom color swatch.

Select foreground color:
Learn more about: Choosing Colors
OK
Cancel
H: 0 °
S: 31 %
B: 75 %
R: 195
G: 132
B: 132
c08484
Only Web Colors

Color Swatches
more
Default

Place in Palette Bin when Closed
Help Contents
Help
New Swatch...
Small Thumbnail
Large Thumbnail
Small List

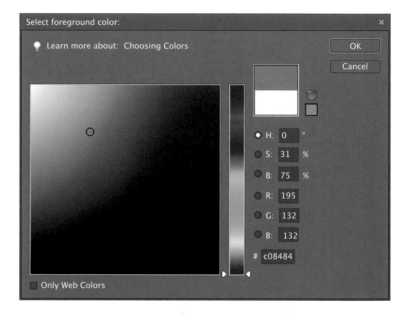

Tip Highly saturated colors rarely look good when combined (although some highly skilled artists are able to pull it off) and often create an amateur feel to the coloring. When you pick colors for your color swatches, choose the less saturated end of the spectrum. When you open up the "color picker" window, you'll see a field of tones for your chosen color, progressing from completely desaturated white and black on the left to fully saturated light and dark colors on the right. Try to avoid the top right corner if possible!

File Edit Image Enhance Layer Select Filter View
Auto Select Layer
Show
P40_PatternFinal.tif
Rotate
Transform
Crop
Divide Scanned Photos
Resize
Mode
Convert Color Profile
Magic Extractor... Alt+Shift+Ctrl+V
Bitmap...
Grayscale
Indexed Color...
RGB Color
8 Bits/Channel
Color Table...

Color Table
Table: Custom
OK
Cancel
Load...
Save...
Help
Preview

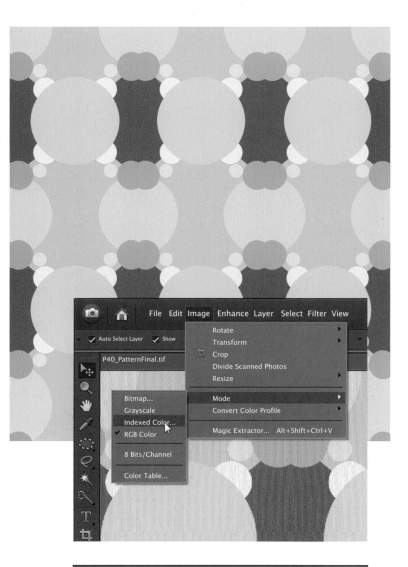

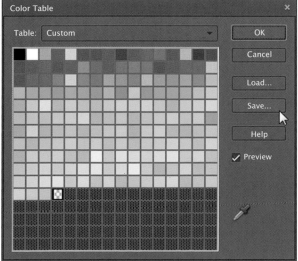

You can also create a custom color palette from a color manga picture you really like. Here's how to do it.

1 Find the image you want to use (normally from the Internet), save it to your computer and open it in Photoshop.

2 To create a custom swatch from an image, we need first to convert it to an indexed palette image. Click Image > Mode > Indexed Color. In the pop-up window, there is a choice of colors. You can put the number of the colors you want on your swatch here. You won't want too many colors as it will be difficult to find what you want if it has too many. A number between 150 and 250 is sensible.

3 Now go to Image > Mode > Color Table to view the color palette extracted from this image. Click on Save to save the color palette, then click Cancel to exit. (Remember where you saved it so that you can load the palette later!)

4 Open the manga page you want to color and go to the swatches palette. Click Replace Swatches from the palette menu. Find the color palette you just generated and saved on your hard drive (it will be saved as an .act file) and load it.

5 Now you can pick any color from the palette and use it on your manga page!

BLOCKING IN BASE COLORS

FILLING IN BASE COLORS IS THE FIRST STEP IN EVERY COLORING PROCESS. IN THE MANGA AND COMICS INDUSTRY, THESE BASIC COLORS ARE KNOWN AS FLATS. BASE COLORS OR FLATS, AS THE NAMES WOULD SUGGEST, PROVIDE A BASE OF FLAT COLOR FOR THE MORE DETAILED COLORING TO FOLLOW. THEY ALLOW YOU TO PLAY WITH COMPLEMENTARY TONES AND COLOR COMPOSITIONS WITHOUT HAVING TO SPEND HOURS SLAVING OVER SHADING ONLY TO REALIZE YOU'VE USED A DARK BLUE INSTEAD OF A LIGHT PURPLE THROUGHOUT. CREATING BLOCKS OF SOLID COLOR ON A SEPARATE LAYER ALSO ALLOWS YOU TO RE-SELECT AREAS OF COLOR WITH THE MAGIC WAND TOOL WITH THE GREATEST OF EASE, WHICH IS VERY HELPFUL WHEN ISOLATING AREAS TO PAINT OVER OR SHADE LATER.

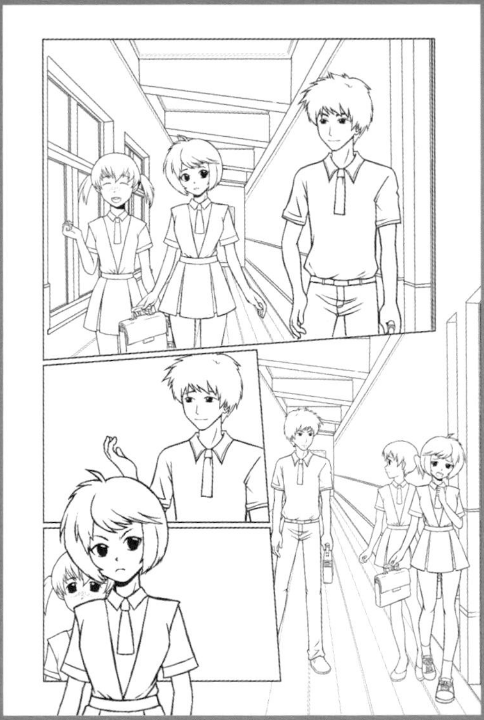

1 Start the base color process by ensuring the line-art is cleaned (filling in gaps between lines that should be solid, and erasing stray lines that may annoy you later)—an important step if you have scanned in your own creations. Copy the line-art to a new layer, name it, and set the mode to Multiply. This will allow colors on layers beneath or above to show through. Delete the information on the original line-art layer, rename it Base and leave the mode as Normal. To help make any gaps in your coloring obvious, create another new layer below your Base layer and flood fill it with a light pastel color (blues and greens are best).

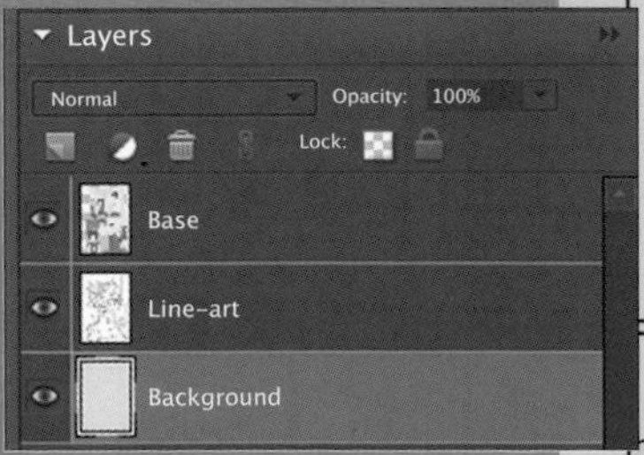
Layers
Normal
Opacity: 100%
Lock:
Base
Line-art
Background

PREPARING THE ARTWORK FOR TONE AND COLOR

When you have completed your character, you should prepare it to be colored or toned. It's important to flatten an image and make sure that no anti-aliasing is present.

Blurry, "anti-aliased" lines can be especially problematic during coloring. Anti-aliasing is the way lines are blurred on screen to make diagonal and curved lines look smoother. While this creates a more pleasing visual effect, it causes difficulties when coloring. Specifically the Paint Bucket tool will fill a white area until it comes to the edge of the next color—so if that's a light gray rather than black, it'll stop there, leaving you with ragged graytone areas around all of your lines.

You can compensate for this to some extent by using a high Threshold value in the Tool Options bar, but a better way is to remove all anti-aliasing and layers at this stage.

1 Choose Layers > Flatten Image from the menu. This will reduce the image to a single layer.

2 Choose Image > Mode > Bitmap. Leave the resolution as it is, but change the method to 50% Threshold. This means that any colors above 50% darkness will become black, and any below will be white. (You will need to convert back to RGB mode before you can color).

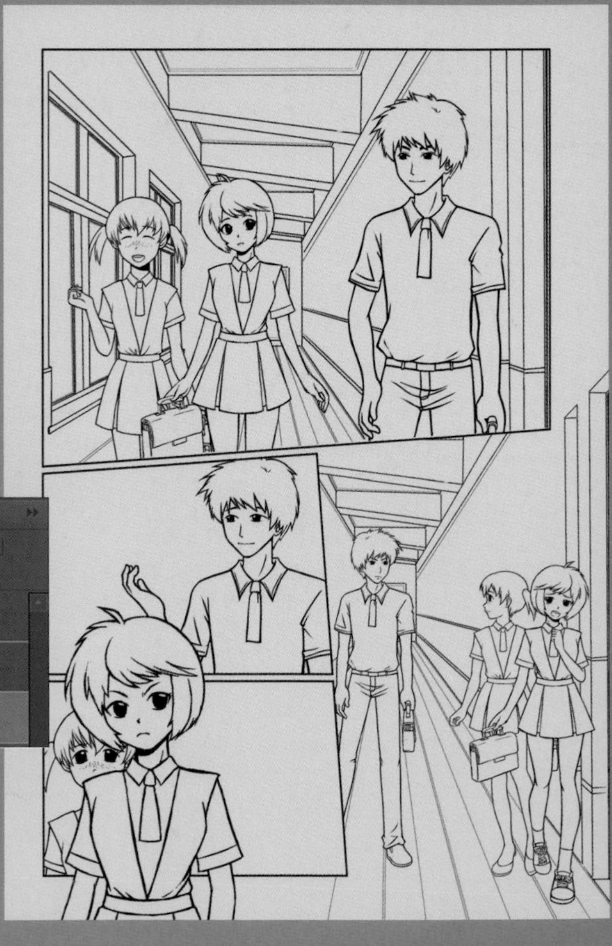

2 On the Base layer, use the Magic Wand tool to select an area you want to block color in. Set the tolerance to about 50, check Contiguous and Sample All Layers, and uncheck Anti-alias. Press and hold the Shift key to select multiple areas (all of one character's skin tones, for instance) or press and hold the Alt key to deselect any areas you may have clicked by accident.

File Edit Image Enhance Layer Select Filter View Window Help
Tolerance: 32
Anti-alias
Contiguo
P48_02.psd @ 50% (base, RGB/8)
All Ctrl+A
Deselect Ctrl+D
Reselect Shift+Ctrl+D
Inverse Shift+Ctrl+I
All Layers
Deselect Layers
Similar Layers
Feather... Alt+Ctrl+D
Refine Edge...
Modify
Grow
Similar
Load Selection...
Save Selection....
Delete Selection...
Border...
Smooth...
Expand...
Contract...

Expand Selection
Learn more about: Expand Selection
OK
Cancel
Expand By: 1 pixels

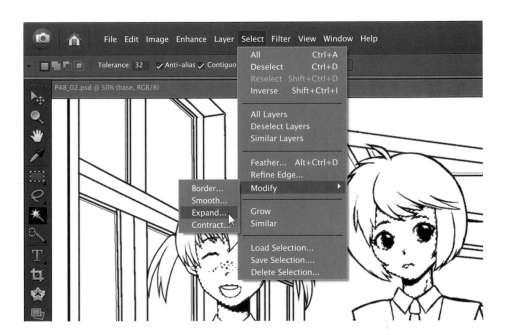

3 Now click Select > Modify > Expand, set the value to 1 and click OK. This expands the area of color out over the linework so that there are no gaps in the color when printed or viewed on screen.

4 Sometimes the line-art is "broken" (i.e. not joined up), which will cause your Magic Wand selection to "spill out" into adjacent areas. You can either Deselect your selection (Ctrl/Cmd + D) and close the line with the Pencil tool on the Line-Art layer, or use Alt and the lasso tool to deselect the excess area. If you have already selected multiple areas and don't want to lose your selection, invert it by pressing Ctrl/Cmd + Shift + I, fix the gap with the Pencil tool, and return to your original selection by pressing Ctrl/Cmd + Shift + I again.

5 Using the Paint Bucket tool, with the mode set to Normal and opacity at 100%, fill the selected area with your chosen color.

SHOUJO

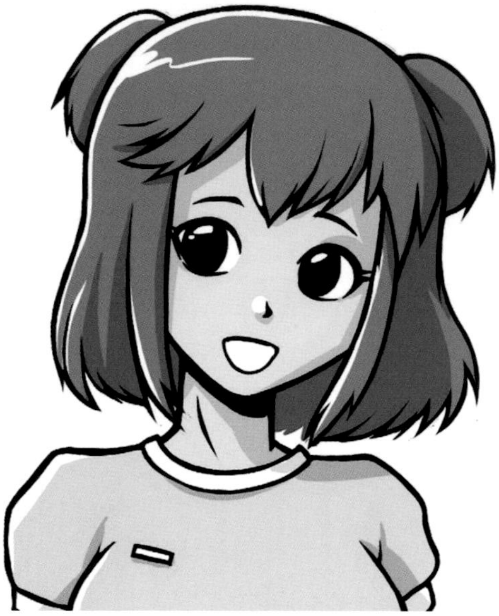

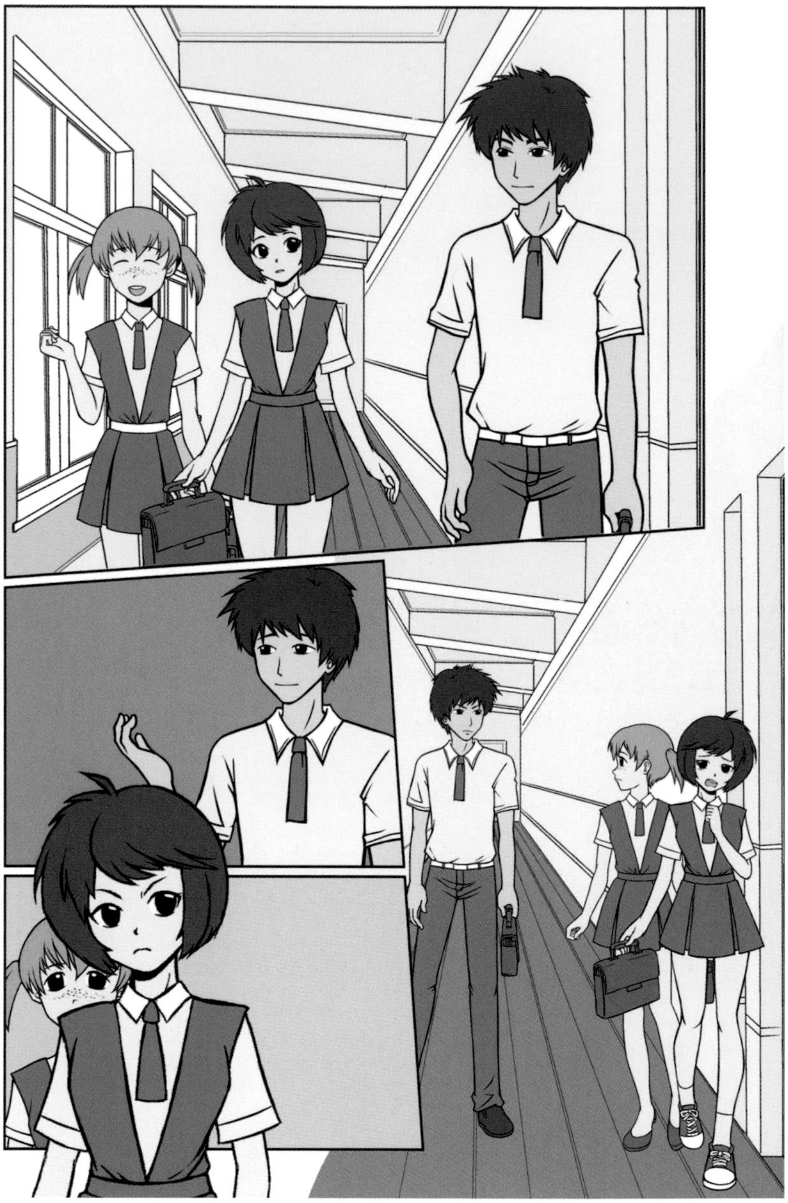

6 Sometimes you will want to use the Pencil tool to fill in small problem areas, or areas not fully enclosed by the line-art (for example, the pupils of your characters' eyes). Use the [and] keys to increase or decrease the brush size.

7 Repeat the above steps to fill in all the colors. Coloring is a time-consuming process, but don't get disheartened if it takes a while—the results are always worth it!

8 If you need to use the Eraser tool at any point, don't forget to change the mode back to Brush from the Pencil tool.

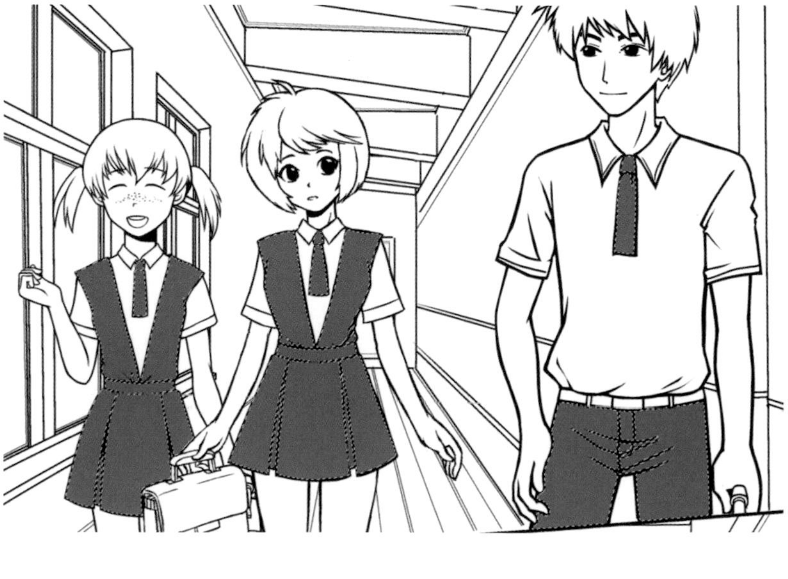

9 If one color you have filled looks out of place next to another, you can adjust it. Use the Magic Wand to select the area of color you want to change (if you've used the color in more than one location on your page, deselect Contiguous and the Wand will select all occurrences of that color), then go to Image > Adjustment > Hue/Saturation and push and pull the sliders until you're happy with the new color.

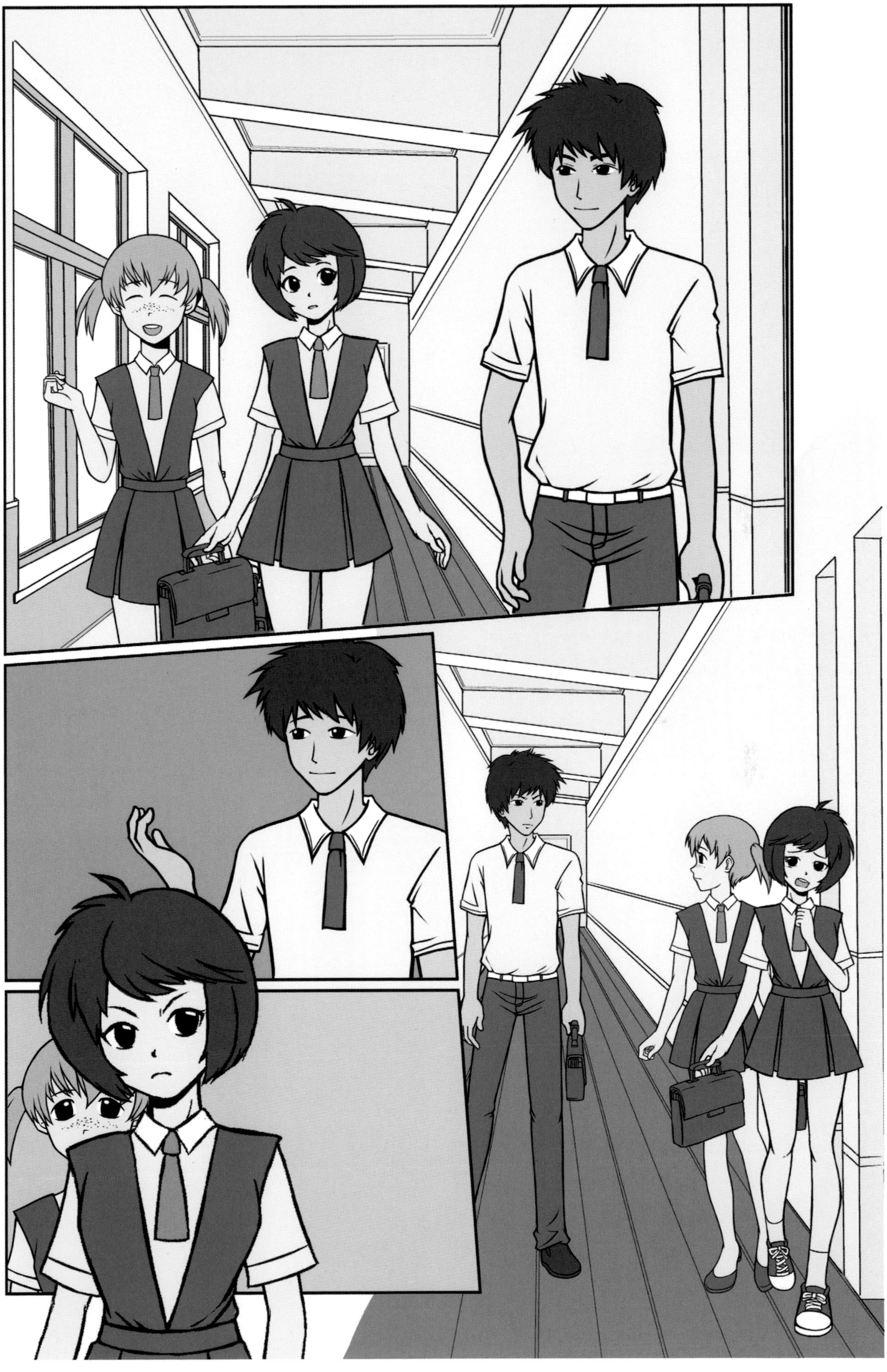

SHOUJO

CEL SHADING

CEL SHADING REFERS TO THE STYLE OF USING FLAT BLOCK COLORS TO REPRESENT AREAS OF LIGHT AND SHADOW ON A PICTURE. THE NAME RELATES TO THE USE OF ANIMATION CELS IN JAPANESE ANIME, AND THE WAY THAT COLORS ARE USED TO DEFINE DEPTH. THE USE OF DARKER AND LIGHTER TONES TO DEFINE SHAPE AND SHADOW WAS SO UNIQUE AND DISTINCTIVE THAT IT BECAME INTRINSICALLY ASSOCIATED WITH JAPANESE ANIMATION. ALTHOUGH SOME WESTERN STUDIOS HAVE ADOPTED THE TECHNIQUE SINCE, IT IS STILL SOMETHING THAT HELPS TO MAKE AUTHENTIC-LOOKING AND AESTHETICALLY PLEASING ANIME-STYLE CHARACTERS.

THE APPEARANCE OF CEL-STYLE SHADING IS VERY EASY TO EMULATE USING PHOTOSHOP. BY MAKING THE MOST OF LAYERS, IT IS POSSIBLE TO ACHIEVE A HIGH-QUALITY LOOK VERY QUICKLY. THE TIME CAN BE SPENT FOCUSING ON THE DETAILS RATHER THAN GETTING THE OVERALL CEL LOOK TO WORK EFFECTIVELY.

FINALLY, CEL SHADING IS OFTEN THE BASIS FOR MANY OTHER VISUAL STYLES, SUCH AS NATURAL MEDIA, AND ACTS AS THE BASIS OF LIGHTING FOR MOST IMAGES. TIME SPENT ON THE CEL SHADING PROCESS WILL IMPROVE THE LOOK OF ANY IMAGE, REGARDLESS OF THE LOOK YOU REQUIRE FOR THE FINAL PIECE.

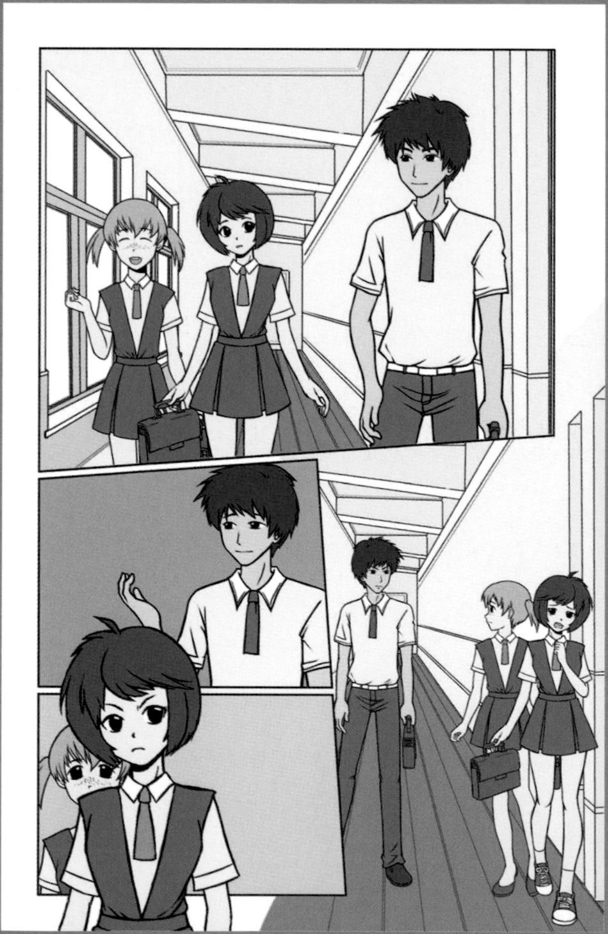

ORIGINAL
This page has no shading, just simple base colors. The most important aspect of cel shading is understanding how light falls, and how the shape of an object will affect the shading.

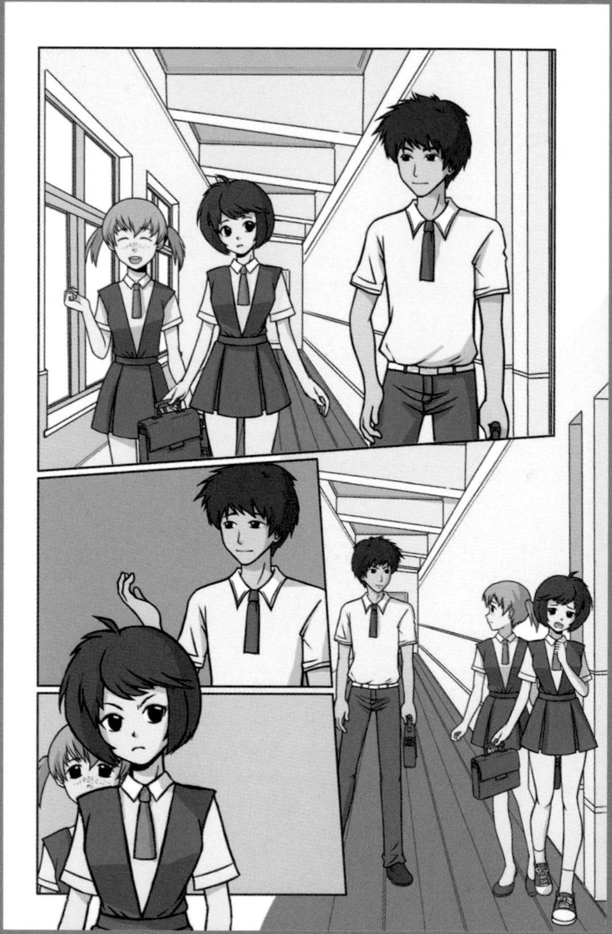

SHADING
The lightest parts of an object are those that face the light source, and the darkest parts are those that face away from the light. Unless the light source is very small and weak (such as the glow from a TV screen or a flickering flame) the light will affect the object equally. In other words, about the same amount of light falls on all the areas that point towards the light.

The light source on this page is originating from the top left, so any areas facing away from there have been shaded more darkly.

SHADOWS

Effective definition of shadows can make all the difference to how "solid" your picture looks. When the objects in the scene are obviously affecting one another, your picture becomes much more believable. Firstly, the characters now cast a shadow onto the floor. Secondly, the characters are also casting shadows on themselves. It's easy for objects to cast shadows on themselves, so you need to be aware of this.

DARK SHADOWS

With shiny materials such as plastic or skin (in some instances), you may wish to further define the shadows. Giving these areas a heavier shadow can help to define the shape of the object more vividly.

HIGHLIGHTS

Highlights are only necessary on shiny materials, and can be used to a greater or lesser degree depending on the effect that is desired. In this image, highlights have been added from the main light source. However, some additional highlights have been added in the opposite direction, implying some sort of other light source nearby. This style of backlight is quite a popular method to give an object more volume.

APPLYING BASIC CEL SHADING

1 Create a new layer on top of your base colors (see page 48), and call it shading. Set the layer's blending mode to Multiply.

Layers
Multiply
Opacity: 100%
Lock:
Shading
Base
Line-art

2 Go to the base layer and use the Magic Wand tool to select the areas you want to color. Set the tolerance to 0 and uncheck Contiguous and Sample All Layers.

3 With the area selected, move back to the shading layer. Normally, permutations of gray are used to shade, as the darker the shadow, the less saturated it is. Using gray not only lowers the lightness of shaded areas, but also decreases the saturation. However, you don't have to use a pure gray—you may want to inject some color, depending on the mood of your page. For example, a night scene might respond well to a purple-gray, while a warm sunny day calls for something more pinkish. To shade, we use the Paint Brush tool. Choose a hard-edged brush and set the opacity and flow to 100%.

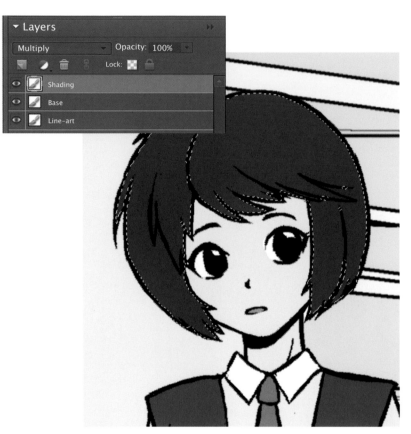

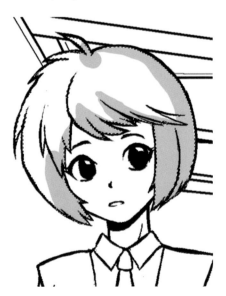

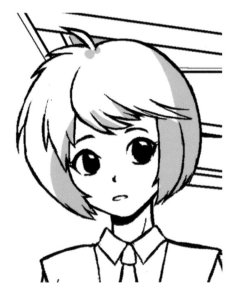

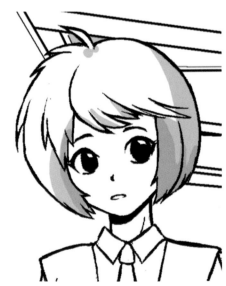

4 Apply the shading, using the Eraser tool to correct any mistakes, and also to sharpen up the end of any lines that you wish to taper to a point. Remember to paint in your shadows consistently, ensuring they all correspond to the same light source.

5 By choosing a darker shade of the same shading color, certain areas can be defined more heavily.

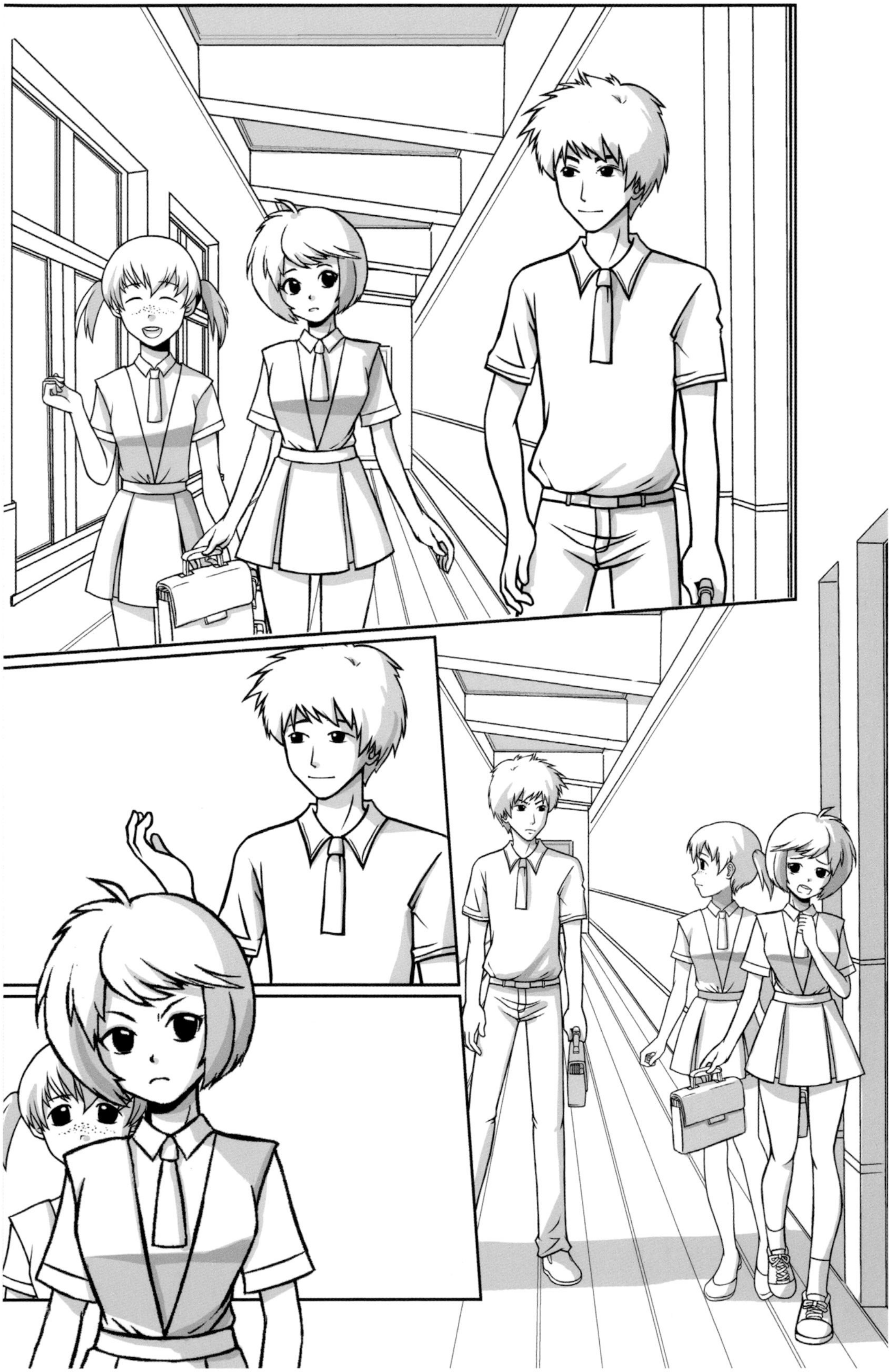

6 Once you have finished, you can use the Hue/Saturation tool to adjust the color of your shadows until you are completely satisfied. This method will save you a lot of time, and is a quick shortcut to professional results!

ADDING HIGHLIGHTS AND DETAIL

1 Create a new layer above the color layer. Label this as highlights. Set the layer to Screen mode, so only that layer will lighten. Set the opacity to about 60%.

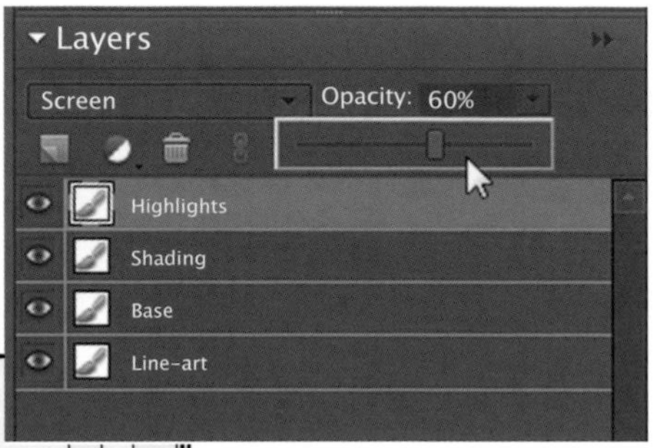
Layers
Screen
Opacity: 60%
Highlights
Shading
Base
Line-art

2 Using a white color, apply areas of light, bearing your light source in mind. Consider the type of material, and whether or not it would in fact have highlights, or would be better left without.

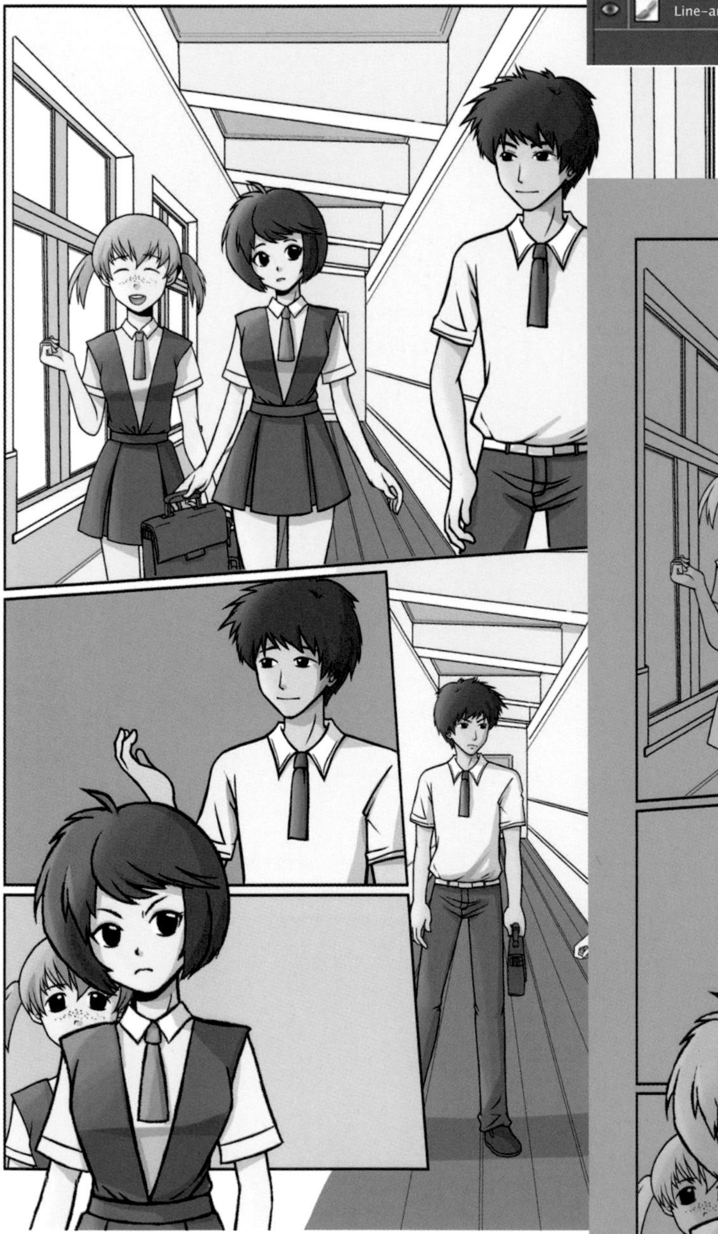

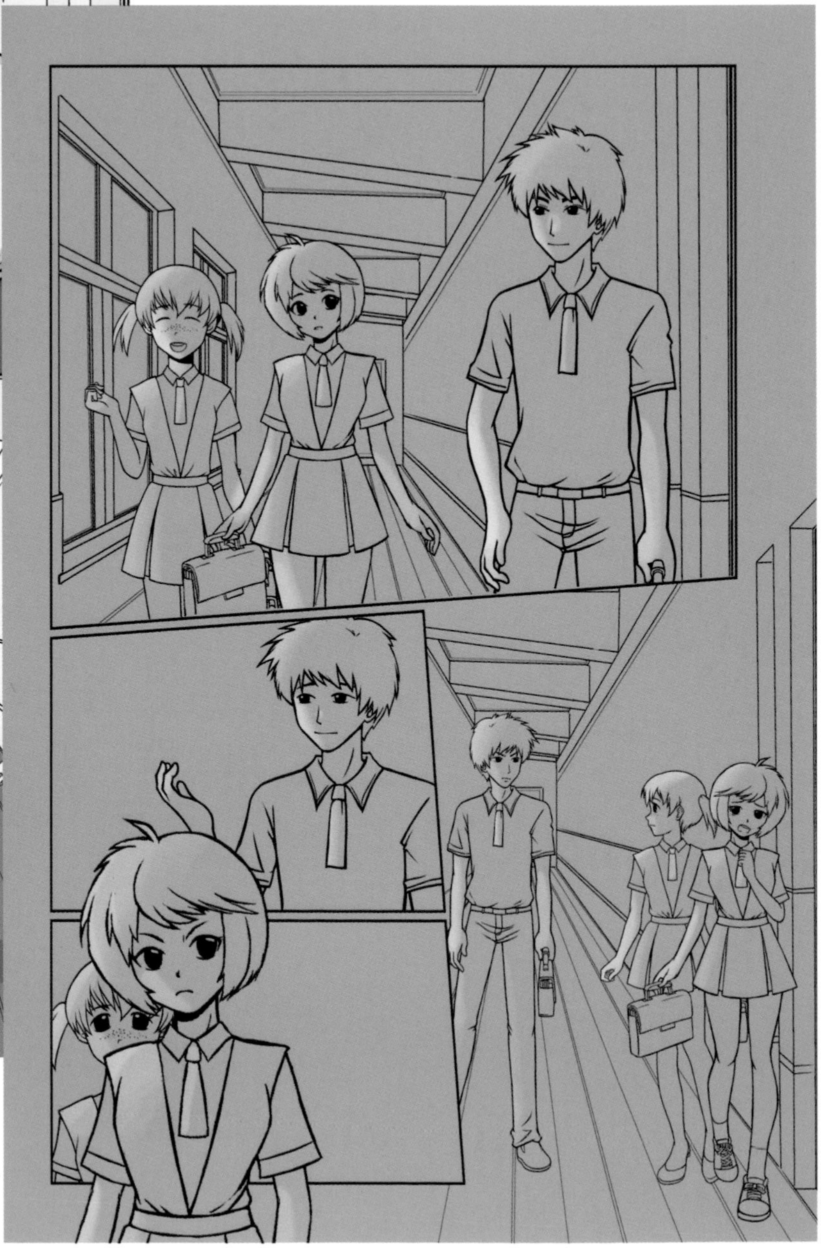

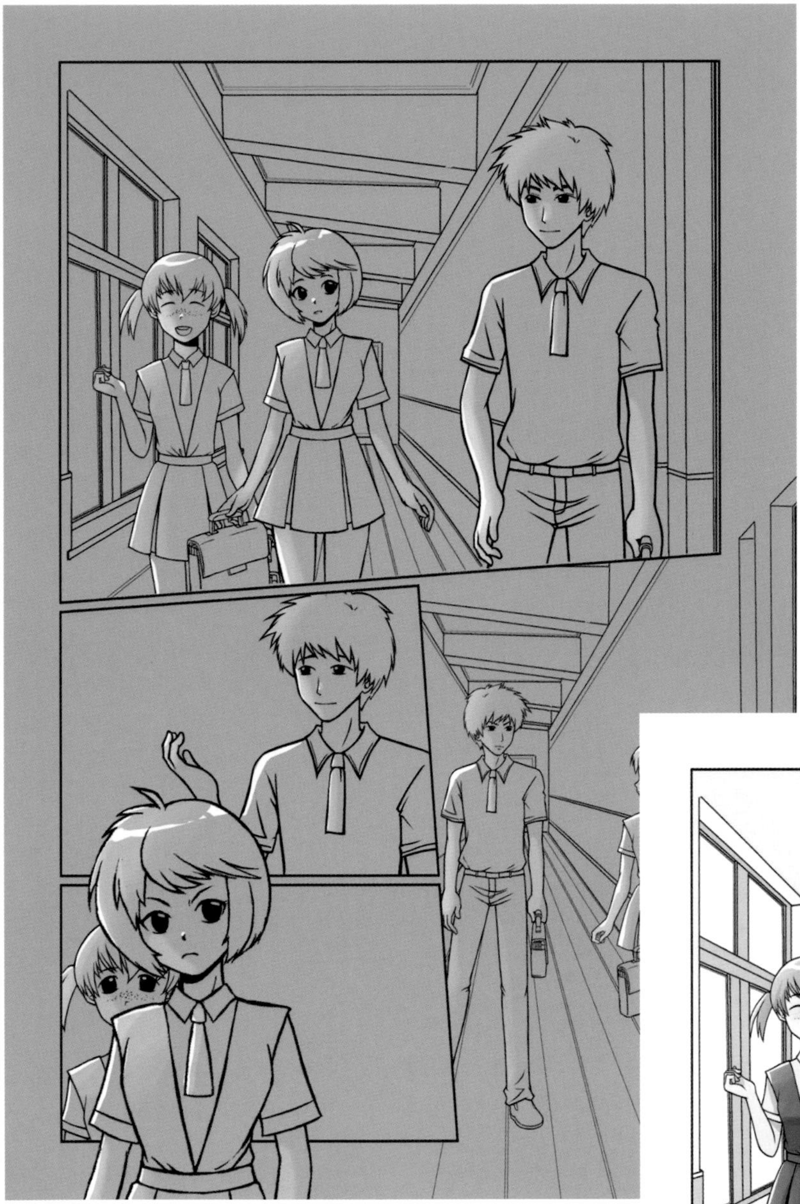

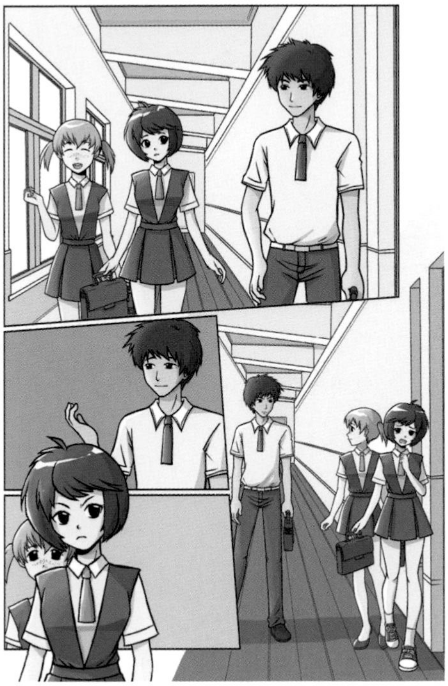

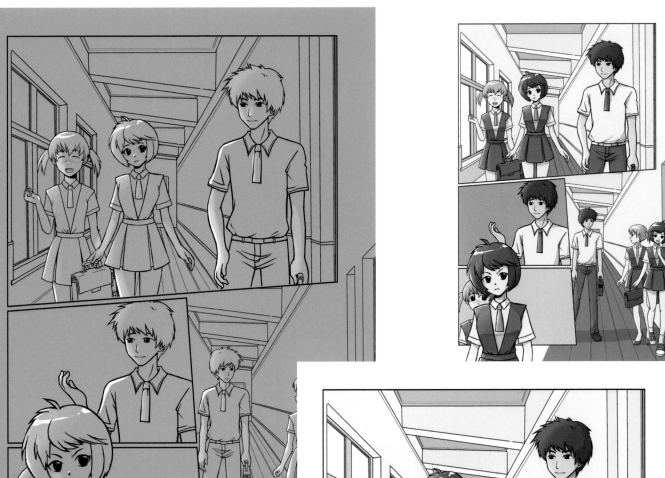

3 Create another layer, labeled strong highlights. Leave this at 100% opacity.

4 We'll now add the brightest highlights to areas such as metal, hair, and shiny areas of skin. Continue using white, and begin to add small dots, lines, and glints of white light to areas which would especially pick up the light.

5 As with the shading, it is possible to turn off the base color layer's visibility to check that your shading is accurate and that no areas have been missed.

6 Finally, add your details like the color of the briefcase clasp, turn on all the layers, and see the finished image.

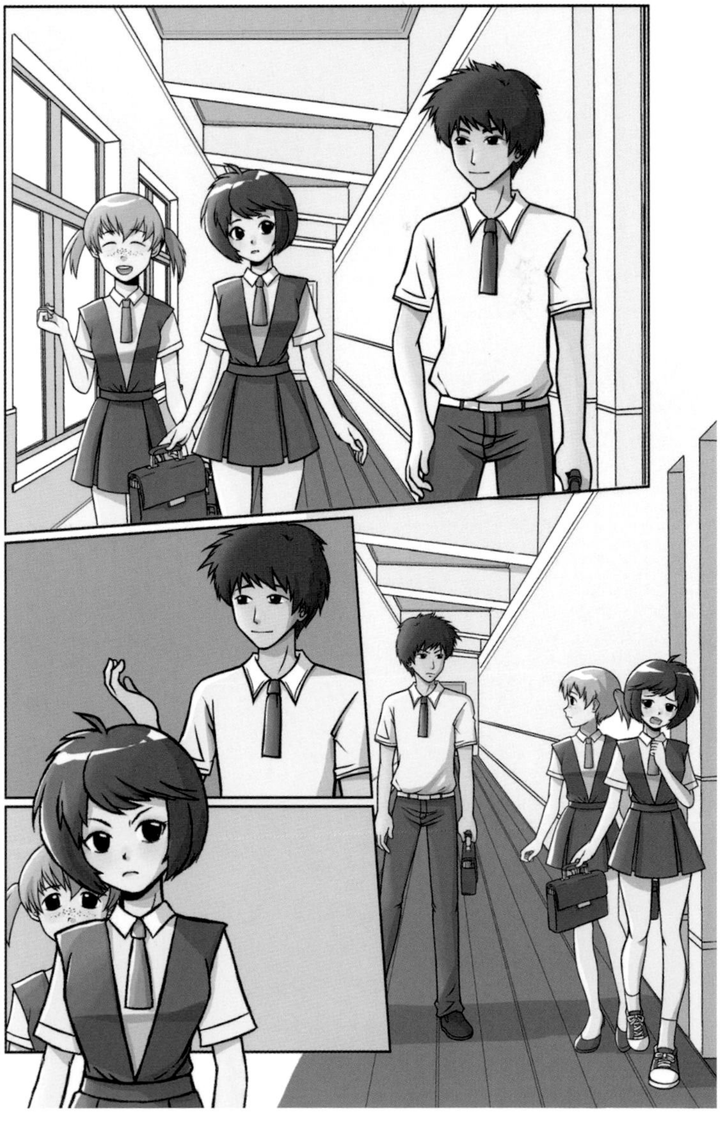

SHOUJO

NATURAL MEDIA

SIMULATED NATURAL-MEDIA COLORING IS POPULAR WITH MANGA ARTISTS IN BOTH JAPAN AND THE WEST. THE EFFECT ADDS BACK TO THE DIGITAL PROCESS THE TEXTURES AND FLAWS OFTEN SEEN IN REAL PAINTINGS, GIVING YOUR ART A MORE FLUID AND WARM LOOK, AS OPPOSED TO DIGITAL PERFECTION. THERE ARE SEVERAL PROGRAMS AVAILABLE SPECIFICALLY FOR NATURAL MEDIA SIMULATION, CHIEF AMONG THEM COREL PAINTER, BUT PHOTOSHOP AND PHOTOSHOP ELEMENTS BOTH RISE TO THE TASK ADMIRABLY.

Layers
Normal
Opacity: 100%
Lock:
line-art
color
base

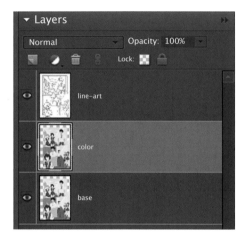

1 After blocking in basic colors in the base layer, duplicate the layer (right-click on the layer and select Duplicate Layer or click Layer > Duplicate Layer). Call the duplicate color and leave its mode on normal. Move the color layer above your base layer. Keep the original base layer, as it will help you select areas of color with the Magic Wand tool later. You will be doing all of your painting work on the new duplicate. Remember not to use the Eraser tool to correct mistakes on the color layer, as it will just erase through to the layer below. If you need to correct mistakes, use the Paint Brush tool to paint over the fault with the original color.

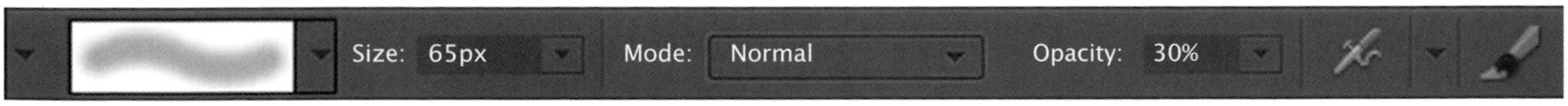
Size: 65px
Mode: Normal
Opacity: 30%

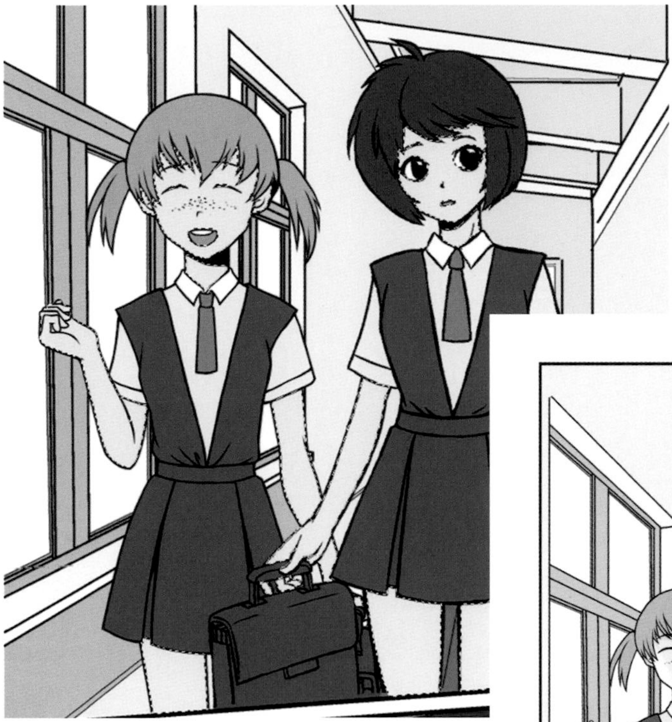

2 Select the skin color using the Magic Wand with Contiguous unchecked. Choose a color that's a few shades darker than the skin tone (not gray!). You will be shading using the Paint Brush tool, so select a soft tip brush and set the opacity to roughly 30%.

3 You can paint directly onto the color layer within your Magic Wand selection (selecting each area of color like this keeps your shading inside the lines). Because the opacity is only 30%, you can build the darker color up gradually, painting more in the places that should have the darker shadows; even adjusting the opacity down further for lighter areas of shadow. Remember to be consistent with your light source. If you think the shadows are not dark enough, simply choose an even darker skin tone. As an alternative working method, you may find it easier to pick the darkest tone you are looking for, and work back to the light, painting over the areas of darkness with each new, lighter color.

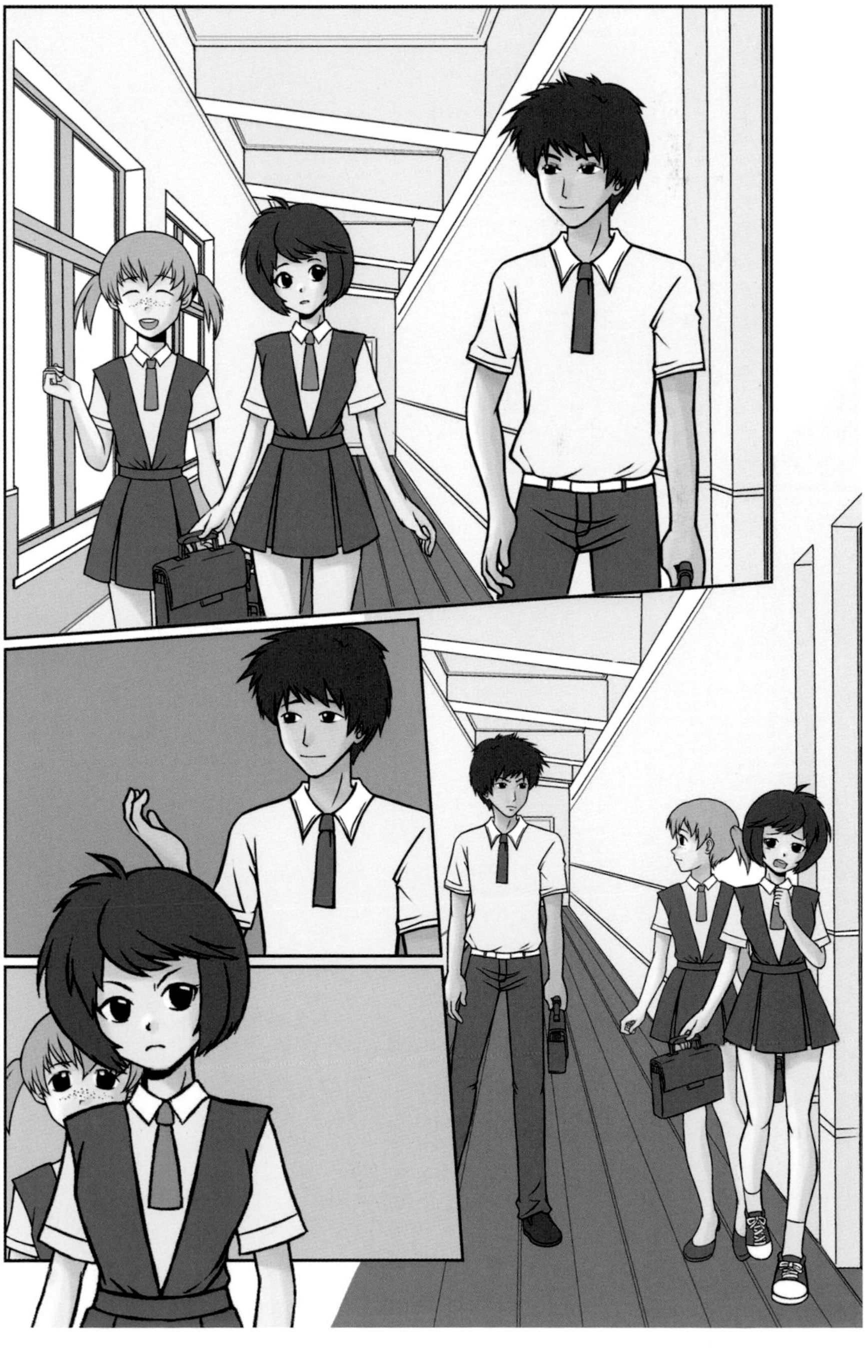

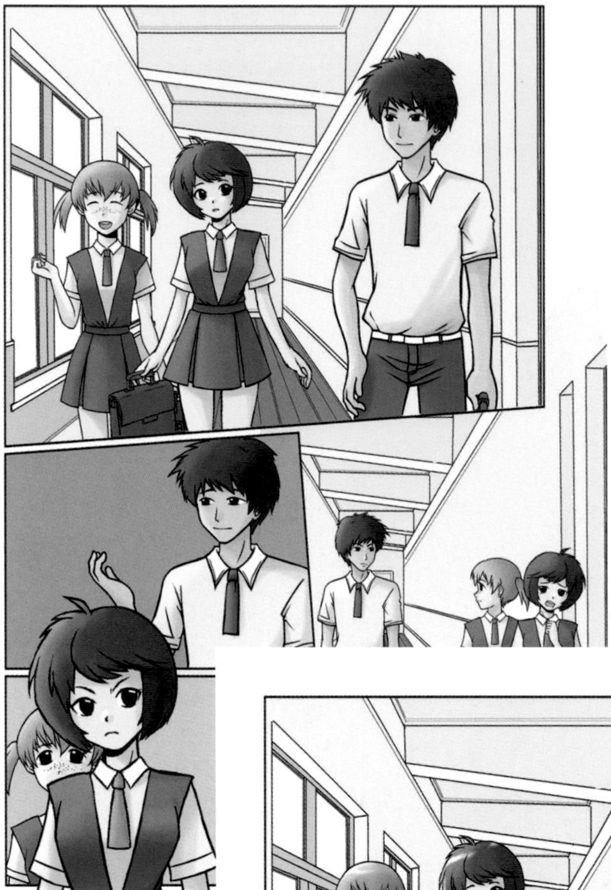

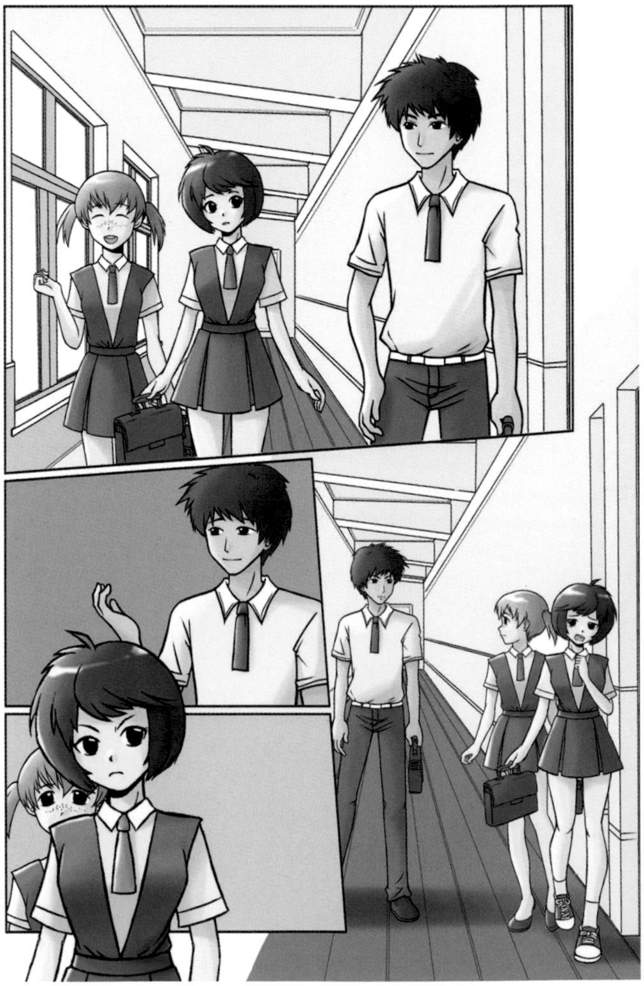

4 Back to our original method. Once the shadows are complete, choose a color lighter than the original skin tone and paint the highlighted parts of the skin, once more using a soft-tipped Brush at low opacity to build the highlights up gradually.

5 Once the skin tones are complete, repeat the process for the other parts of the picture, paying attention to the types of material you are painting, and how reflective or shiny they might be. Don't forget to adjust the Hue/Saturation on areas of color to tweak them until you're satisfied. This is where keeping your base color layer comes in handy, as your painted areas of color will now be difficult to accurately select with the Magic Wand. Just click back to the base layer, select the area of flat color you want to adjust, then flip back to the color layer and alter as necessary.

6 When you finish coloring your image, you can add your strong highlights. Create a new layer on top of the color layer, name it highlights, and leave the mode as Normal. Pick a hard-tipped Brush and set the opacity to 80%–100%, then paint in the bright highlights to finish off your piece.

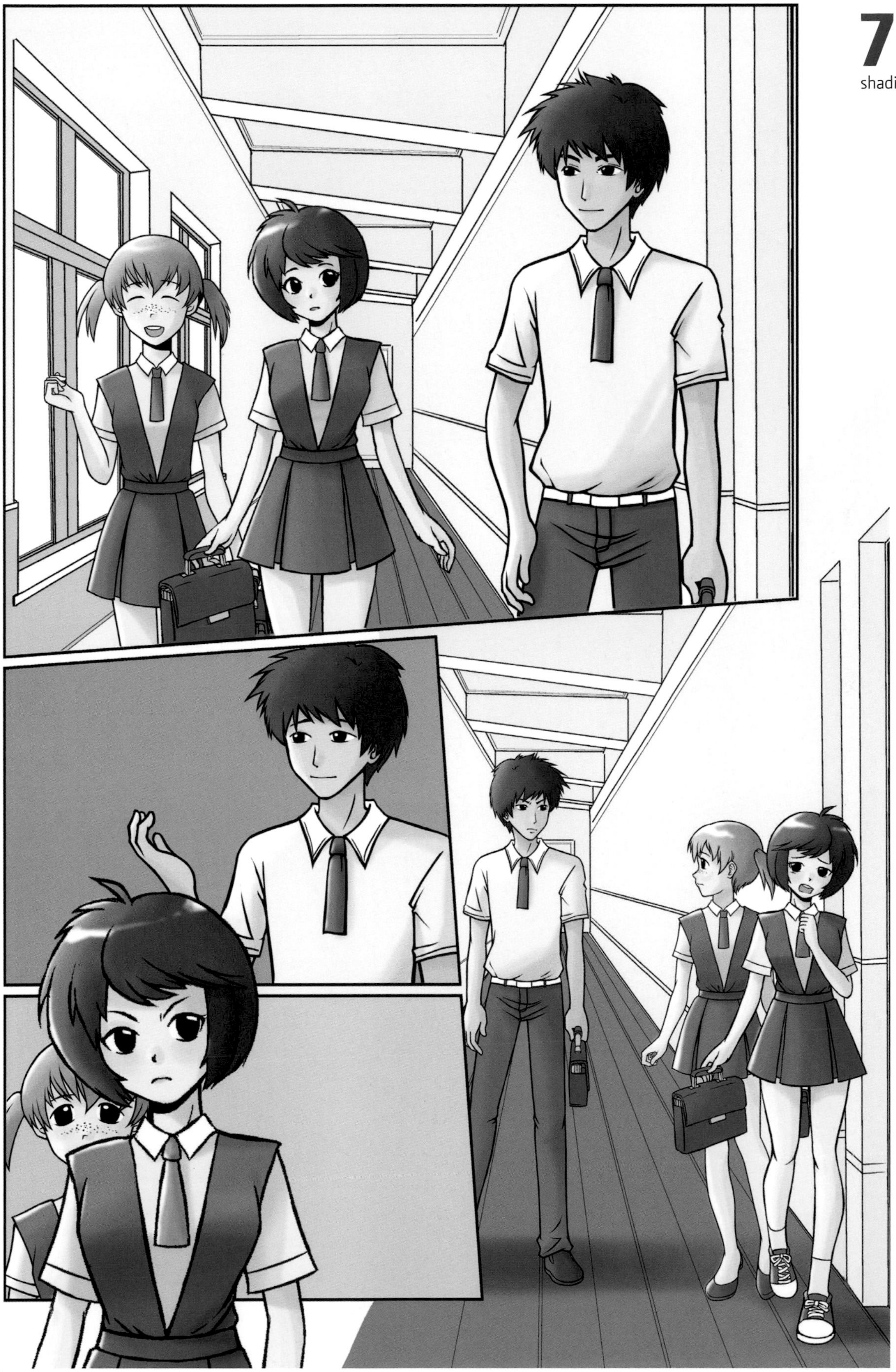

7 Finally, as before with cel shading, add the small details.

SHOUJO
DESIGNING COVER ART

THE COVER OF YOUR SHOUJO MANGA MASTERPIECE WILL TELL PROSPECTIVE READERS A LOT ABOUT YOUR BOOK, JUST BY LOOKING AT IT, AND HOW WELL YOUR COVER CAPTURES THEIR ATTENTION IS THE DIFFERENCE BETWEEN THEM PICKING IT UP, AND THEM DECIDING TO READ SOMETHING ELSE. WHEN YOUR STORY IS COMPLETE, YOUR PAGES ARE TONED, COLORED, AND LETTERED, AND THE BOOK IS ALL READY TO GO, IT'S STILL WORTH SPENDING THAT EXTRA BIT OF TIME PERFECTING YOUR COVER.

The most common cover design for manga is a pin-up image of your main characters. Your cover should suggest some of the relationships between your cast, although you don't have much space in which to do so, and no panel-to-panel action by which to communicate it. This is a perfect opportunity to really hone your characters' expressions—is your female lead rolling her eyes at the attention she's getting from two goofy boys, or is she casting longing glances at a boy whose attention is caught by a flashy sports car? To suggest emotional states or add some humor, you may want to add some chibi characters jumping behind your serious leads. You may be surprised how much of a story you can tell with a single image!

Some manga books may get away with blank backgrounds on the covers, but the majority of them get a little more creative. The background doesn't have to be complicated—often an abstract pattern or a single solid color will be sufficient—but you may want to anchor your characters in real location with a drawing of a building or place. Why not add excitement to your picture by placing your illustrated characters into a photographic background you have taken? To create a background, simply add another layer underneath the base layer and either paint on it or import an image into the space.

FINISHING OFF!

NOW YOUR VERY OWN MANGA BOOK IS ALMOST DONE, CONGRATULATIONS! IT'S TIME TO PUBLISH YOUR MASTERWORK AND START SCOURING FOR READERS.

File
Edit
Image
Enhance
Layer
Select
Tolerance: 32
P60_01.-sd @ 33.3% (bas
Image Size... Alt+Ctrl+I
Canvas Size...
Reveal All
Scale
Rotate
Transform
Crop
Divide Scanned Photos
Resize
Mode
Convert Color Profile
Magic Extractor... Alt+Shi

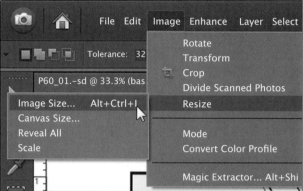

1 If you want to publish your title online, you'll need to save your pages as JPEGs. Open the PSD file and click File > Save as and choose JPEG as the saving format. If the JPEG file is too big to upload (you'll probably want a file size of between 500K and 1MB), change the image size by clicking Image > Resize> Image Size and set the resolution to a lower number. Screen resolution is 72 dpi. Now you can upload it online and share it with your friends!

Image Size
Learn more about: Image Size
OK
Cancel
Help
Pixel Dimensions: 41.8M
Width: 3160 pixels
Height: 4618 pixels
Document Size:
Width: 111.48 cm
Height: 162.91 cm
Resolution: 72 pixels/inch
Scale Styles
Constrain Proportions
Resample Image: Bicubic

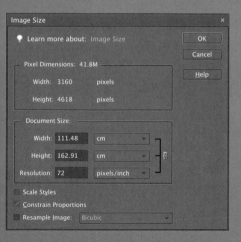

2 If you want to print your book out, simply open the PSD file you want to print and click File > Print. In the pop up window, set the scale to 100% and select Print on the right. Don't try to resize these manga pages, as this might create moiré patterns with your graytones.

SHOJO

02 //
THE CATALOG

ONCE YOU HAVE DECIDED ON YOUR STORY AND
SCRIPT, YOU NEED TO PICK YOUR CHARACTERS AND
THE COMPONENTS FOR YOUR STRIP. THE CATALOG ACTS
AS A GALLERY OF IMAGES FOR YOU TO CHOOSE FROM,
AND THE CHARACTERS SECTION LISTS WHICH OF THE
PHOTOSHOP LAYERS HAVE BEEN USED TO CREATE EACH
VARIATION, IN BOTH FRONT AND SIDE PROFILES.

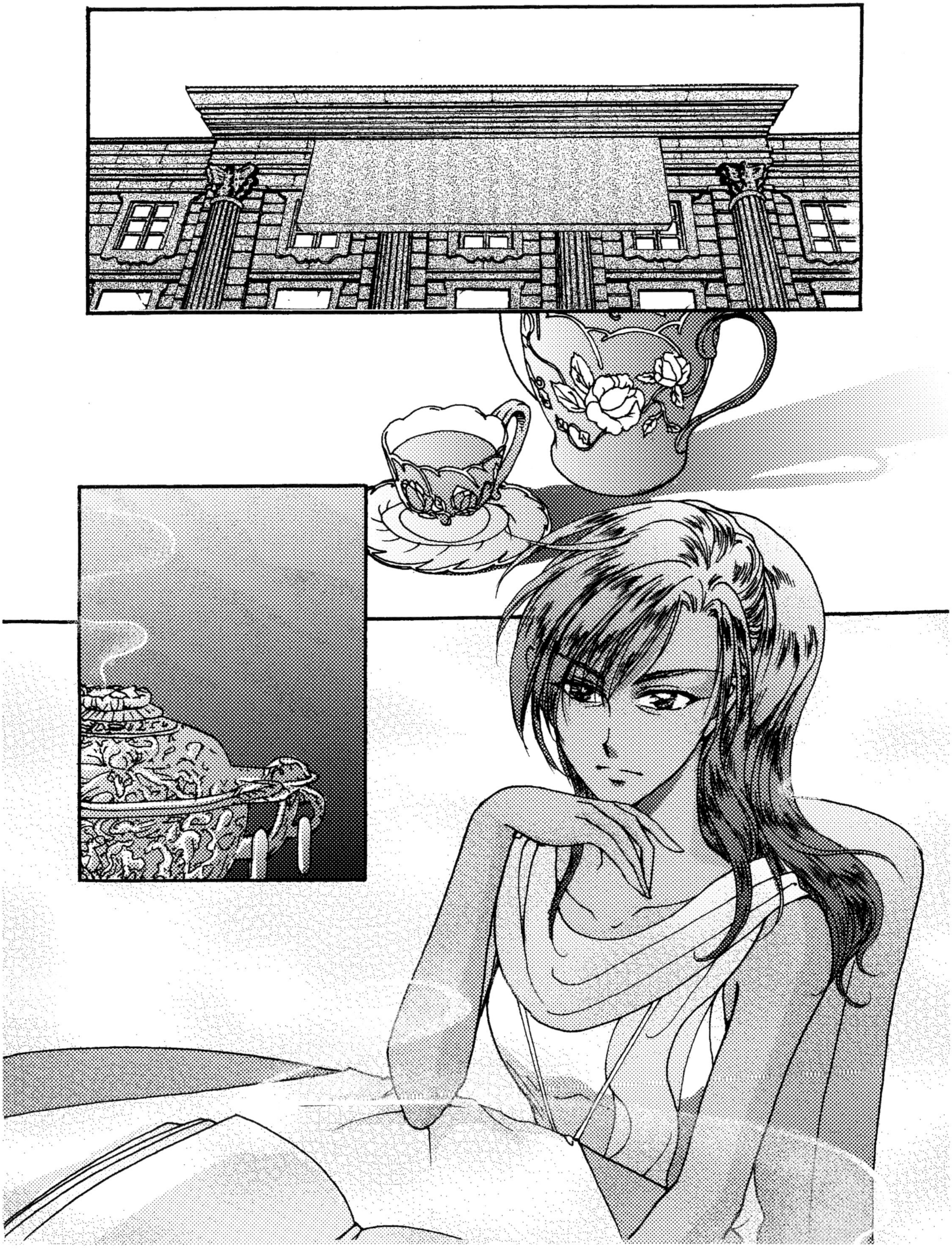

SHOUJO
FEMALE LEAD CHARACTERS

THE FEMALE LEAD IS THE MOST IMPORTANT CHARACTER IN YOUR STORY. YOU CAN CUSTOMIZE HER INTO MANY DIFFERENT LOOKS USING THE DOZENS OF LAYERS INCLUDED—COMBINING VARIOUS ACCESSORIES, HAIRSTYLES, OUTFITS, AND EXPRESSIONS.

FRONT LAYERS

- accessory1
- accessory2
- accessory3
- accessory4
- hair1
- hair2
- hair3
- eyes1
- eyes2
- eyes3
- eyes4
- mouth1
- mouth2
- mouth3
- mouth4
- mouth5
- head
- right arm1
- right arm2
- right arm3
- left arm1
- left arm2
- left arm3
- arms4
- bicycle
- outfit1
- outfit2
- outfit3
- outfit4
- outfit5
- outfit6
- outfit7
- outfit8
- outfit9
- outfit sitting1
- outfit sitting2
- outfit sitting3
- outfit sitting4
- outfit sitting5
- legs1
- legs2
- legs3
- legs4
- legs5
- legs6
- legs7
- legs8
- body

SIDE LAYERS

- accessory1
- accessory2
- accessory3
- accessory4
- hair1
- hair2
- hair3
- eyes1
- eyes2
- eyes3
- eyes4
- mouth1
- mouth2
- mouth3
- mouth4
- mouth5
- head
- outfit sleeve1
- outfit sleeve2
- outfit sleeve3
- outfit sleeve4
- left arm1
- left arm2
- left arm3
- left arm4
- outfit1
- outfit2
- outfit3
- outfit4
- outfit5
- outfit6
- outfit7
- outfit8
- outfit9
- outfit sitting1
- outfit sitting2
- outfit sitting3
- outfit sitting4
- outfit sitting5

- legs1
- legs2
- legs3
- legs4
- legs5
- legs6
- legs7
- legs8
- body
- right arm1
- right arm2
- bicycle

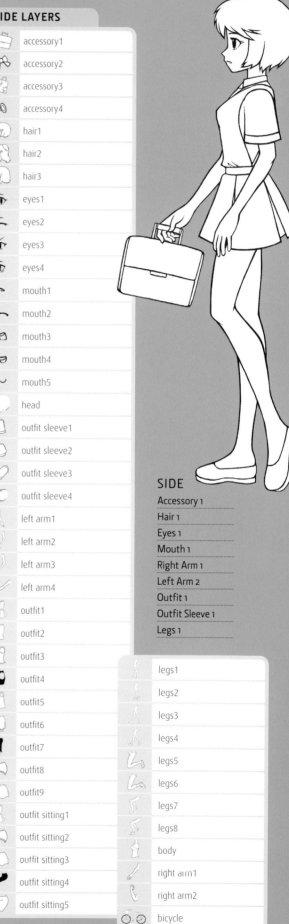

SCHOOLGIRL
FRONT

Accessory	1
Hair	1
Eyes	1
Mouth	1
Right Arm	1
Left Arm	1
Outfit	1
Legs	1

SIDE

Accessory	1
Hair	1
Eyes	1
Mouth	1
Right Arm	1
Left Arm	2
Outfit	1
Outfit Sleeve	1
Legs	1

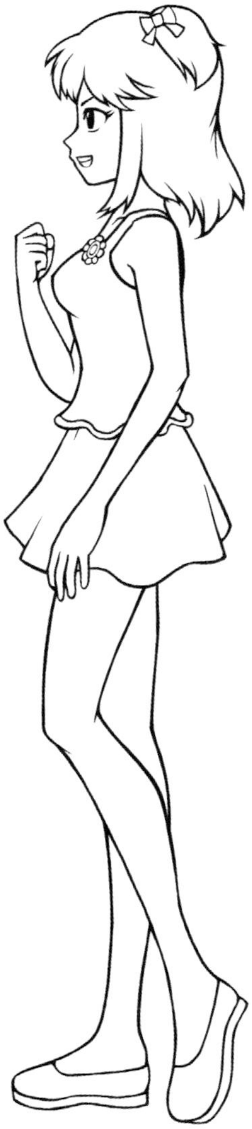

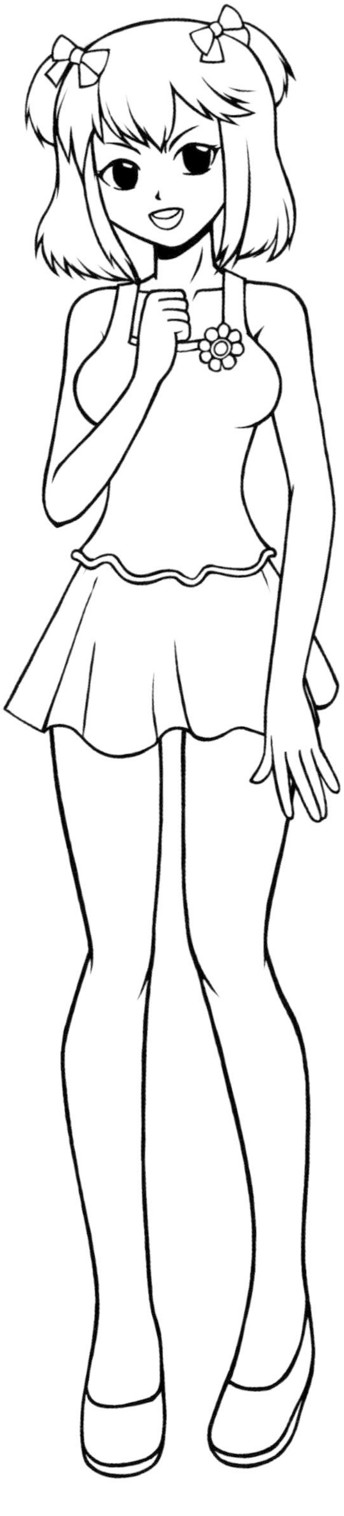

FEMININE

FRONT

- Accessory 2
- Hair 2
- Eyes 3
- Mouth 5
- Right Arm 2
- Left Arm 2
- Outfit 3 + 9
- Legs 1

SIDE

- Accessory 2
- Hair 2
- Eyes 3
- Mouth 4
- Right Arm 2
- Left Arm 2
- Outfit 3 + 9
- Legs 1

NETBALL KIT

FRONT

- Accessory 4
- Hair 3
- Eyes 4
- Mouth 2
- Arms 4
- Outfit 2 + 9
- Legs 2

SIDE

- Accessory 4
- Hair 3
- Eyes 4
- Mouth 2
- Left Arm 3
- Outfit 2 + 9
- Outfit Sleeve 4
- Legs 4

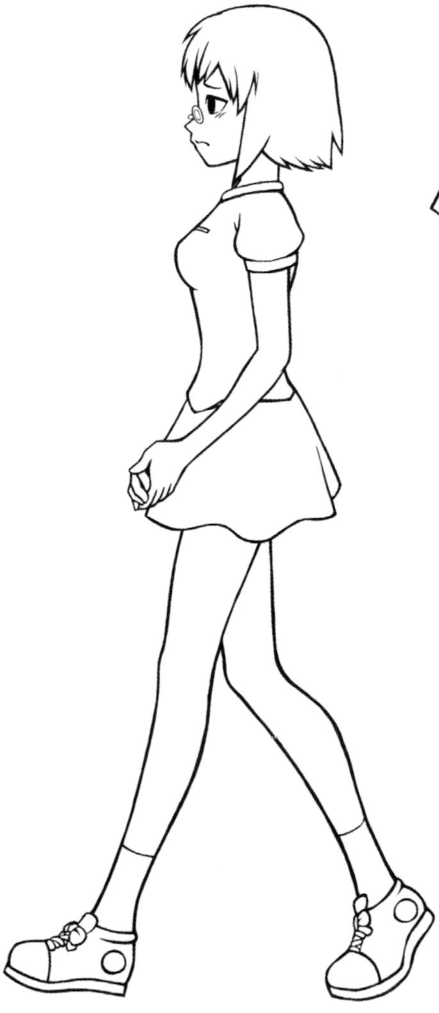

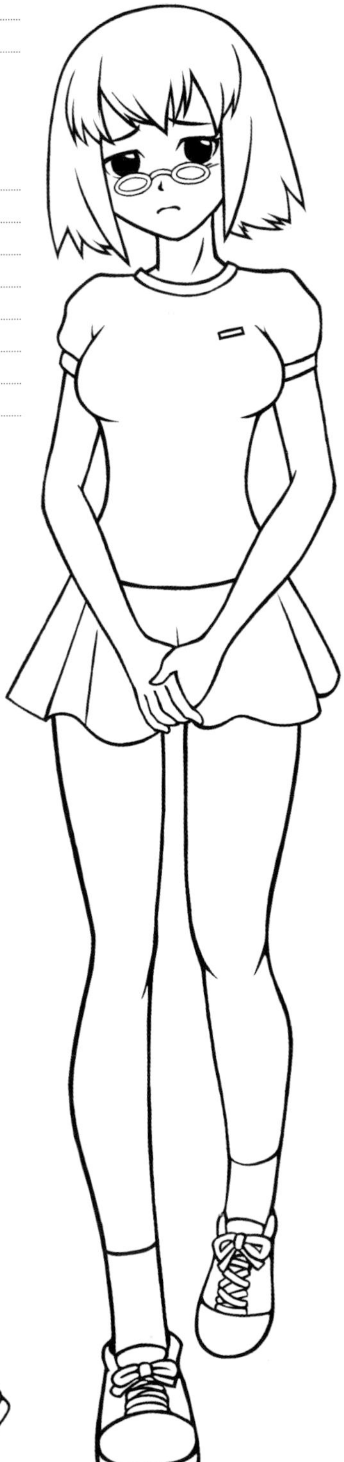

SHOUO

**SUMMER
CLOTHES**

FRONT

Hair 3

Eyes 2

Mouth 3

Arms 4

Outfit 5+ 7

Legs 2

SIDE

Hair 3

Eyes 2

Mouth 3

Left Arm 3

Outfit 5 + 7

Legs 1

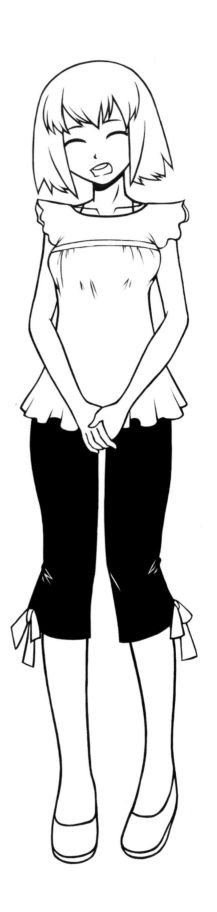

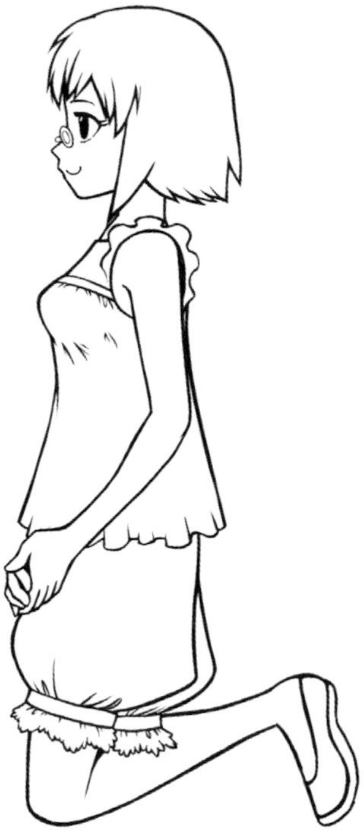

BEDTIME

FRONT

Accessory 4
Hair 3
Eyes 1
Mouth 4
Arms 4
Outfit 5 + 6
Legs 5

SIDE

Accessory 4
Hair 3
Eyes 1
Mouth 5
Left Arm 3
Outfit 5 + 6
Legs 5

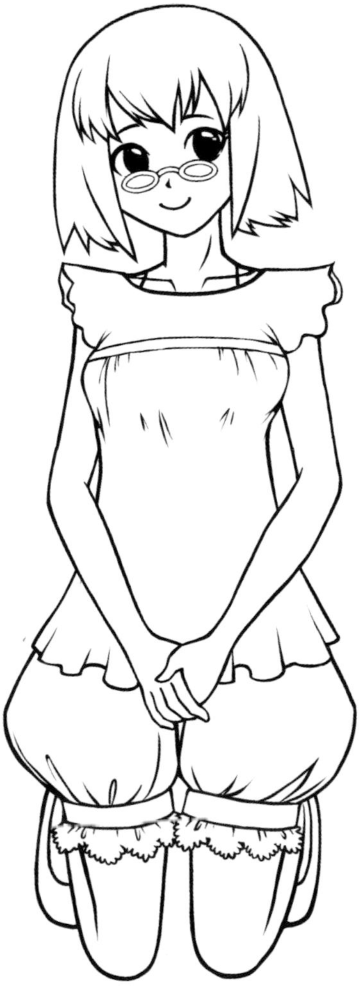

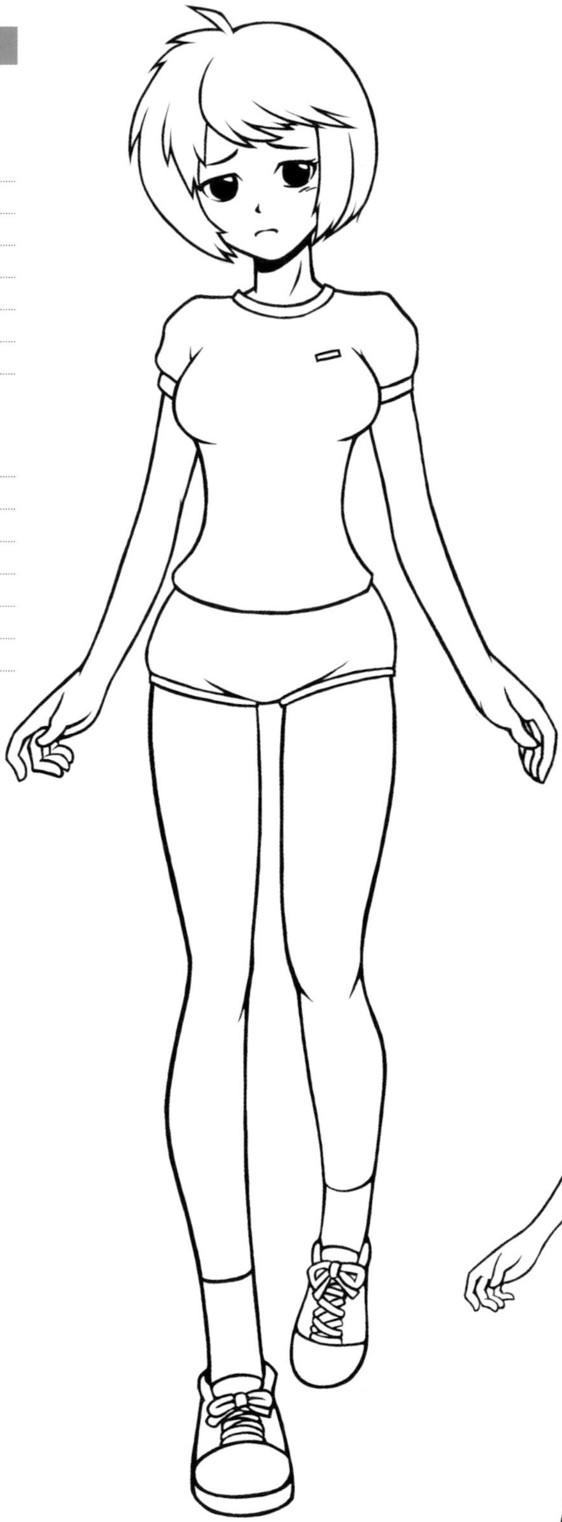

GYM GEAR

FRONT

Hair 1
Eyes 4
Mouth 2
Right Arm 1
Left Arm 1
Outfit 2 + 8
Legs 2

SIDE

Hair 1
Eyes 4
Mouth 2
Right Arm 1
Left Arm 1
Outfit 2 + 8
Outfit Sleeve 2
Legs 4

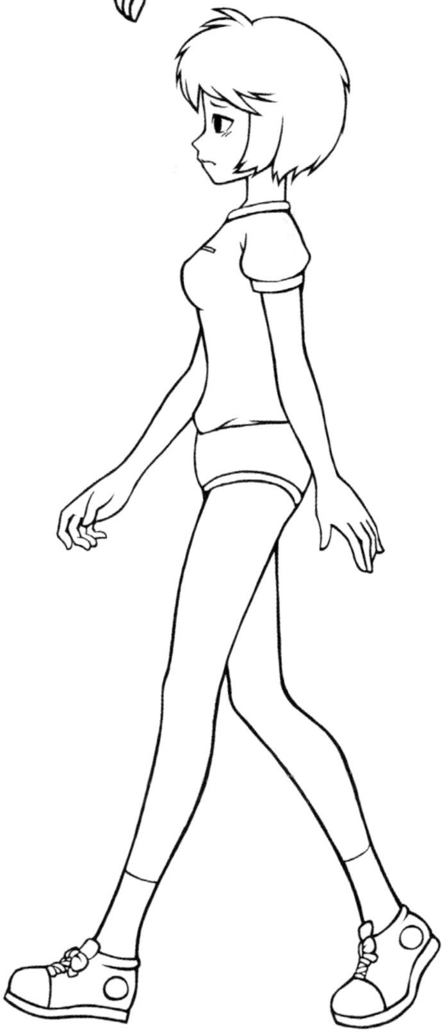

SHOUJO

WORKOUT

FRONT

- Accessory 2
- Hair 1
- Eyes 3
- Mouth 5
- Right Arm 1
- Left Arm 2
- Outfit 3 + 8
- Legs 2

SIDE

- Accessory 2
- Hair 1
- Eyes 3
- Mouth 4
- Right Arm 1
- Left Arm 2
- Outfit 3 + 8
- Legs 2

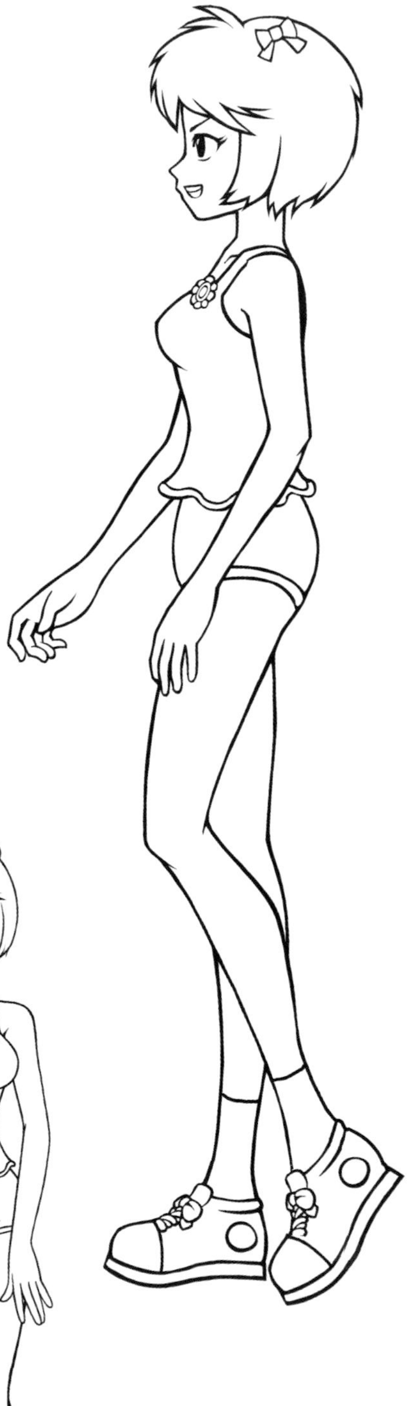

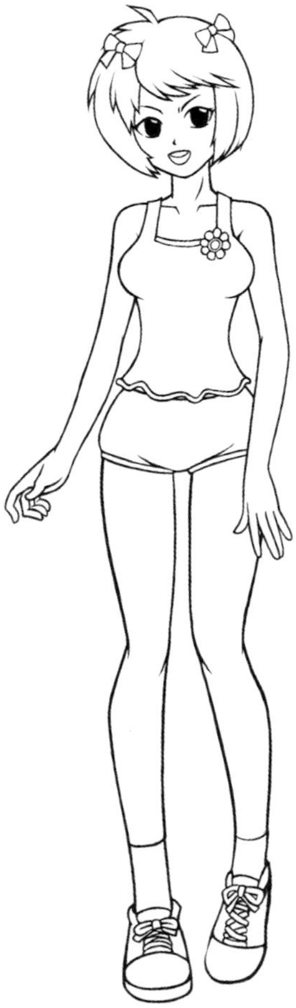

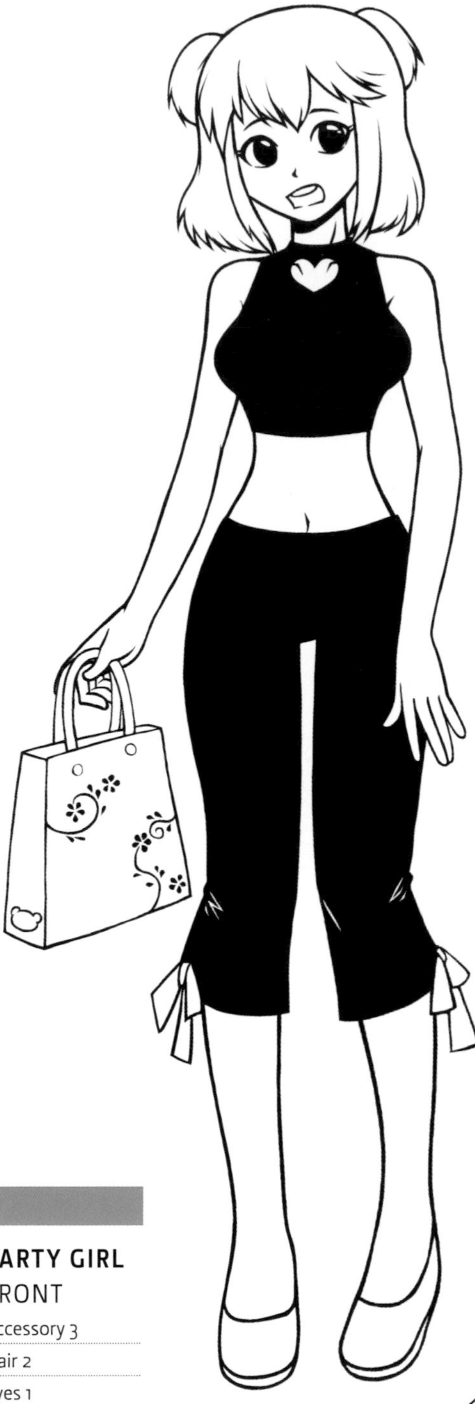

PARTY GIRL

FRONT

- Accessory 3
- Hair 2
- Eyes 1
- Mouth 3
- Right Arm 1
- Left Arm 2
- Outfit 4 + 7
- Legs 1

SIDE

- Accessory 3
- Hair 2
- Eyes 1
- Mouth 3
- Right Arm 1
- Left Arm 2
- Outfit 4 + 7
- Legs 1

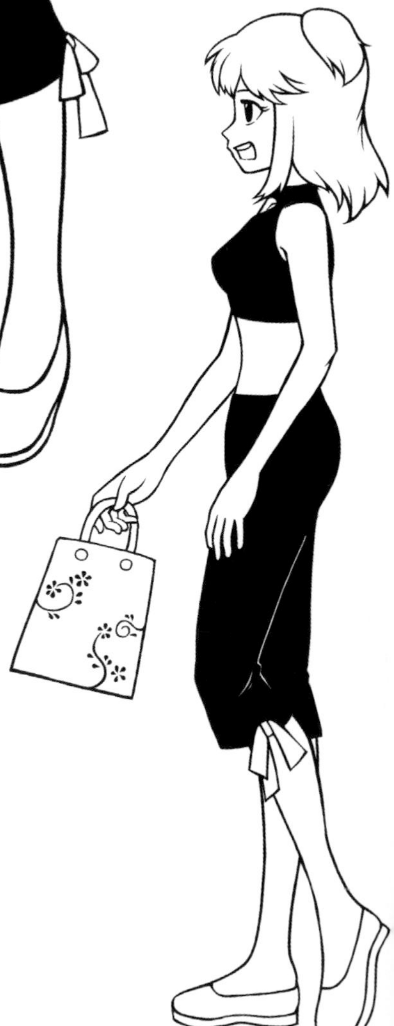

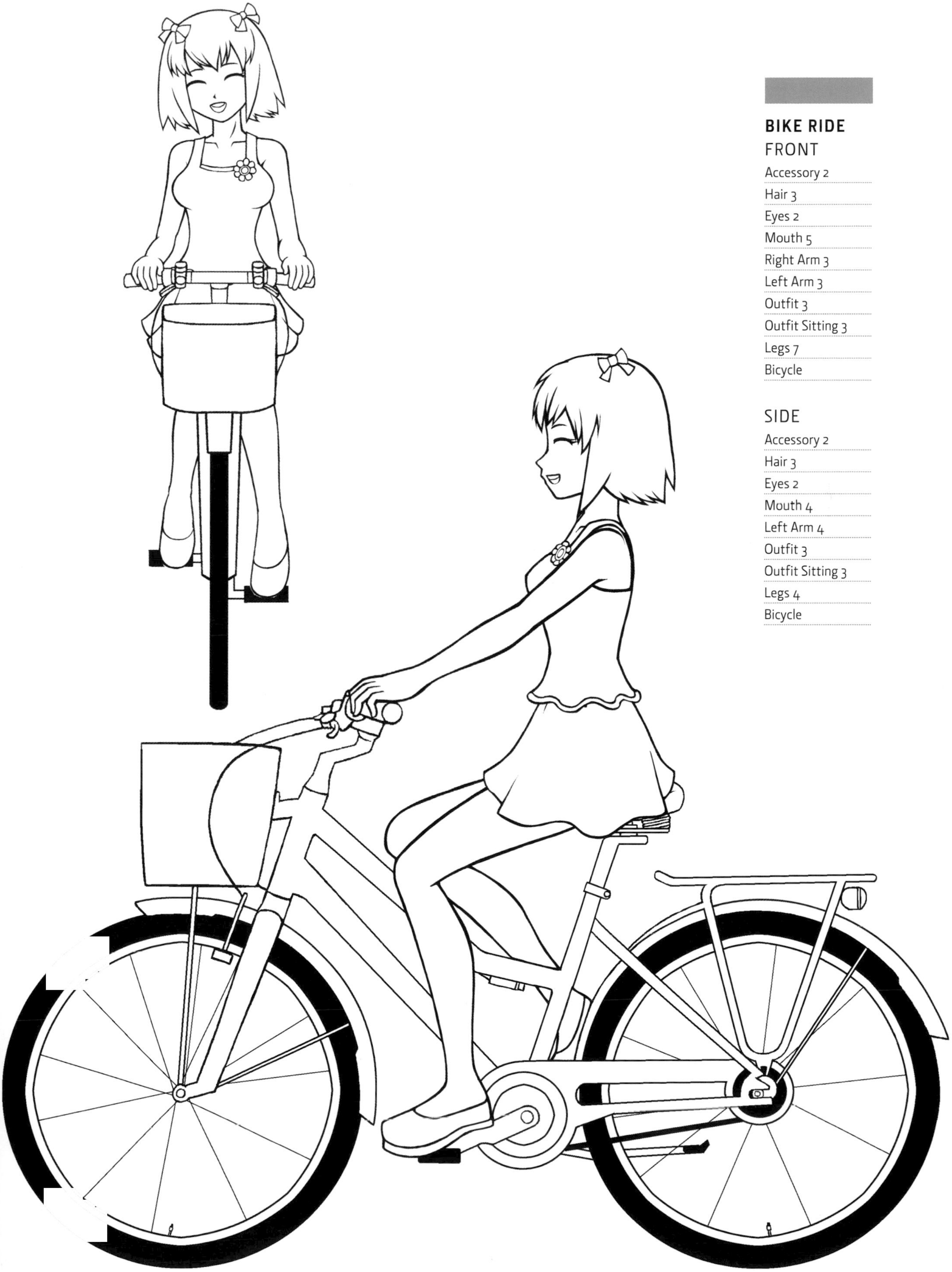

BIKE RIDE

FRONT

- Accessory 2
- Hair 3
- Eyes 2
- Mouth 5
- Right Arm 3
- Left Arm 3
- Outfit 3
- Outfit Sitting 3
- Legs 7
- Bicycle

SIDE

- Accessory 2
- Hair 3
- Eyes 2
- Mouth 4
- Left Arm 4
- Outfit 3
- Outfit Sitting 3
- Legs 4
- Bicycle

76 SHOUJO
MALE LEAD CHARACTERS

WHETHER YOUR MALE LEAD IS SPORTY, GEEKY, OR THE SINGER OF A GARAGE ROCK BAND, YOU'LL FIND THE CLOTHING AND HAIRSTYLES YOU NEED RIGHT HERE. MIX AND MATCH THE LAYERS TO CREATE THE PERFECT LOVE INTEREST FOR YOUR LEADING LADY.

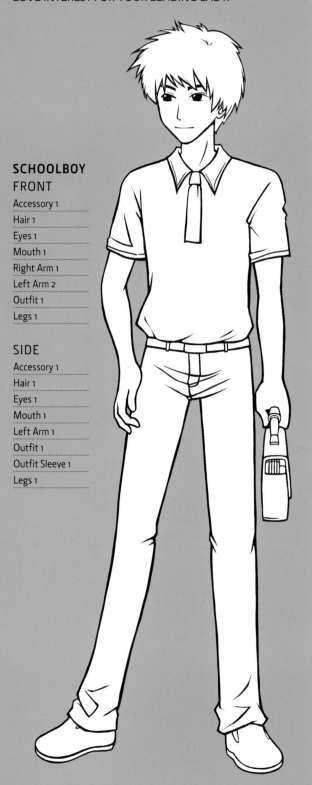

SCHOOLBOY
FRONT

Accessory 1
Hair 1
Eyes 1
Mouth 1
Right Arm 1
Left Arm 2
Outfit 1
Legs 1

SIDE

Accessory 1
Hair 1
Eyes 1
Mouth 1
Left Arm 1
Outfit 1
Outfit Sleeve 1
Legs 1

FRONT LAYERS

	bike
	accessory1
	accessory2
	accessory3
	accessory4
	hair1
	hair2
	hair3
	eyes1
	eyes2
	eyes3
	eyes4
	mouth1
	mouth2
	mouth3
	mouth4
	mouth5
	head
	outfit1
	outfit2
	outfit3
	right arm1
	right arm2
	right arm3
	left arm1
	left arm2
	left arm3
	arms4
	legs1
	legs2
	legs3
	legs4
	legs5
	legs6
	legs7
	legs8
	body

SIDE LAYERS

	accessory1
	accessory2
	accessory3
	hair1
	hair2
	hair3
	eyes1
	eyes2
	eyes3
	eyes4
	mouth1
	mouth2
	mouth3
	mouth4
	mouth5
	head
	outfit sleeve1
	outfit sleeve2
	left arm1
	left arm2
	left arm3
	left arm4
	outfit1
	outfit2
	outfit3
	legs1
	legs2
	legs3
	legs4
	legs5
	legs6
	legs7
	legs8
	body
	bike

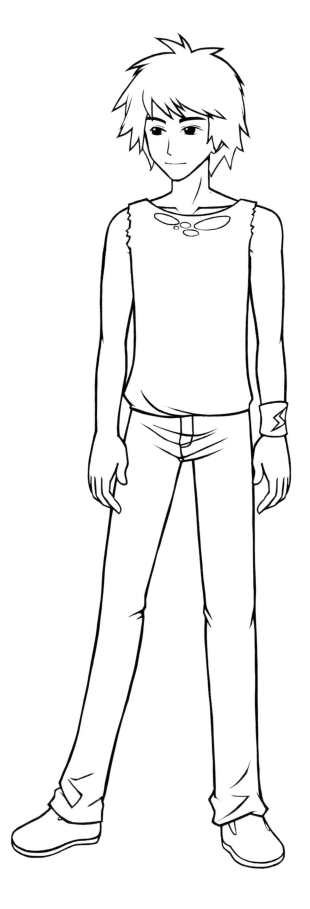

FLASH
FRONT
Accessory 2
Hair 2
Eyes 1
Mouth 1
Right Arm 2
Left Arm 1
Outfit 3
Legs 1

SIDE
Accessory 2
Hair 2
Eyes 1
Mouth 1
Left Arm 4
Outfit 3
Legs 1

SHOuJO

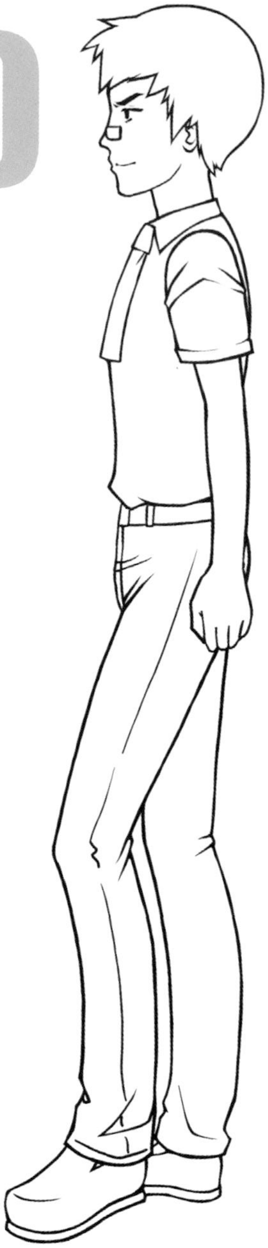

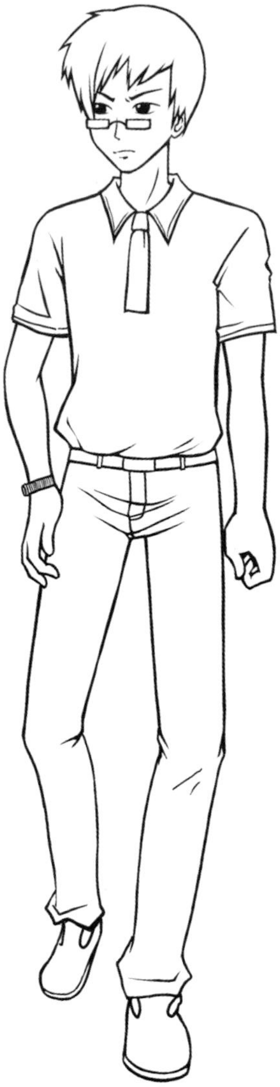

CASUAL

FRONT

- Hair 2
- Eyes 4
- Mouth 5
- Right Arm 3
- Left Arm 3
- Outfit 2
- Legs 2

SIDE

- Hair 2
- Eyes 4
- Mouth 5
- Left Arm 3
- Outfit 2
- Outfit Sleeve 2
- Legs 4

PREP

FRONT

- Accessory 3 + 4
- Hair 3
- Eyes 3
- Mouth 2
- Right Arm 1
- Left Arm 2
- Outfit 1
- Legs 3

SIDE

- Accessory 3
- Hair 3
- Eyes 3
- Mouth 1
- Left Arm 1
- Outfit 1
- Outfit Sleeve 1
- Legs 1

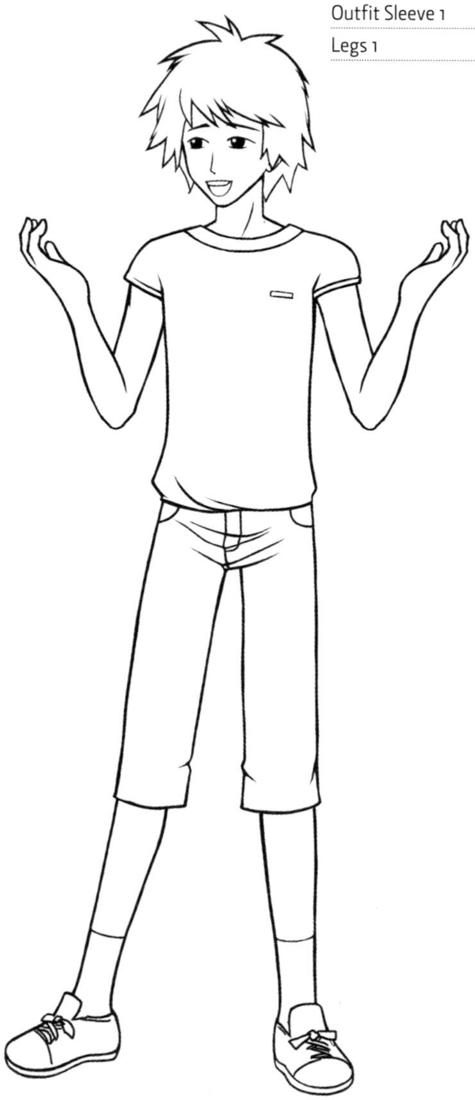

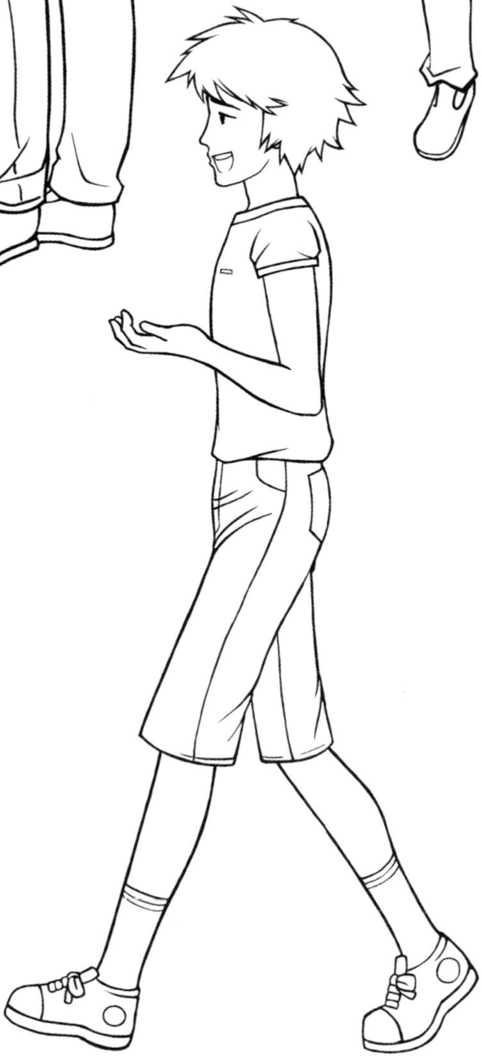

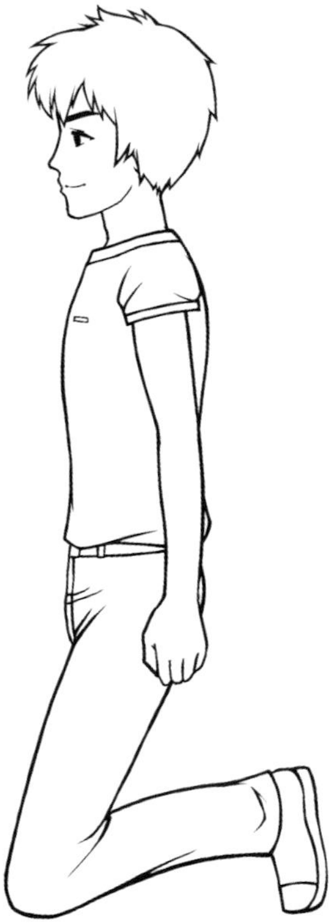

KNEELING

FRONT

- Hair 1
- Eyes 2
- Mouth 1
- Right Arm 1
- Left Arm 2
- Outfit 2
- Legs 5

SIDE

- Hair 1
- Eyes 1
- Mouth 1
- Left Arm 1
- Outfit 2
- Outfit Sleeve 2
- Legs 5

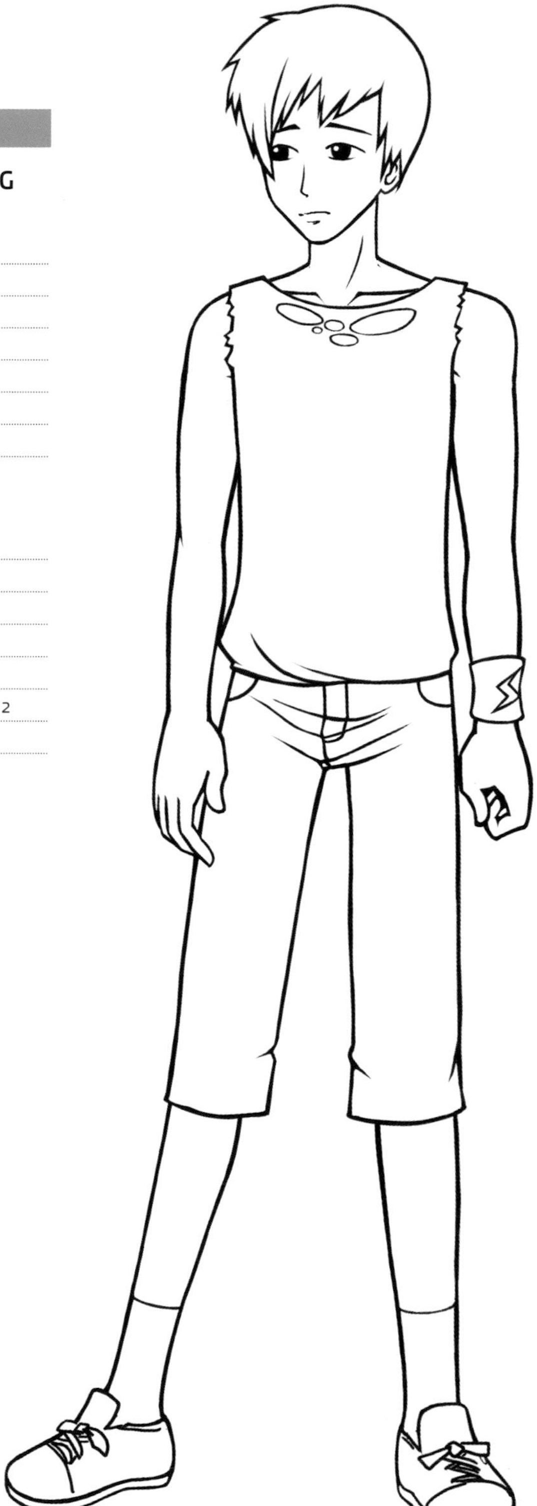

SPORTY

FRONT

- Accessory 2
- Hair 3
- Eyes 4
- Mouth 2
- Right Arm 2
- Left Arm 2
- Outfit 3
- Legs 2

SIDE

- Accessory 2
- Hair 3
- Eyes 4
- Mouth 2
- Left Arm 1
- Outfit 3
- Legs 4

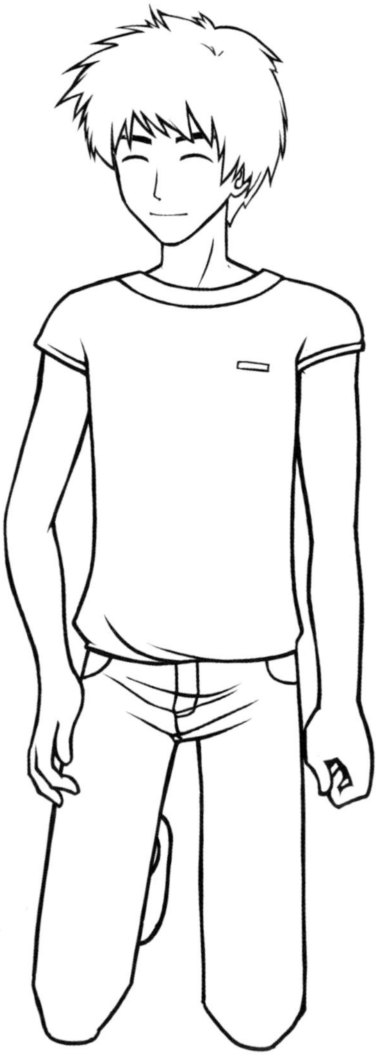

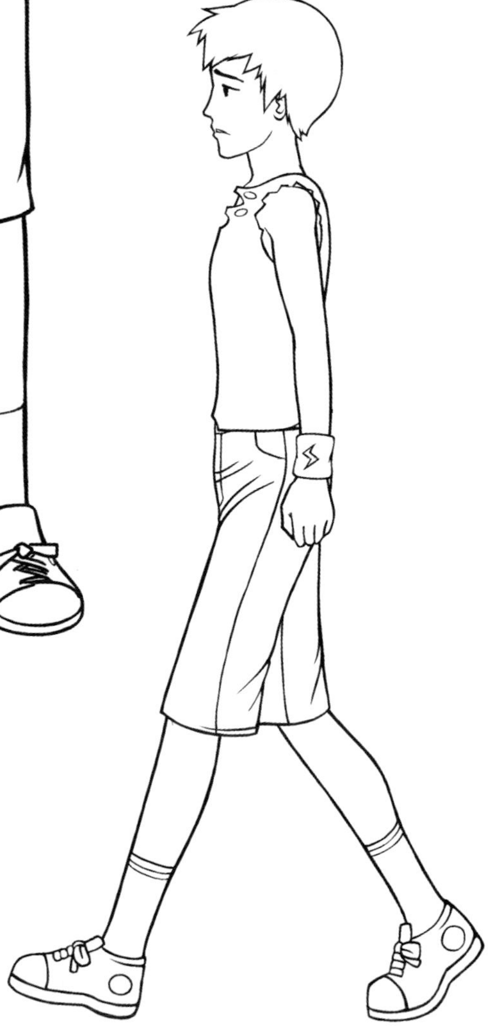

SHOJO

GEEKY
FRONT

Accessory 4

Hair 1

Eyes 4

Mouth 4

Right Arm 2

Left Arm 2

Outfit 2 + 3

Legs 4

SIDE

Accessory 3

Hair 1

Eyes 4

Mouth 4

Left Arm 1

Outfit 3

Outfit Sleeve 2

Legs 4

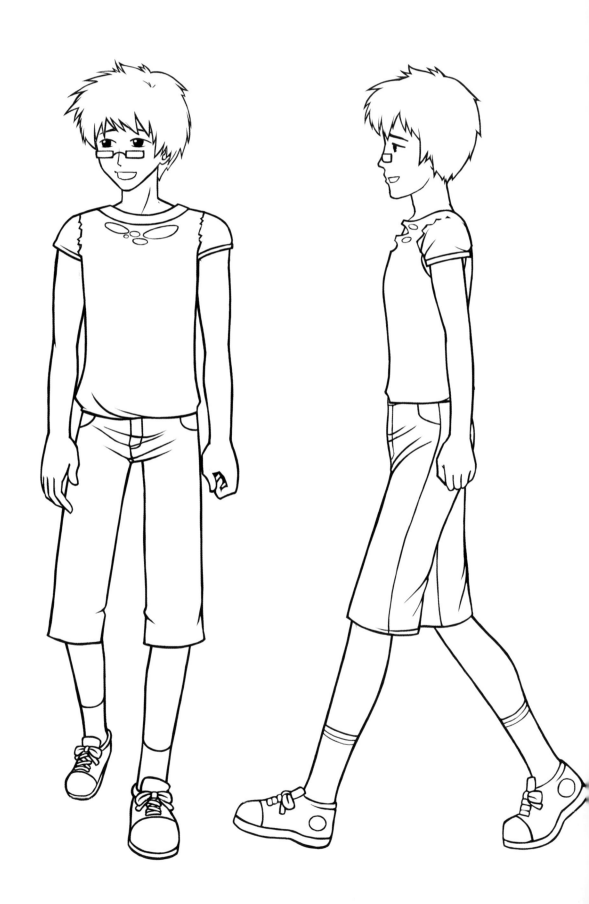

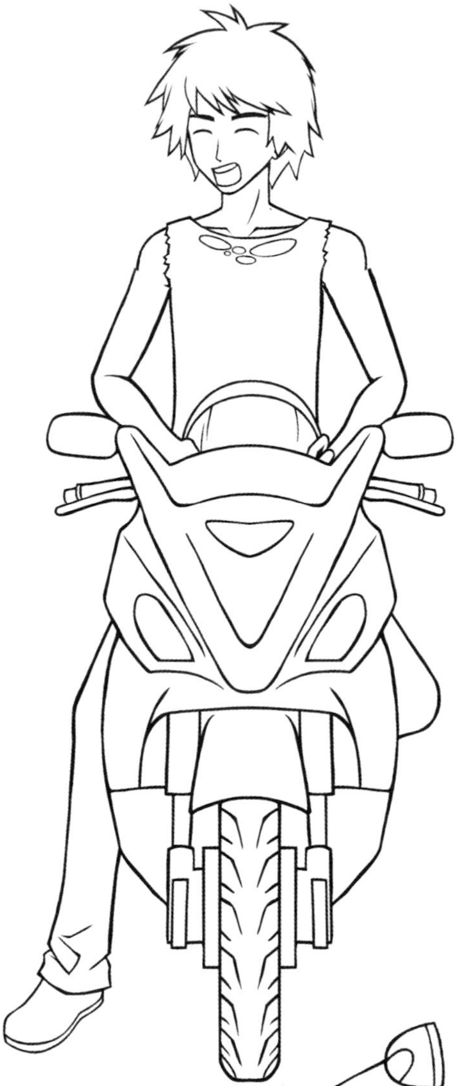

BIKER

FRONT

- Hair 2
- Eyes 2
- Mouth 3
- Arms 4
- Outfit 3
- Legs 7

SIDE

- Hair 2
- Eyes 2
- Mouth 5
- Left Arm 2
- Outfit 3
- Legs 7
- Bike

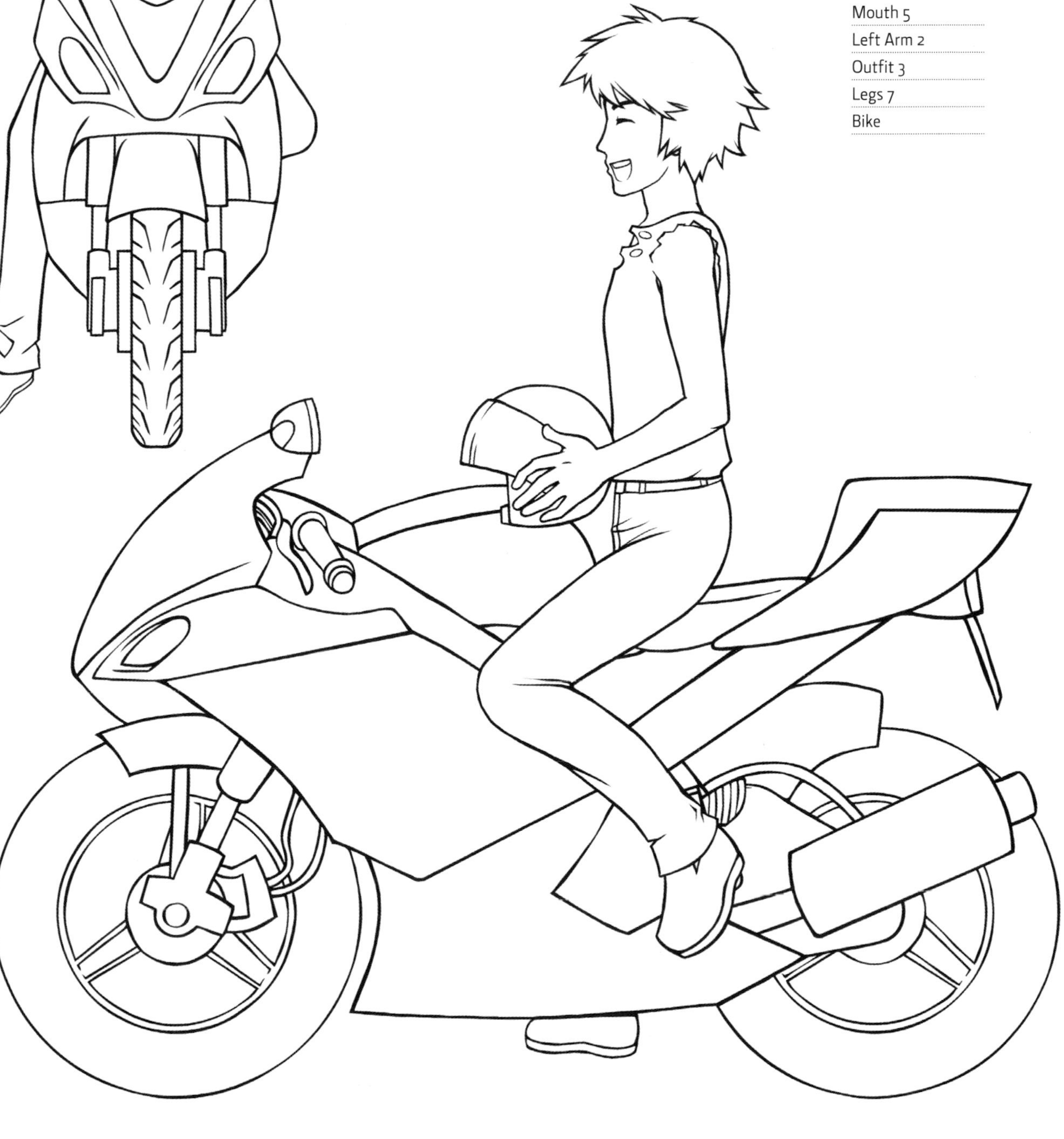

SHOUJO
SUPPORTING CHARACTERS

THE SUPPORTING CHARACTERS' FILES OFFER A RANGE OF GREAT OPTIONS FOR YOUR SECONDARY CHARACTERS. PEPPER YOUR SHOUJO STORY WITH A LOVE RIVAL FOR YOUR MAIN MALE LEAD, A YOUNG SCHOOLGIRL OR BEST FRIEND TO THE MAIN FEMALE, AND TWO PARENTAL/ SCHOOLTEACHER FIGURES, ALL WITH MIX AND MATCH ACCESSORIES AND EXPRESSIONS!

FRONT LAYERS

	accessory1
	accessory2
	eyes1
	eyes2
	eyes3
	mouth1
	mouth2
	mouth3
	mouth4
	body
	right arm1
	right arm2
	left arm1
	left arm2
	legs1
	legs2

SIDE LAYERS

	accessory1
	accessory2
	eyes1
	eyes2
	eyes3
	mouth1
	mouth2
	mouth3
	mouth4
	left arm1
	left arm2
	body
	legs1
	legs2

AT WORK
FRONT
Accessory 1
Eyes 3
Mouth 4
Right Arm 2
Left Arm 1
Legs 2

SIDE
Accessory 1
Eyes 2
Mouth 2
Left Arm 1
Legs 2

ON A DATE
FRONT
Accessory 2
Eyes 1
Mouth 1
Right Arm 1
Left Arm 2
Legs 1

SIDE
Accessory 2
Eyes 1
Mouth 1
Left Arm 2
Legs 1

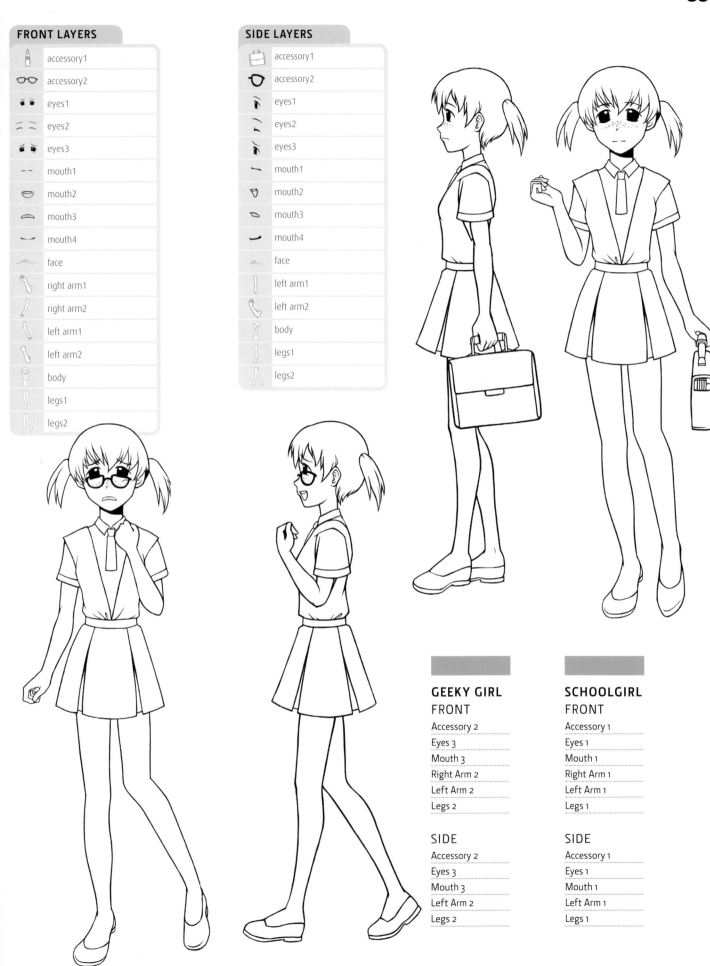

FRONT LAYERS

	accessory1
	accessory2
	eyes1
	eyes2
	eyes3
	mouth1
	mouth2
	mouth3
	mouth4
	face
	right arm1
	right arm2
	left arm1
	left arm2
	body
	legs1
	legs2

SIDE LAYERS

	accessory1
	accessory2
	eyes1
	eyes2
	eyes3
	mouth1
	mouth2
	mouth3
	mouth4
	face
	left arm1
	left arm2
	body
	legs1
	legs2

GEEKY GIRL

FRONT

Accessory 2	
Eyes 3	
Mouth 3	
Right Arm 2	
Left Arm 2	
Legs 2	

SIDE

Accessory 2	
Eyes 3	
Mouth 3	
Left Arm 2	
Legs 2	

SCHOOLGIRL

FRONT

Accessory 1	
Eyes 1	
Mouth 1	
Right Arm 1	
Left Arm 1	
Legs 1	

SIDE

Accessory 1	
Eyes 1	
Mouth 1	
Left Arm 1	
Legs 1	

SHOUJO

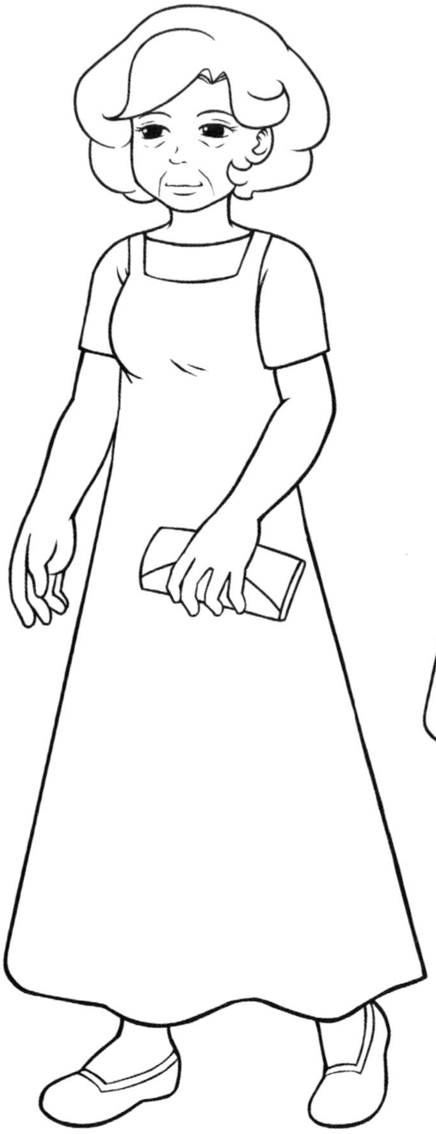

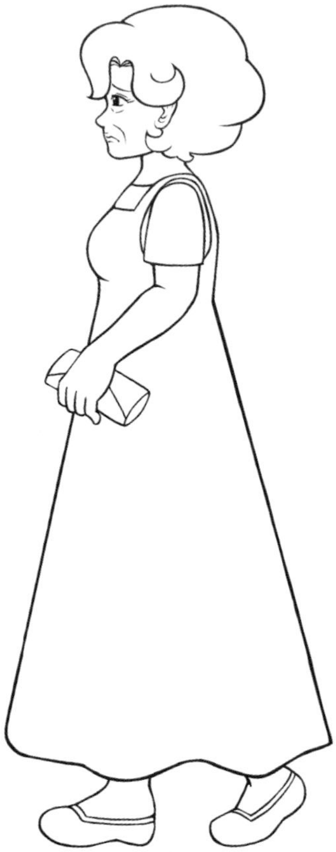

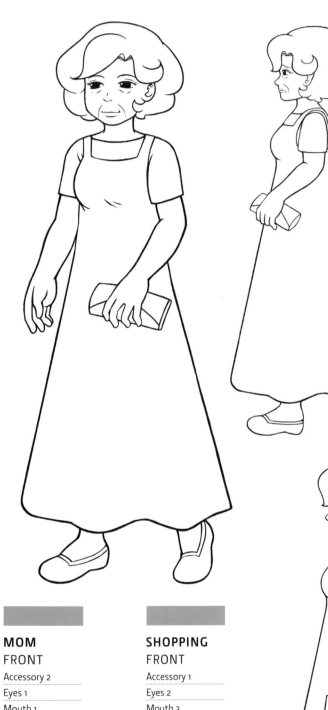

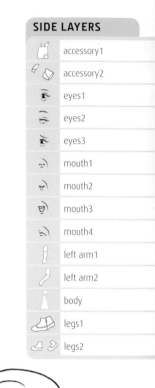

FRONT LAYERS

accessory1
accessory2
eyes1
eyes2
eyes3
mouth1
mouth2
mouth3
mouth4
right arm1
right arm2
left arm1
left arm2
body
legs1
legs2

SIDE LAYERS

accessory1
accessory2
eyes1
eyes2
eyes3
mouth1
mouth2
mouth3
mouth4
left arm1
left arm2
body
legs1
legs2

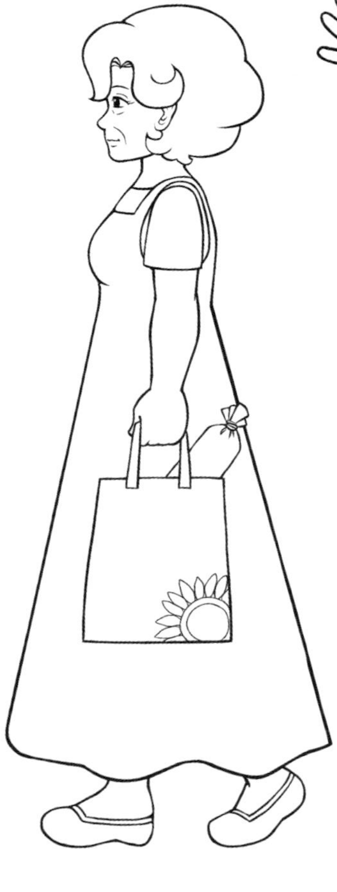

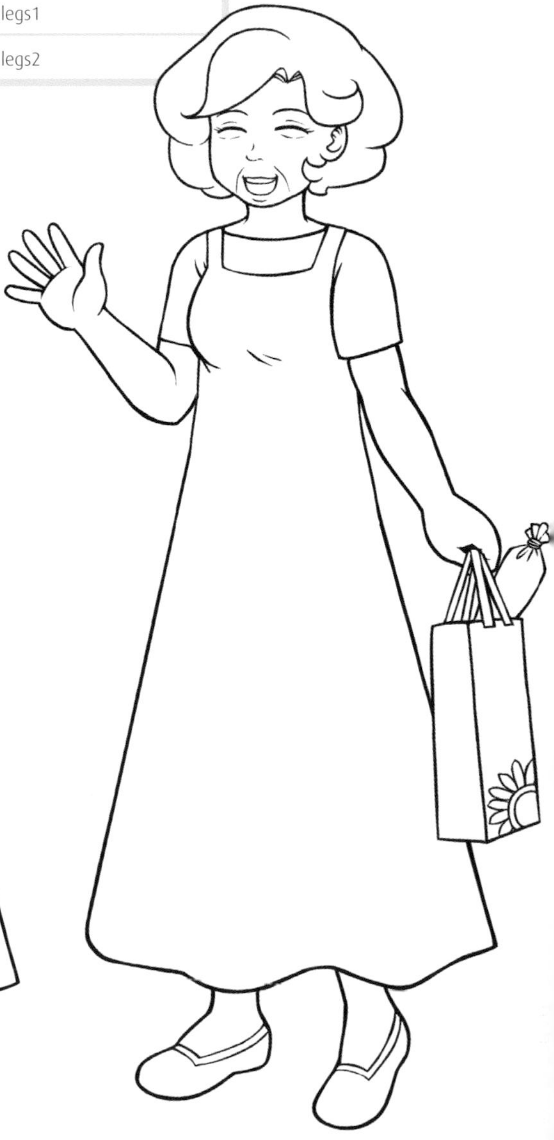

MOM

FRONT

- Accessory 2
- Eyes 1
- Mouth 1
- Right Arm 2
- Left Arm 2
- Legs 2

SIDE

- Accessory 2
- Eyes 3
- Mouth 4
- Left Arm 2
- Legs 2

SHOPPING

FRONT

- Accessory 1
- Eyes 2
- Mouth 3
- Right Arm 1
- Left Arm 1
- Legs 1

SIDE

- Accessory 1
- Eyes 1
- Mouth 1
- Left Arm 1
- Legs 2

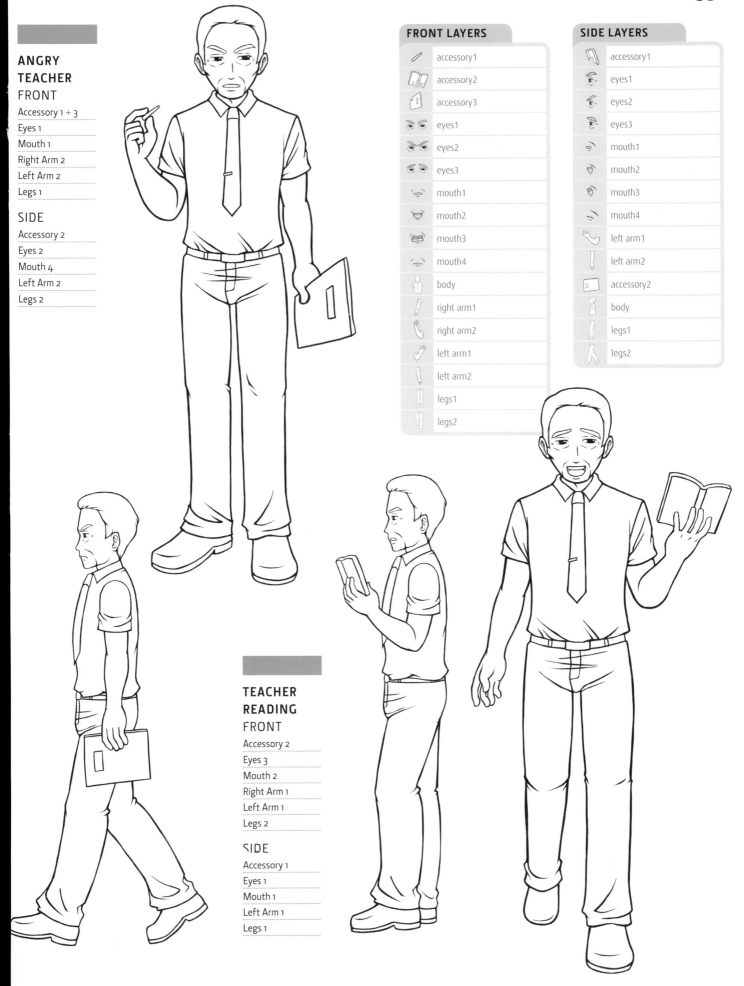

ANGRY TEACHER

FRONT

- Accessory 1 + 3
- Eyes 1
- Mouth 1
- Right Arm 2
- Left Arm 2
- Legs 1

SIDE

- Accessory 2
- Eyes 2
- Mouth 4
- Left Arm 2
- Legs 2

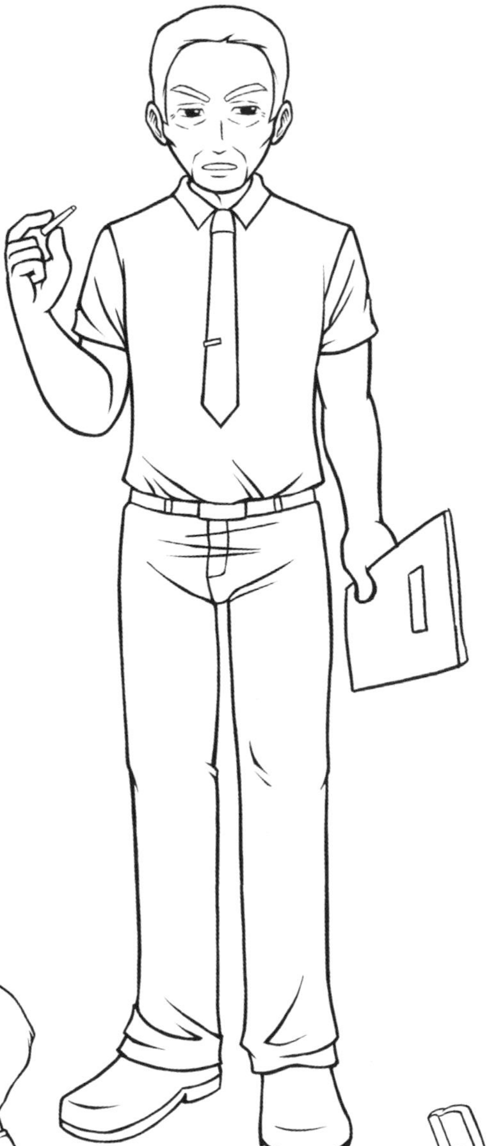

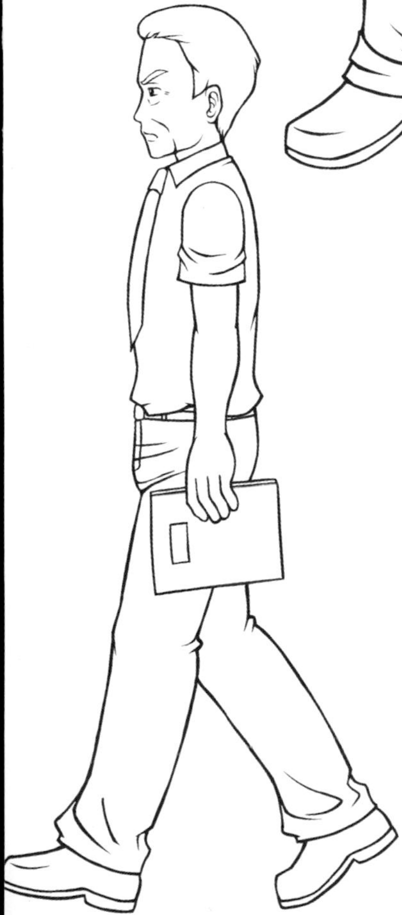

FRONT LAYERS
accessory1
accessory2
accessory3
eyes1
eyes2
eyes3
mouth1
mouth2
mouth3
mouth4
body
right arm1
right arm2
left arm1
left arm2
legs1
legs2

SIDE LAYERS
accessory1
eyes1
eyes2
eyes3
mouth1
mouth2
mouth3
mouth4
left arm1
left arm2
accessory2
body
legs1
legs2

TEACHER READING

FRONT

- Accessory 2
- Eyes 3
- Mouth 2
- Right Arm 1
- Left Arm 1
- Legs 2

SIDE

- Accessory 1
- Eyes 1
- Mouth 1
- Left Arm 1
- Legs 1

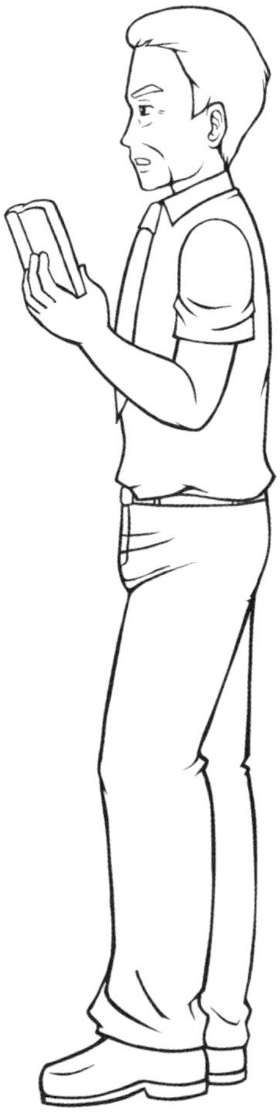

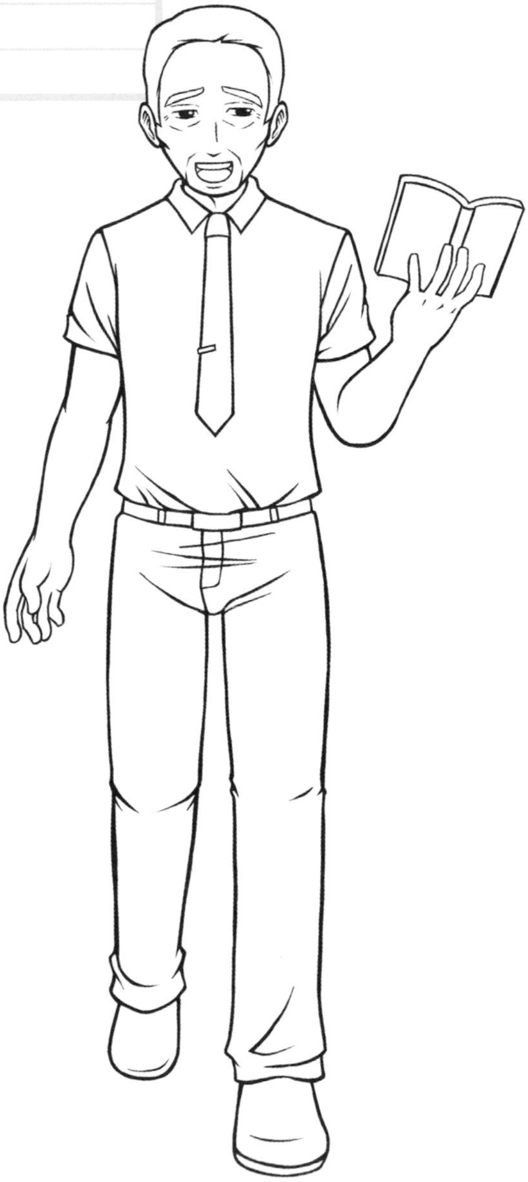

SHOUJO

PAGE LAYOUT TEMPLATES

THE PRODUCTION OF EVERY PAGE STARTS WITH
THE LAYOUT OF PANELS. THESE TEMPLATES OFFER
A WIDE NUMBER OF VARIATIONS, ALL PERFECTLY
SIZED FOR PROFESSIONAL MANGA, AND INCREASING
INCREMENTALLY IN THE NUMBER OF PANELS AND
COMPLEXITY OF LAYOUT. YOU CAN FLIP THE LAYOUTS
HORIZONTALLY AND VERTICALLY TO INCREASE YOUR
VISUAL VARIETY.

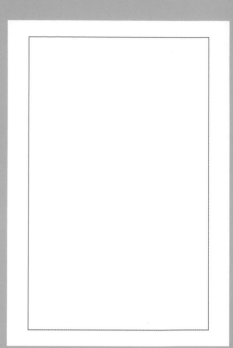

PAGE LAYOUT 1

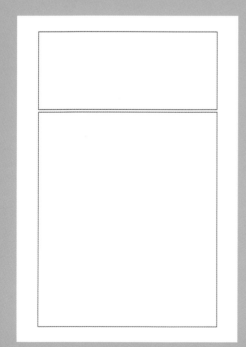

PAGE LAYOUT 2.1

PAGE LAYOUT 2.2

PAGE LAYOUT 2.3

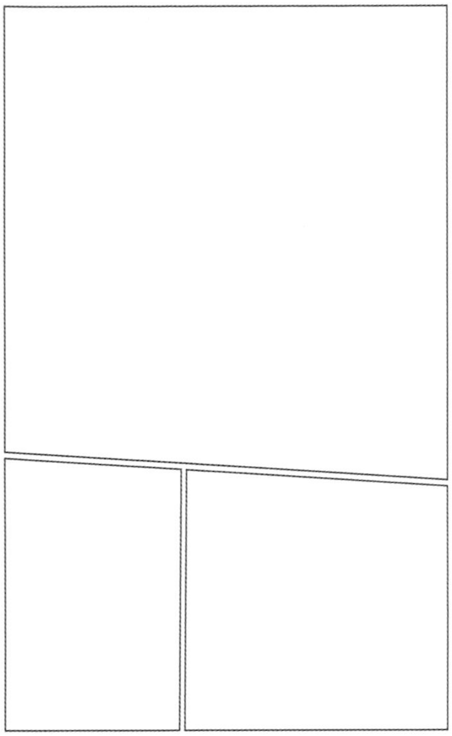

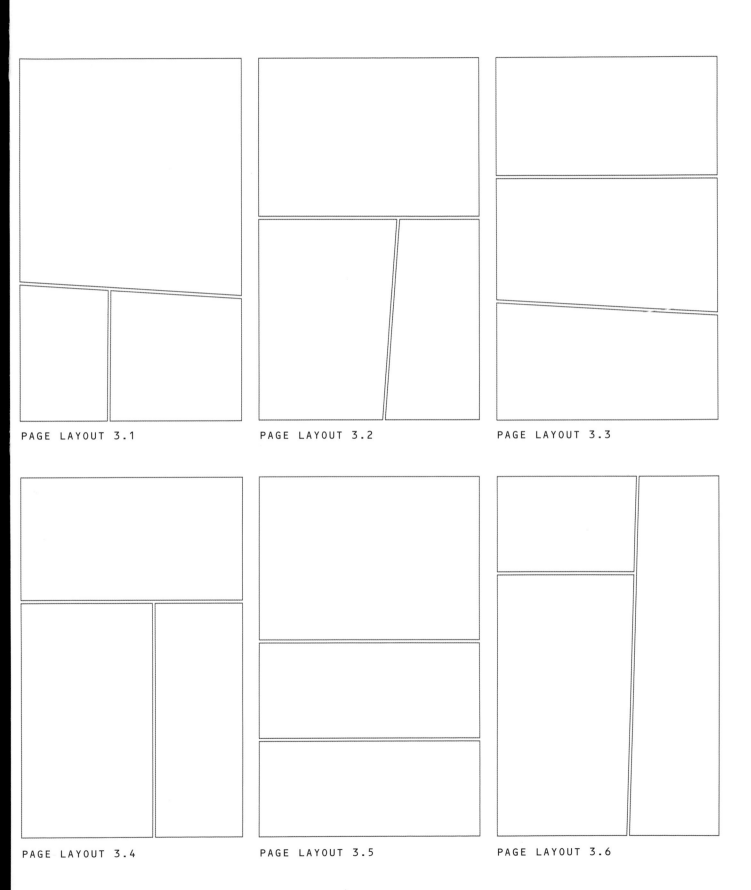

PAGE LAYOUT 3.1

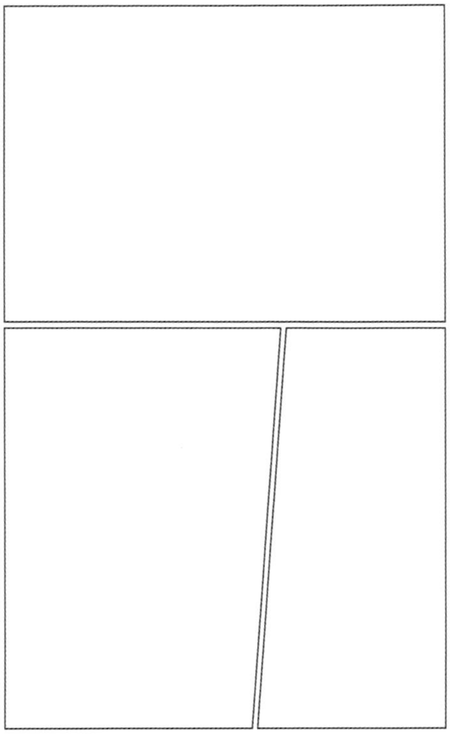

PAGE LAYOUT 3.2

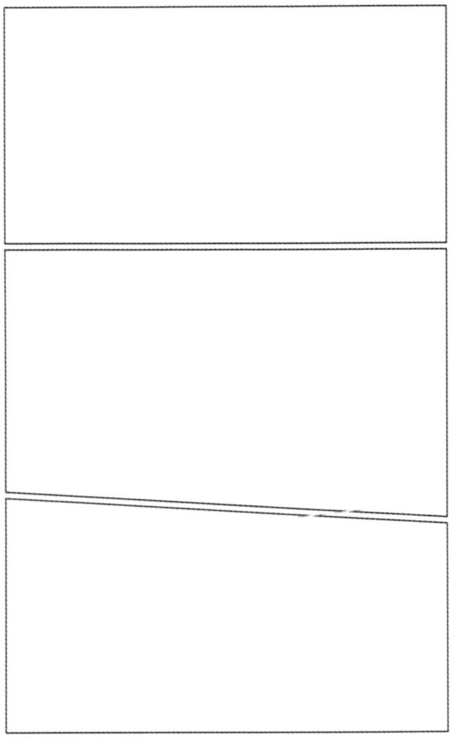

PAGE LAYOUT 3.3

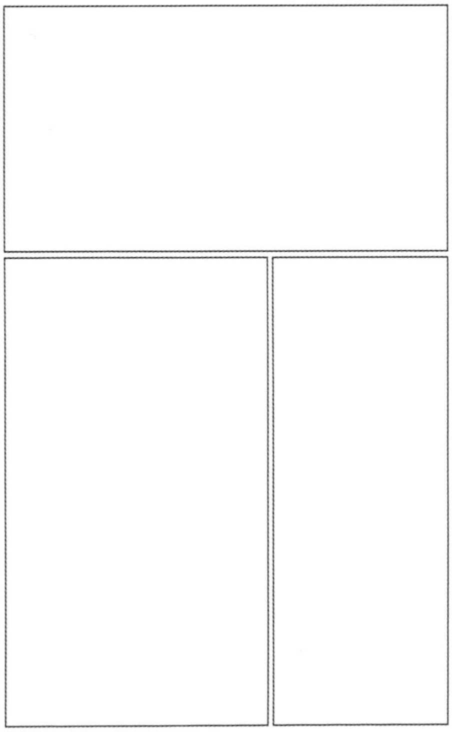

PAGE LAYOUT 3.4

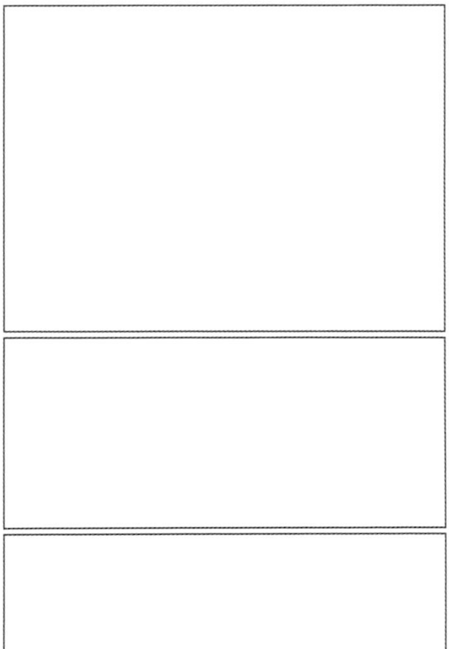

PAGE LAYOUT 3.5

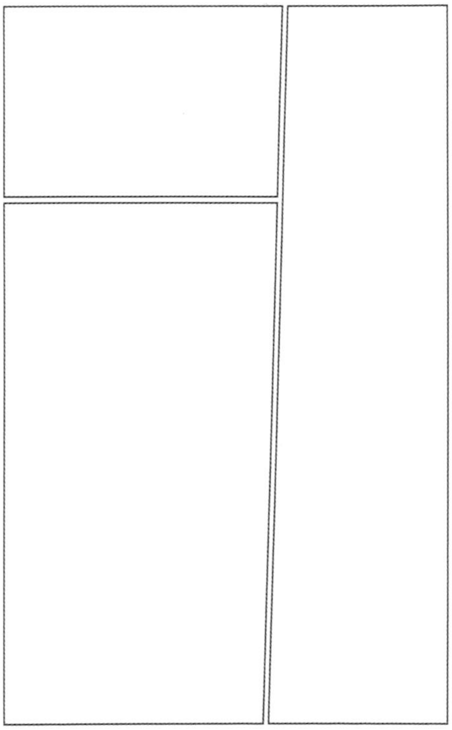

PAGE LAYOUT 3.6

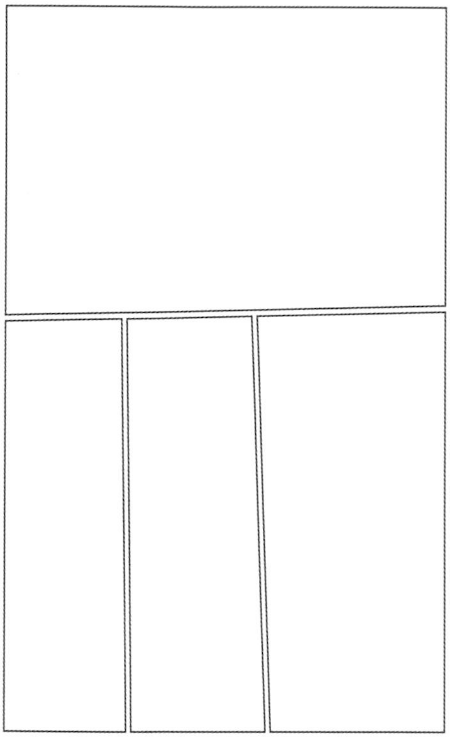

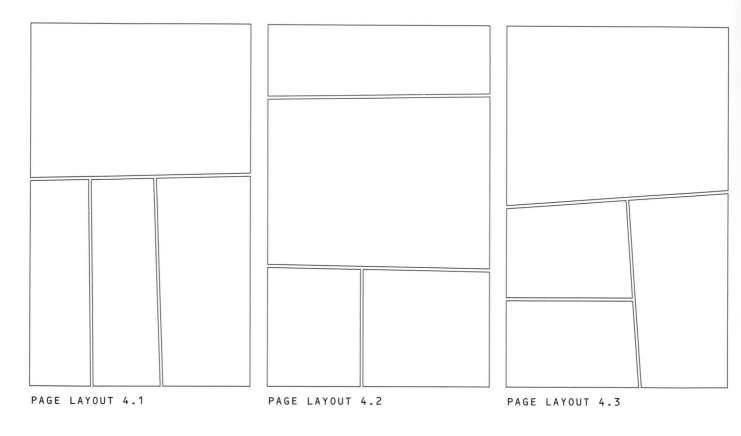

PAGE LAYOUT 4.1

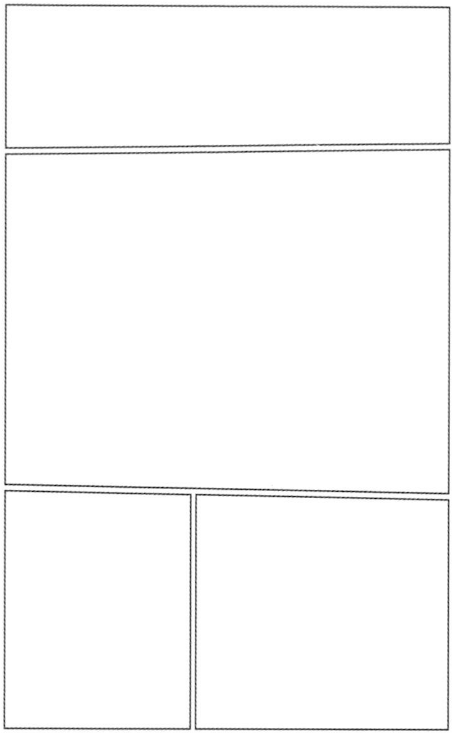

PAGE LAYOUT 4.2

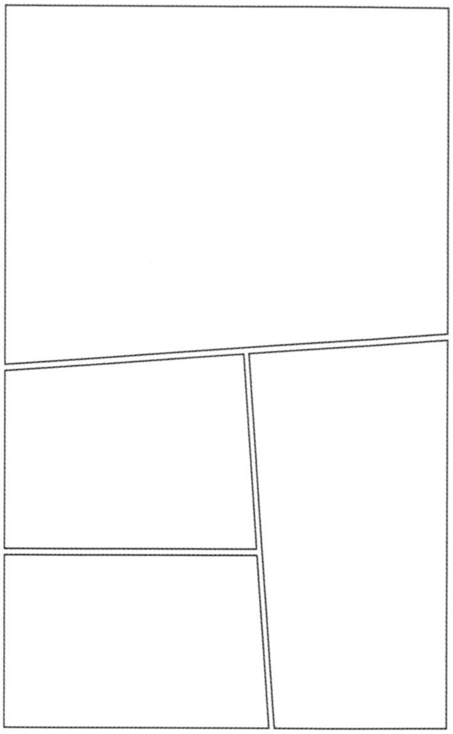

PAGE LAYOUT 4.3

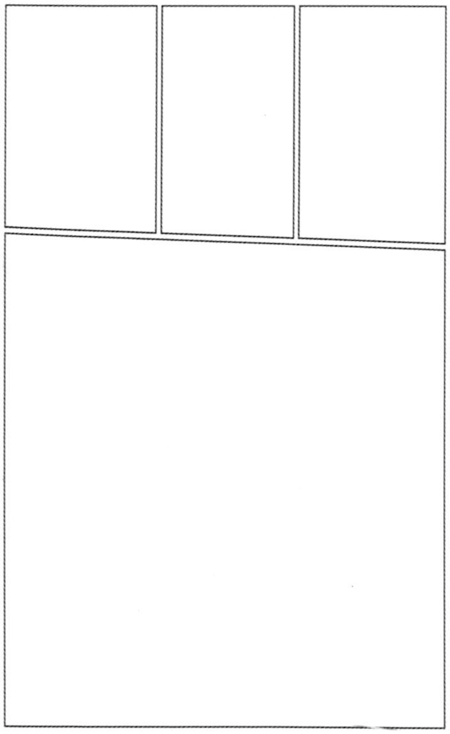

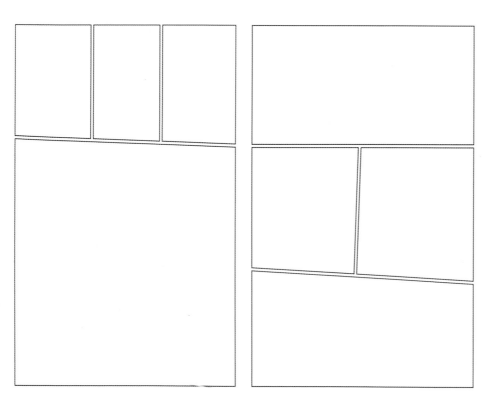

PAGE LAYOUT 4.4

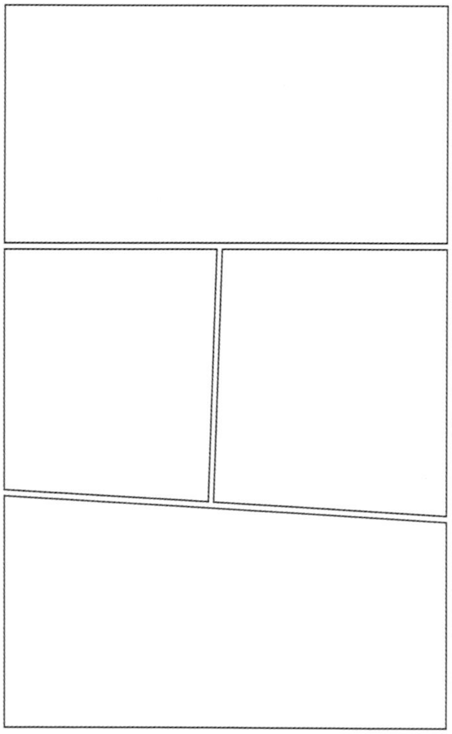

PAGE LAYOUT 4.5

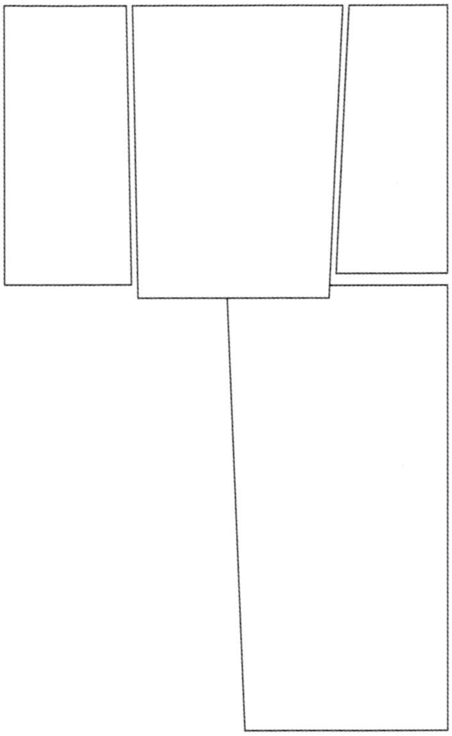

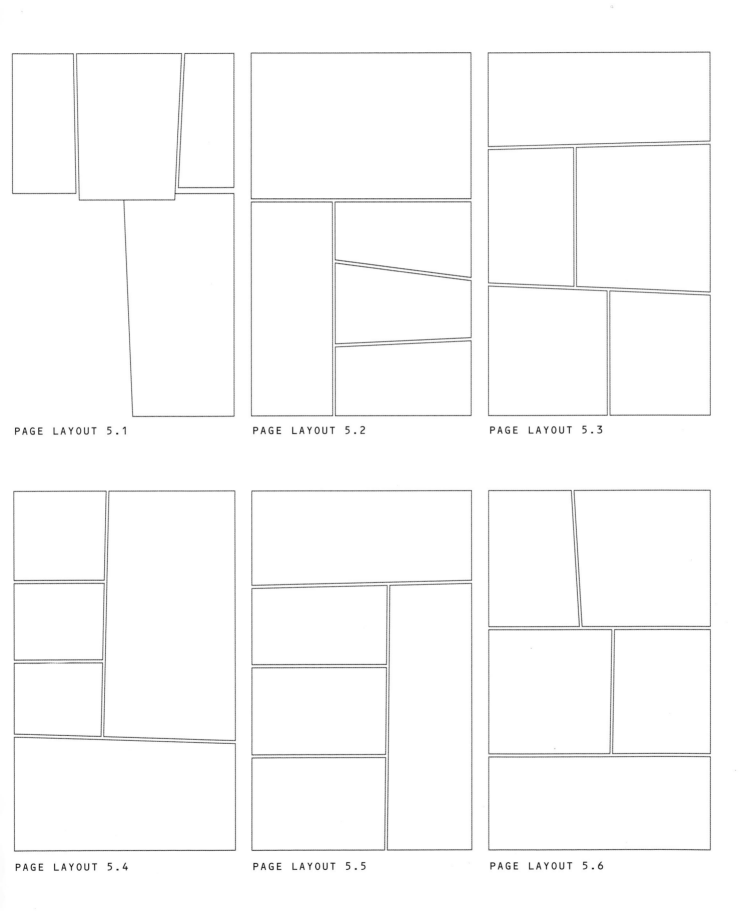

PAGE LAYOUT 5.1

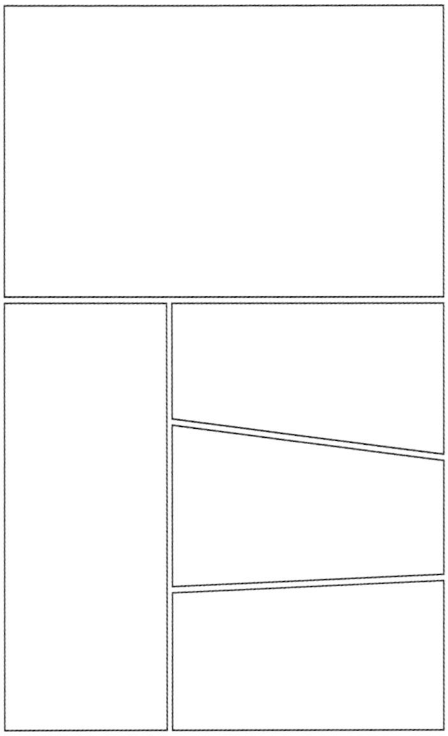

PAGE LAYOUT 5.2

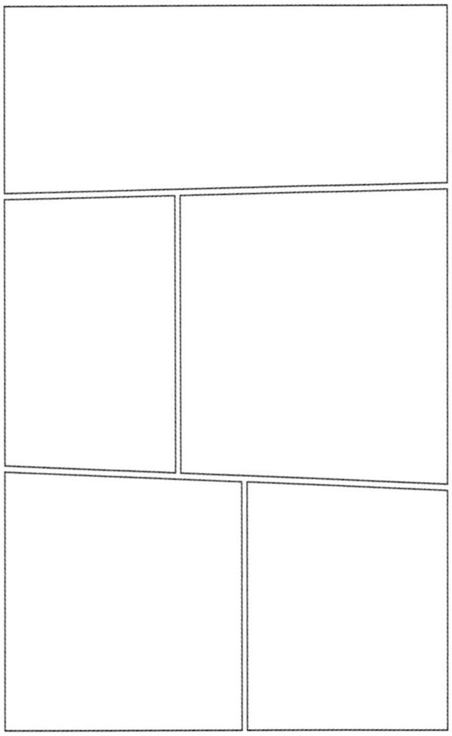

PAGE LAYOUT 5.3

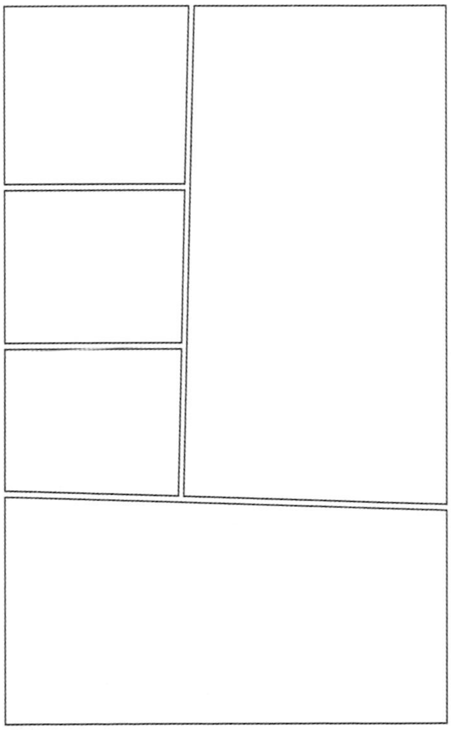

PAGE LAYOUT 5.4

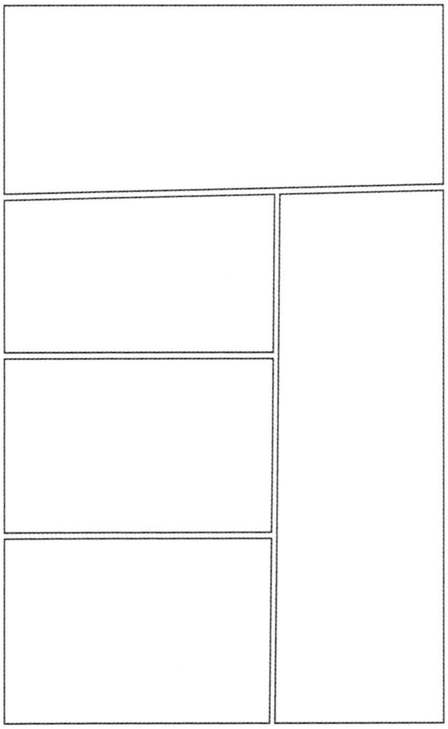

PAGE LAYOUT 5.5

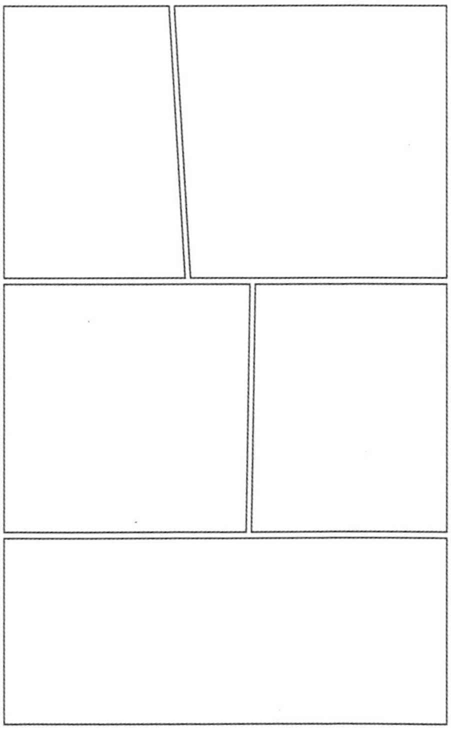

PAGE LAYOUT 5.6

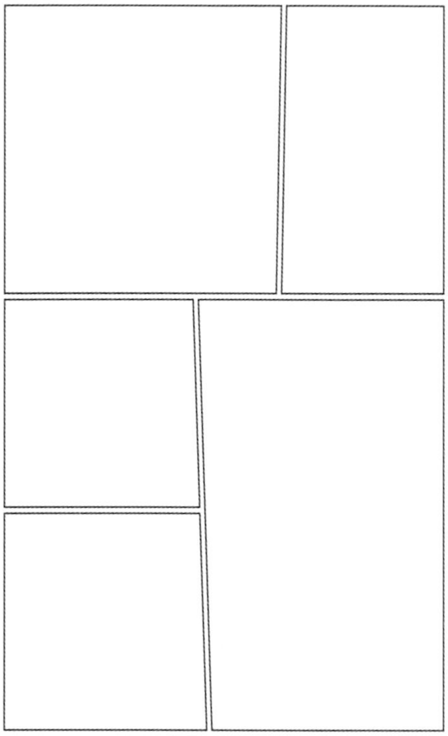

PAGE LAYOUT 5.7

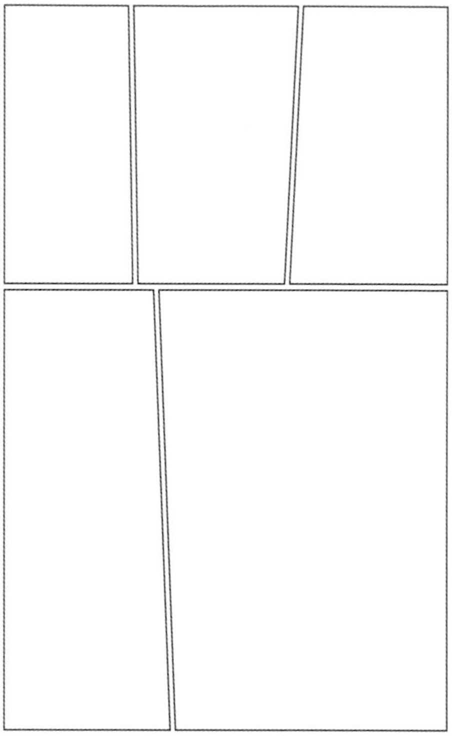

PAGE LAYOUT 5.8

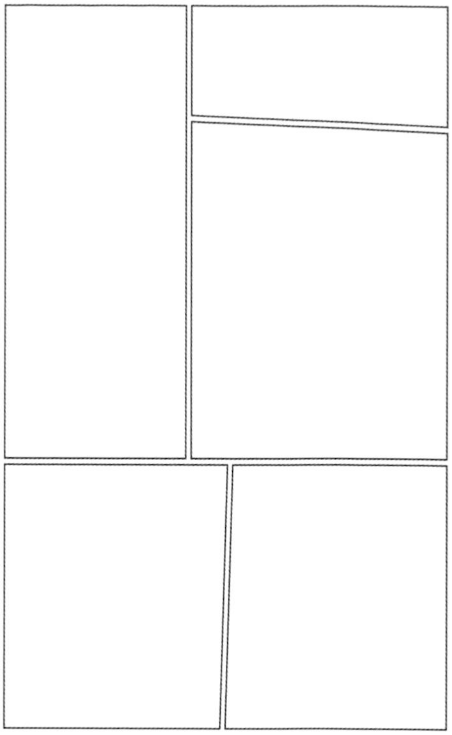

PAGE LAYOUT 5.9

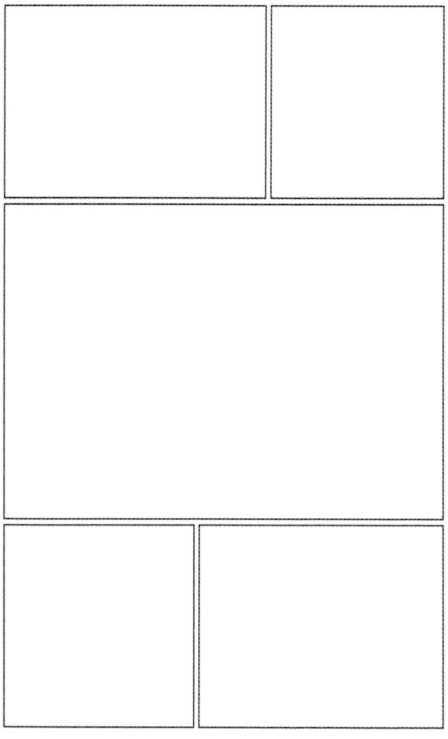

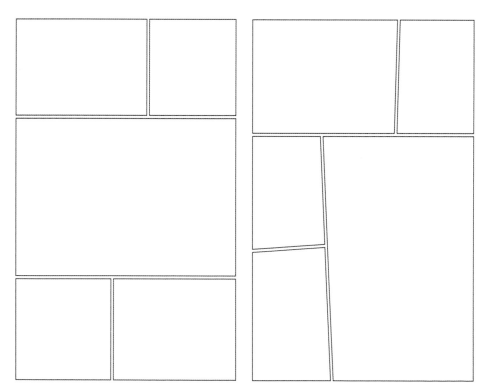

PAGE LAYOUT 5.10

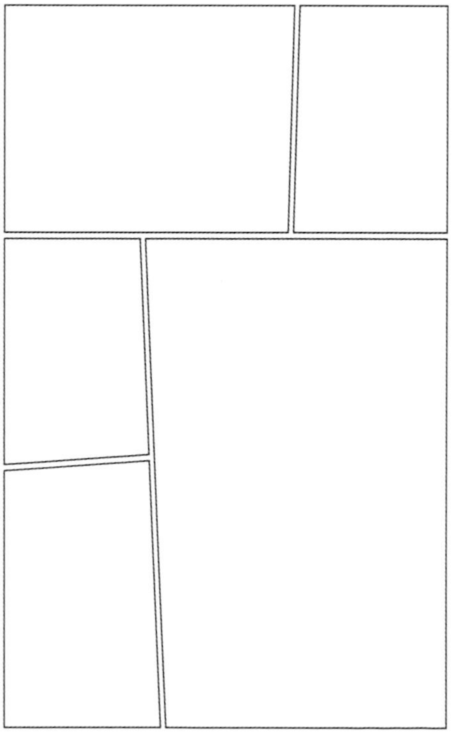

PAGE LAYOUT 5.11

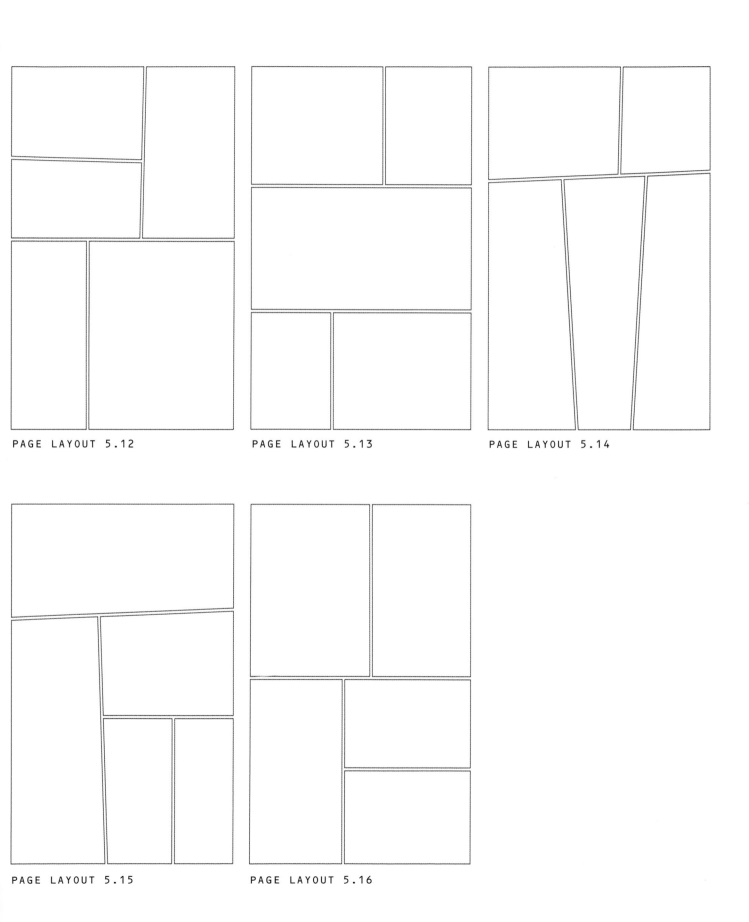

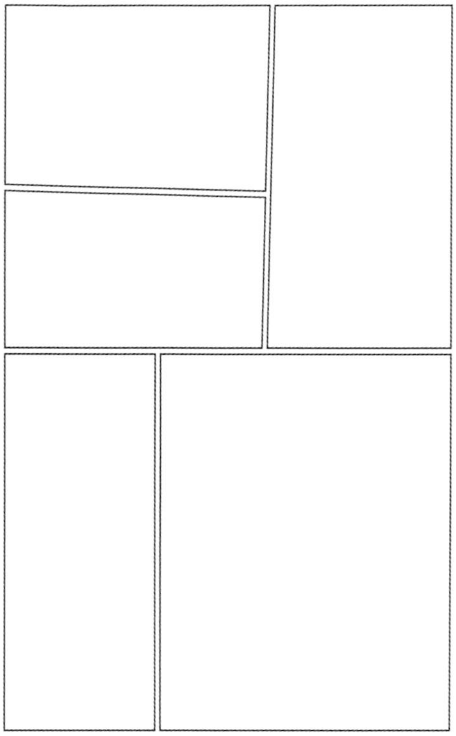
PAGE LAYOUT 5.12

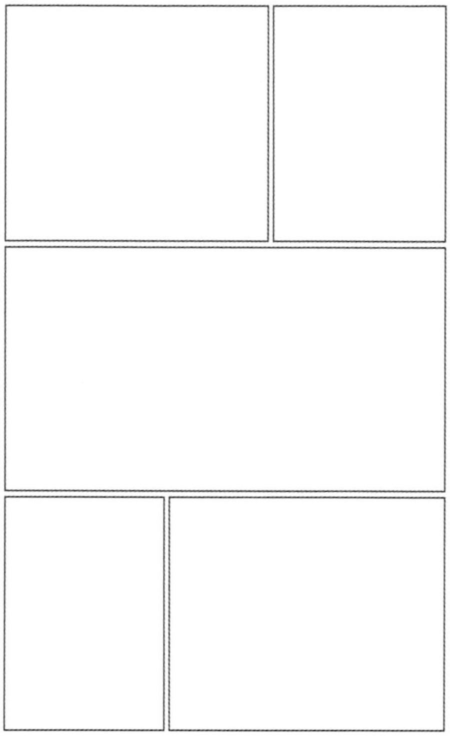
PAGE LAYOUT 5.13

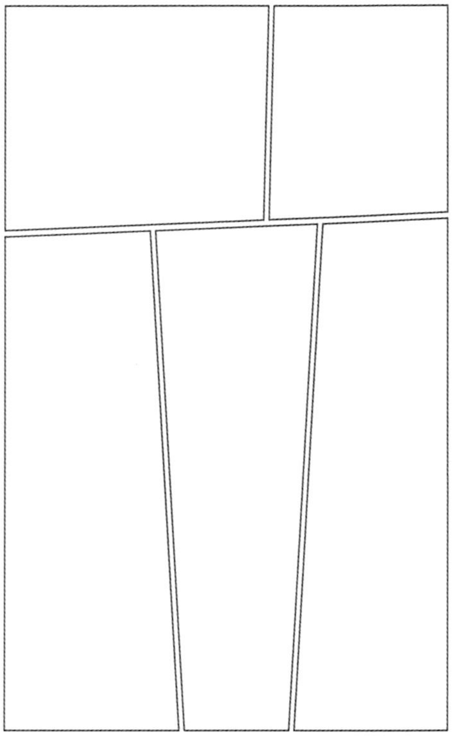
PAGE LAYOUT 5.14

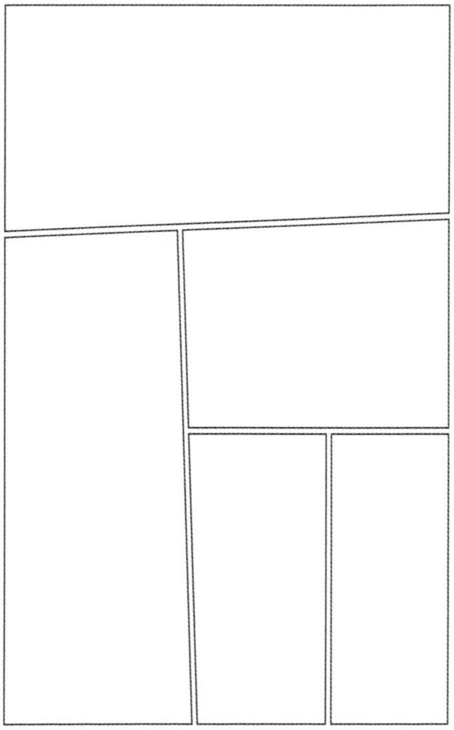
PAGE LAYOUT 5.15

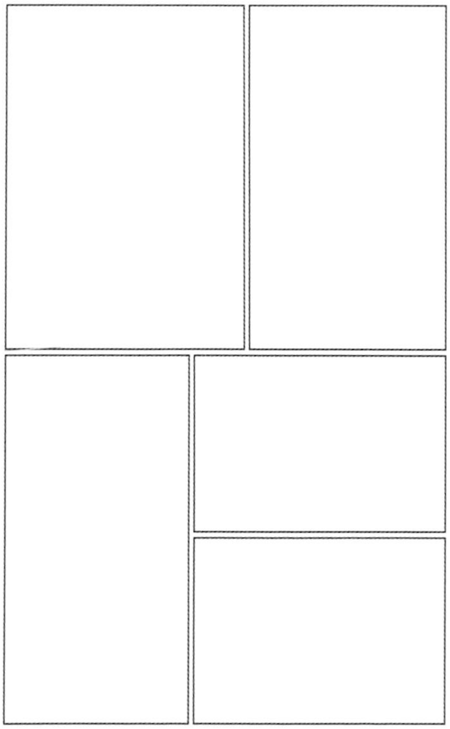
PAGE LAYOUT 5.16

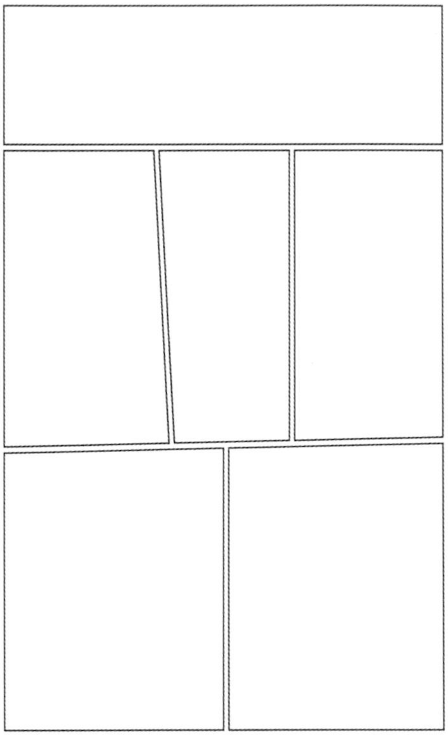

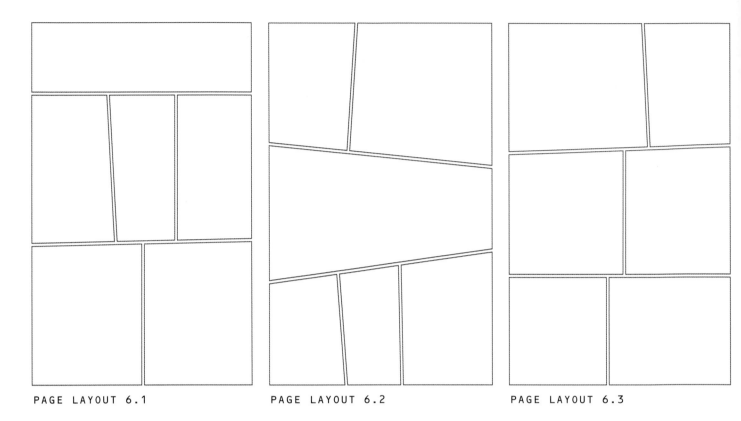

PAGE LAYOUT 6.1

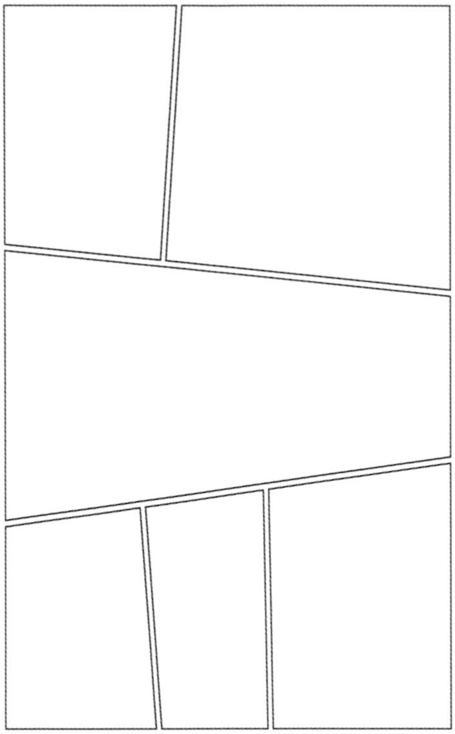

PAGE LAYOUT 6.2

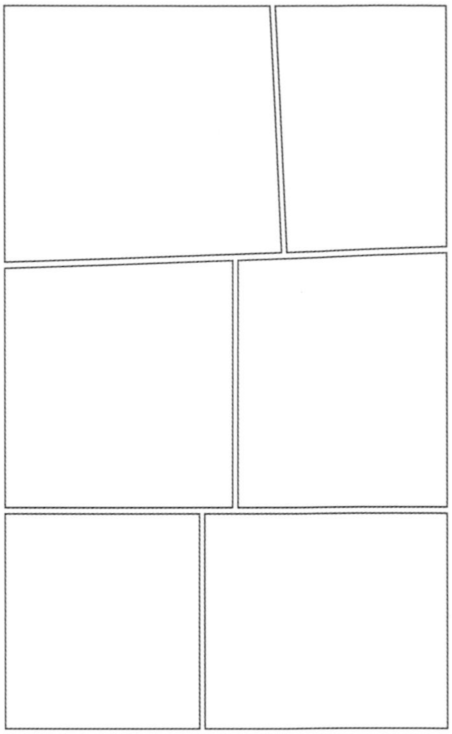

PAGE LAYOUT 6.3

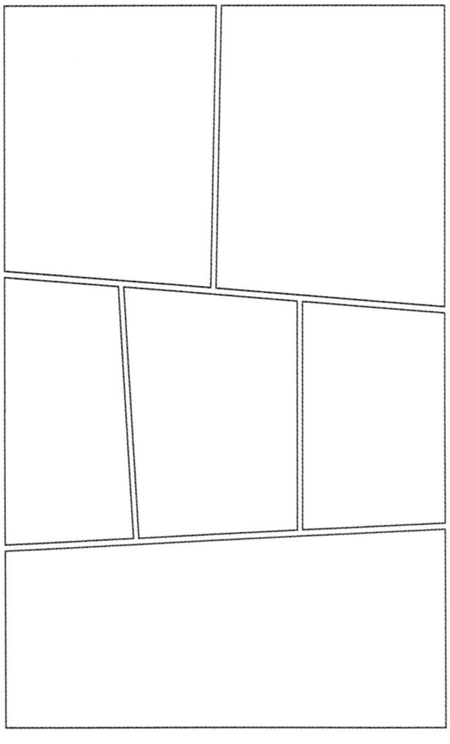

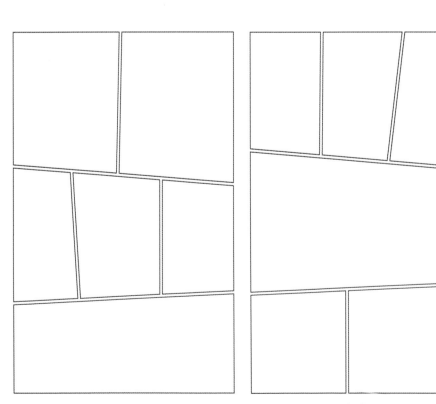

PAGE LAYOUT 6.4

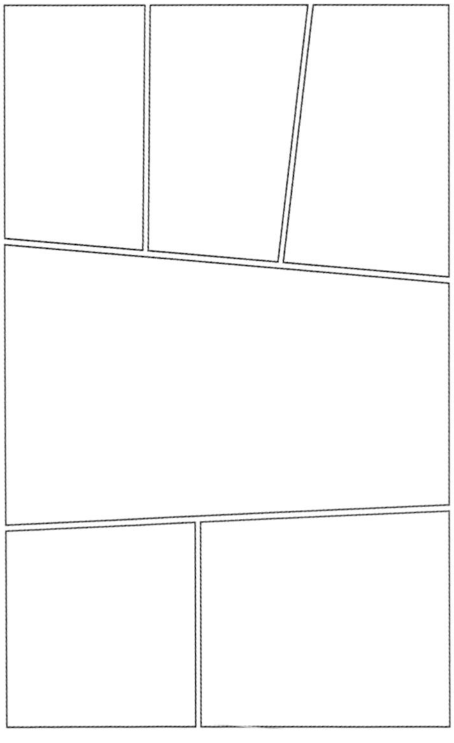

PAGE LAYOUT 6.5

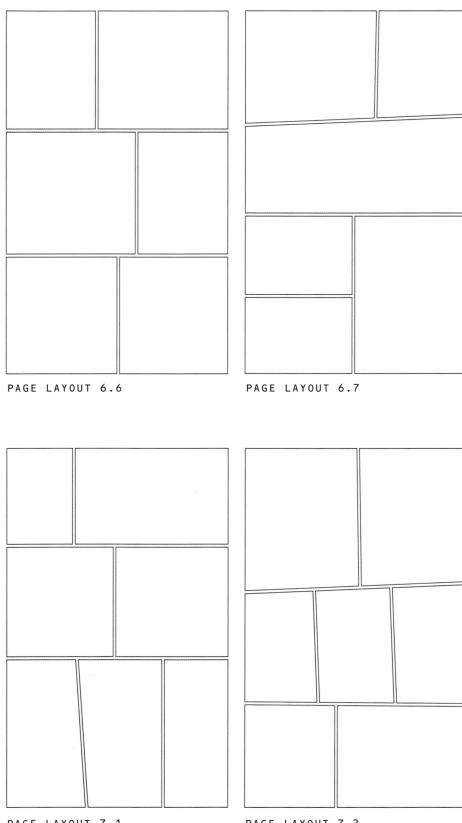

PAGE LAYOUT 6.6

PAGE LAYOUT 6.7

PAGE LAYOUT 7.1

PAGE LAYOUT 7.2

WORD BALLOONS AND CAPTION BOXES

YOUR CHARACTERS WOULD BE NOTHING WITHOUT WORDS TO SAY, AND BALLOONS TO SAY THEM IN. HERE ARE A WEALTH OF BALLOONS FOR EVERY OCCASION, FROM CURVED ELLIPSES TO RECTANGULAR AND JAGGED ITERATIONS. SQUASH AND STRETCH THESE BALLOONS BY RESIZING THEM IN PHOTOSHOP TO ENSURE YOUR WORDS WILL ALWAYS BE A PERFECT FIT.

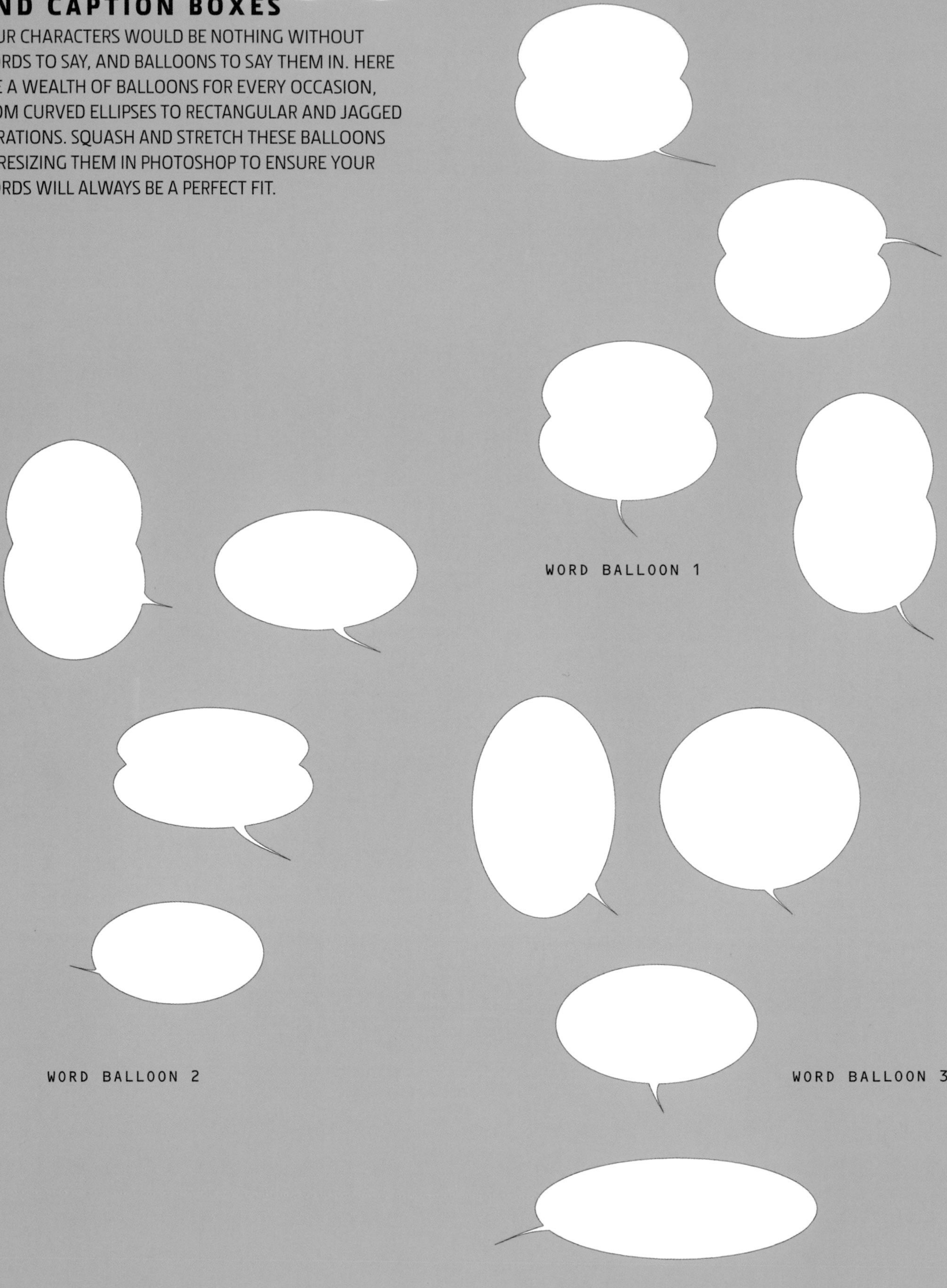

WORD BALLOON 1

WORD BALLOON 2

WORD BALLOON 3

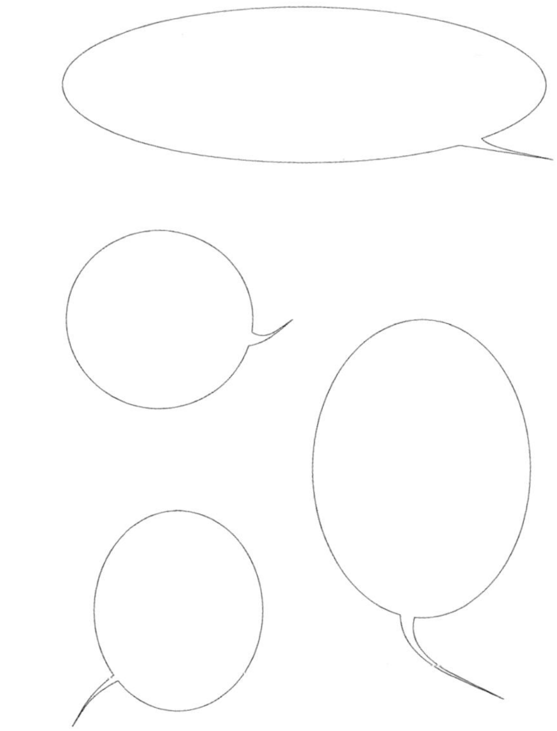

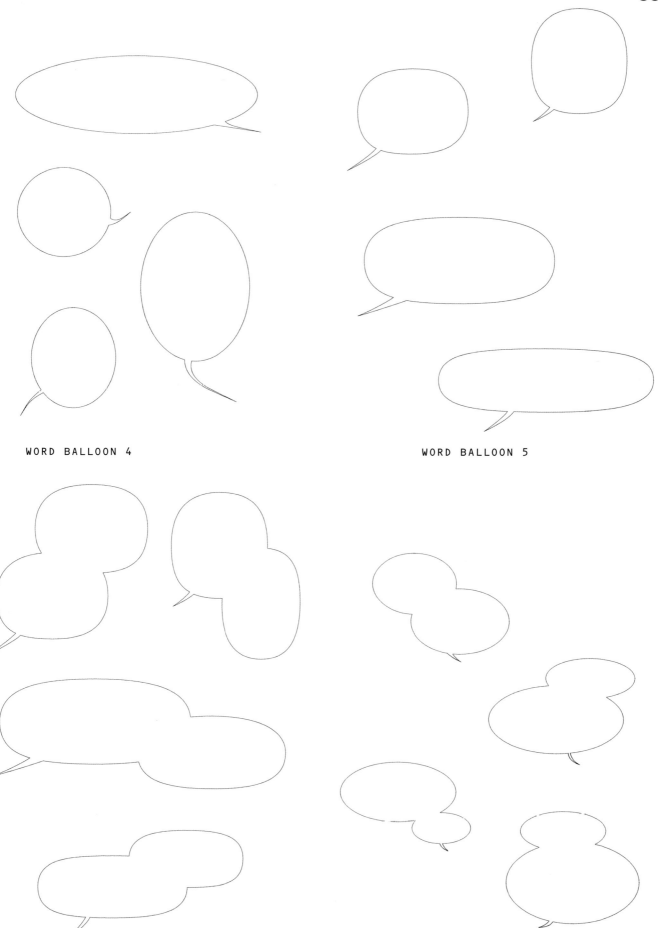

WORD BALLOON 4

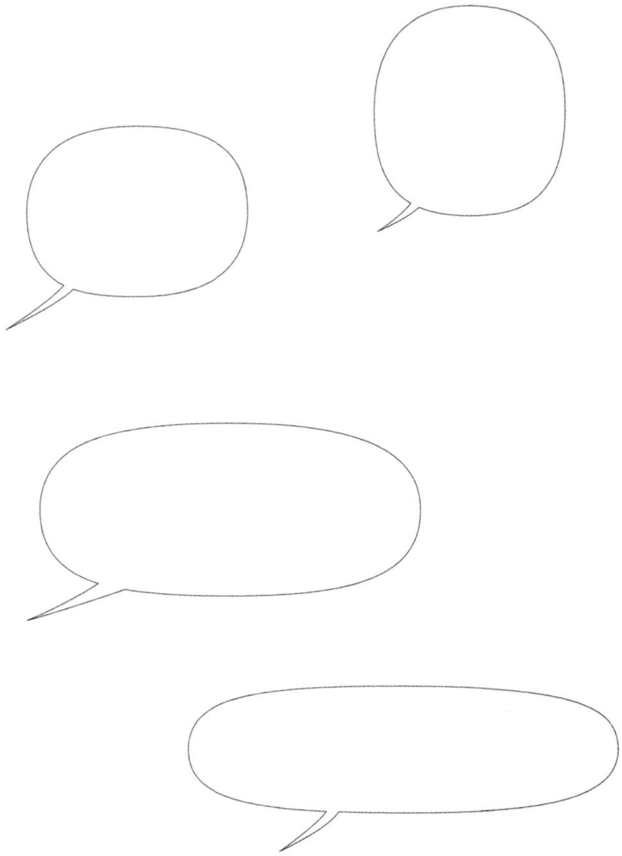

WORD BALLOON 5

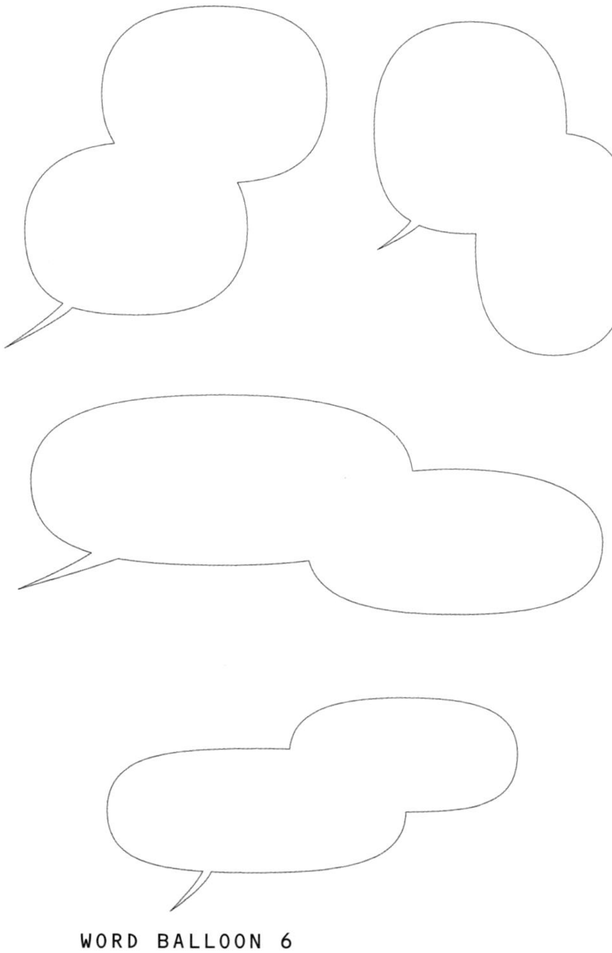

WORD BALLOON 6

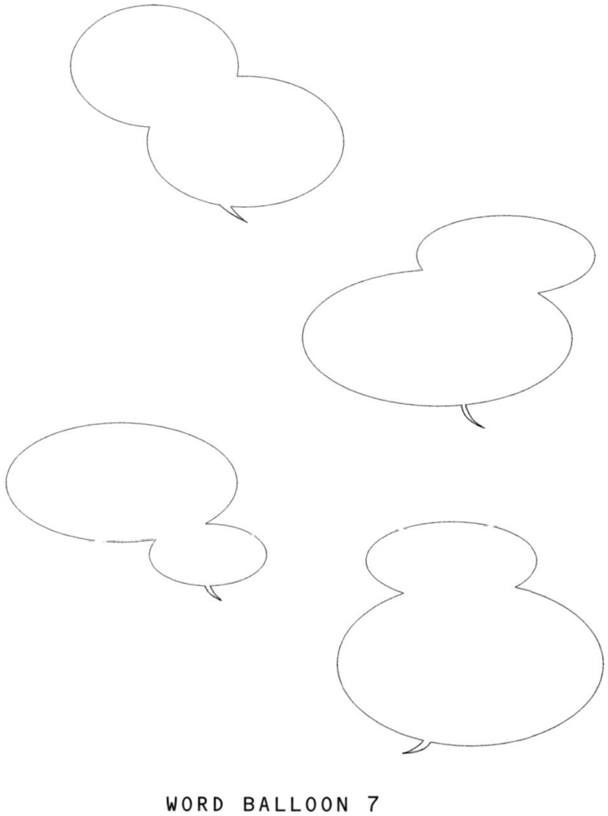

WORD BALLOON 7

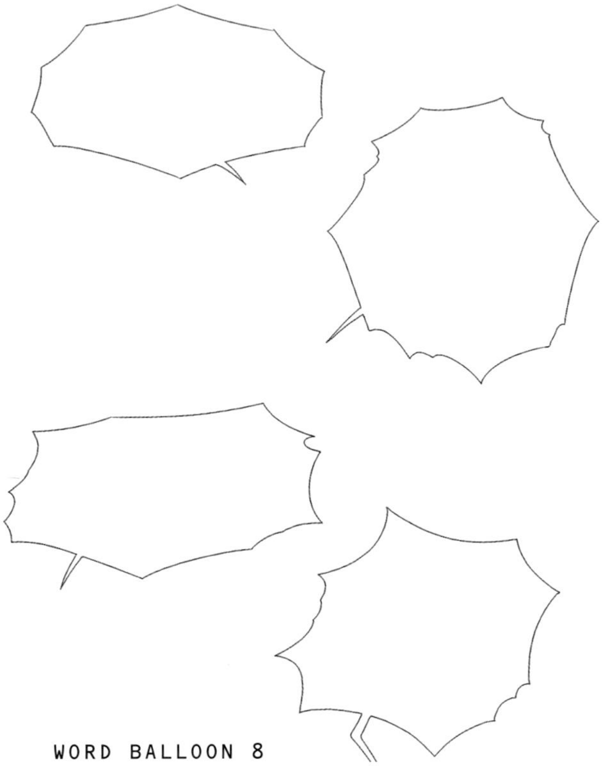

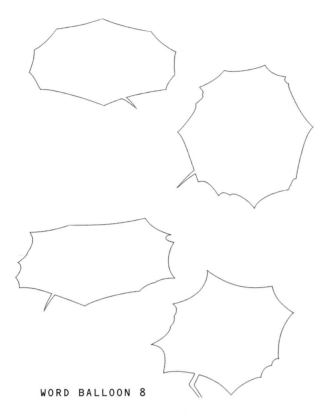

WORD BALLOON 8

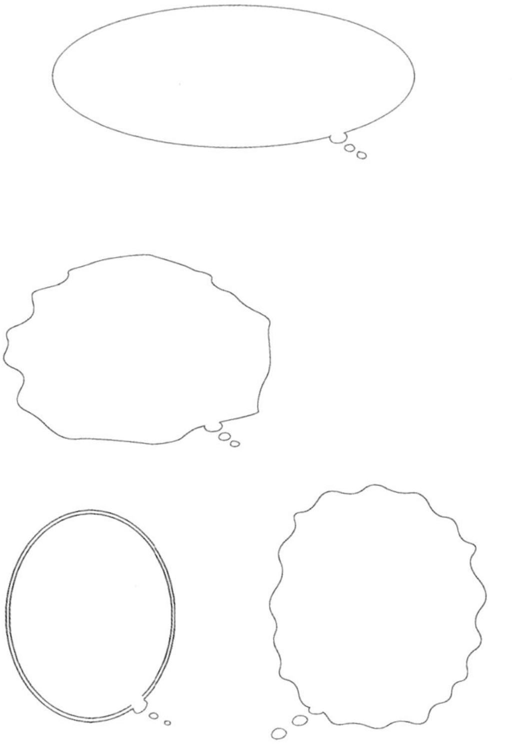

WORD BALLOON 9

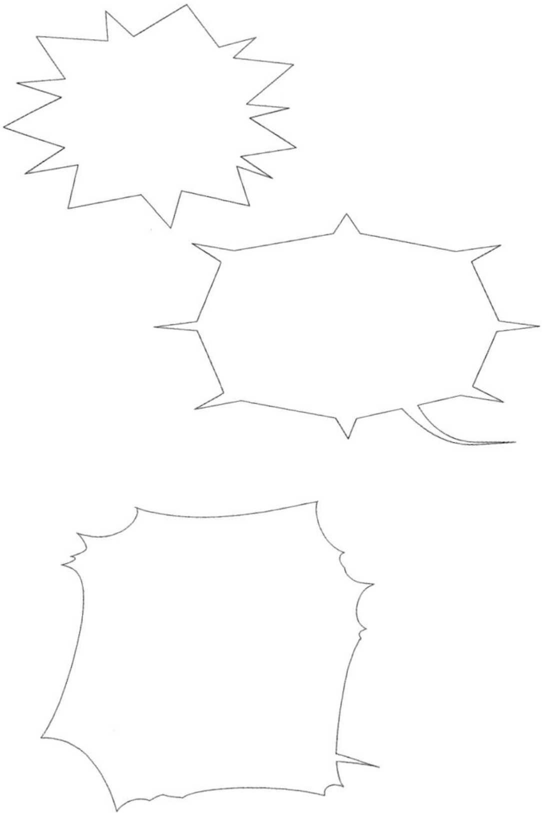

WORD BALLOON 10

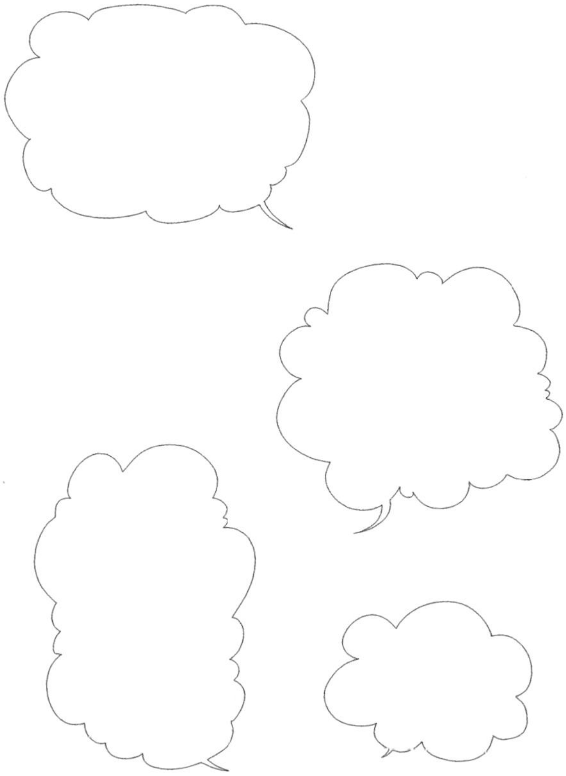

WORD BALLOON 11

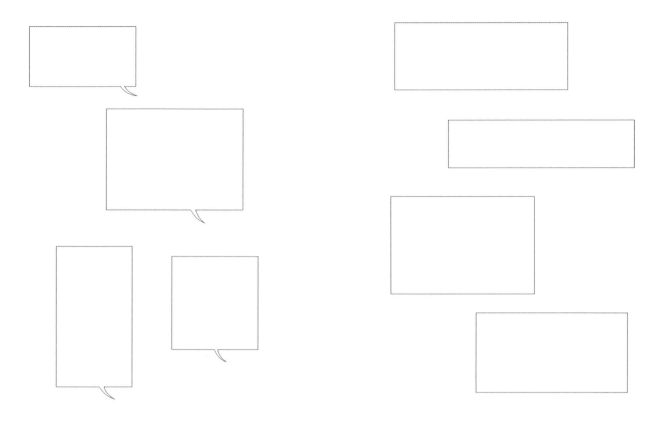

WORD BALLOON 12

WORD BALLOON 13

WORD BALLOON 14

SHOJO

SPEEDLINES
AND FOCUS LINES

SPEEDLINES AND FOCUS LINES ADD DRAMA AND
DYNAMISM TO ANY PAGE, DRAWING ATTENTION TO AN
EMOTIONAL MOMENT, OR AMPING UP A CHASE SCENE.
THE PATTERNS ON THE DISC CAN BE CUT, CROPPED,
ROTATED, AND PLACED ONTO YOUR PAGES HOWEVER
YOU SEE FIT. TRY OVERLAPPING THEM WITH YOUR ART
ON A SEPARATE LAYER.

SPEEDLINE 1

SPEEDLINE 2

SPEEDLINE 3

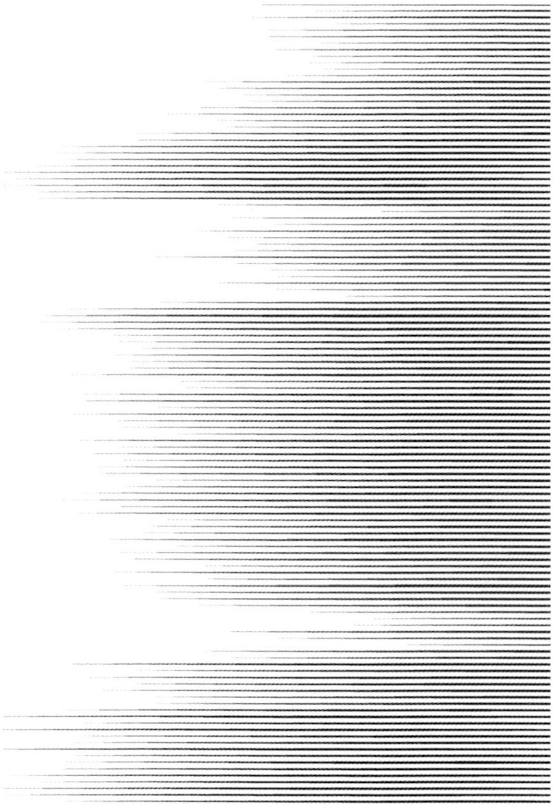

SPEEDLINE 4

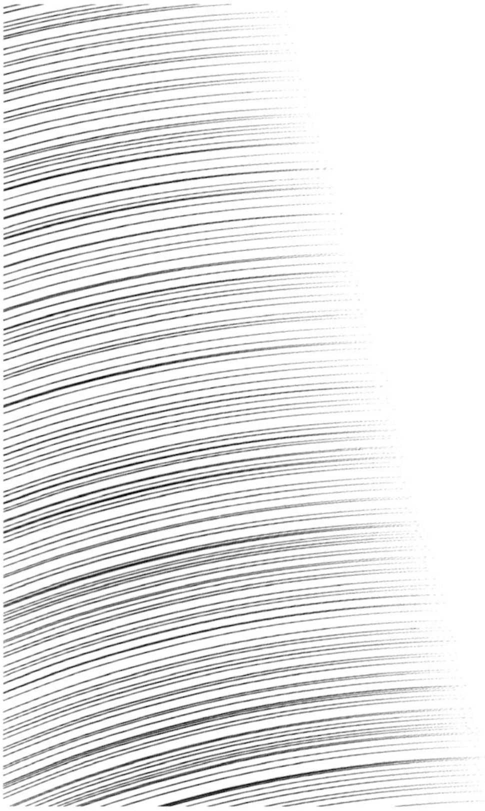

SPEEDLINE 5

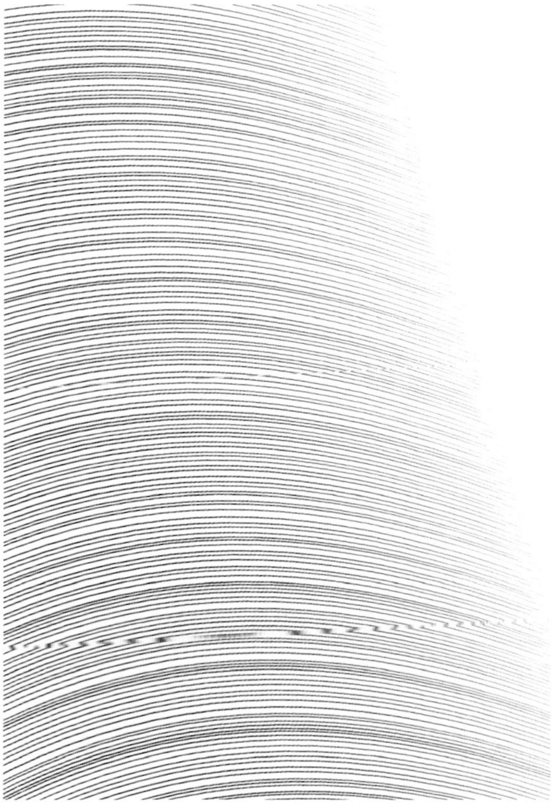

SPEEDLINE 6

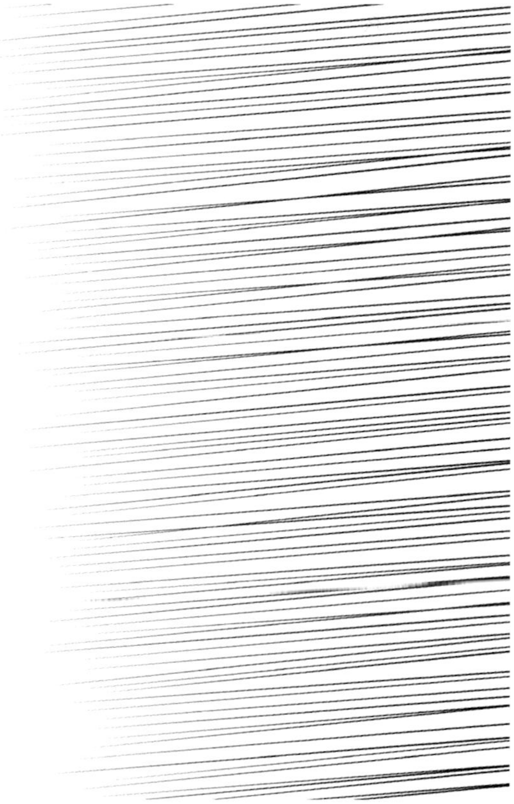

SPEEDLINE 7

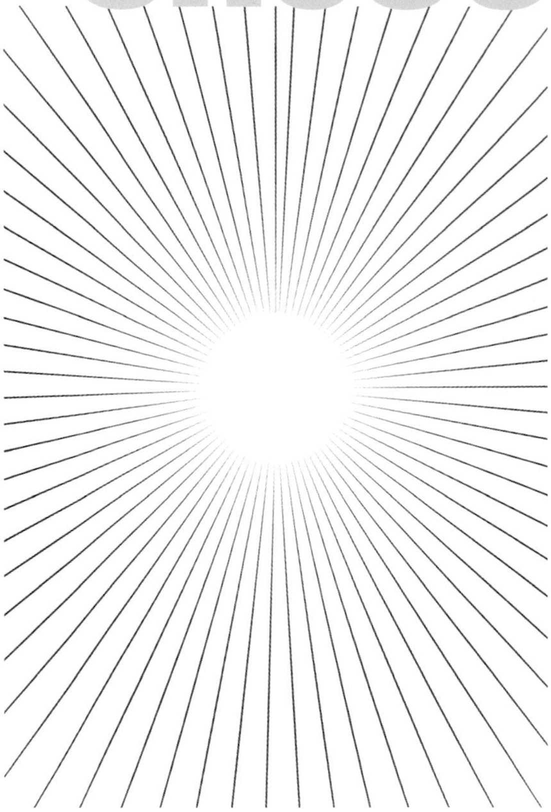

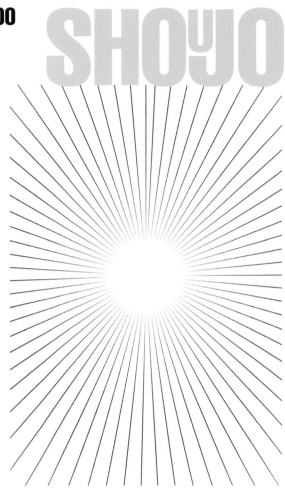

FOCUS LINE 1

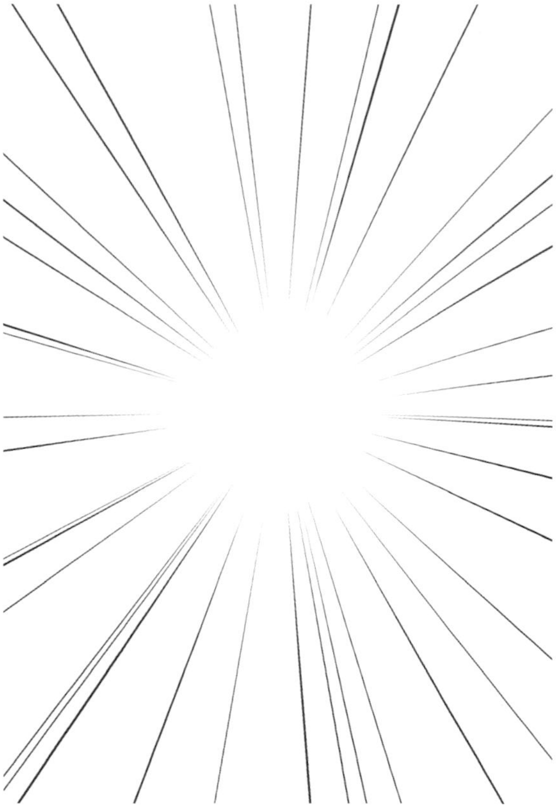

FOCUS LINE 2

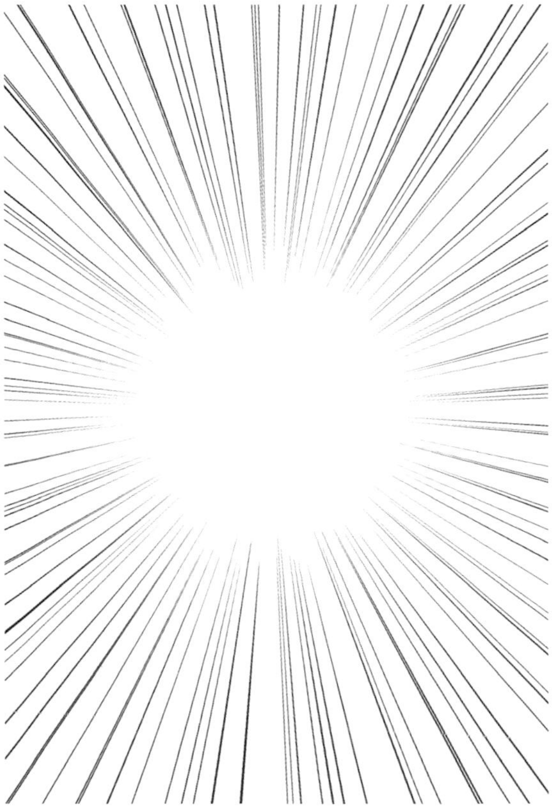

FOCUS LINE 3

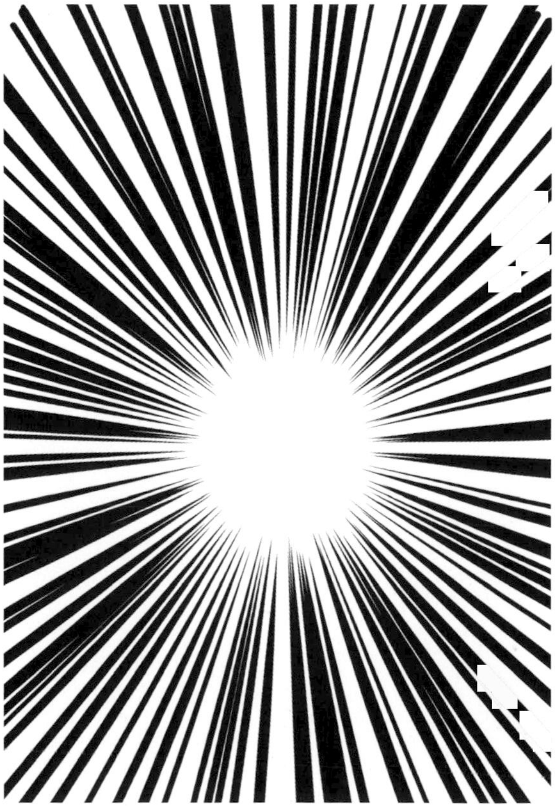

FOCUS LINE 4

FOCUS LINE 5

FOCUS LINE 6

FOCUS LINE 7

TONES SHOUJO

BLACK AND WHITE MANGA THRIVES ON TONES, AND YOU'LL FIND AN UNMATCHED SELECTION HERE: EVERYTHING FROM SIMPLE GRADATIONS TO STARBURSTS, ELECTRICAL ARCS, AND MORE! LOAD A TONE INTO THE PATTERN FILL TOOL IN PHOTOSHOP AND FILL TARGETED AREAS, OR PASTE A PATTERN TO A NEW LAYER FOR MIX-AND-MATCH OR BACKGROUND EFFECTS.

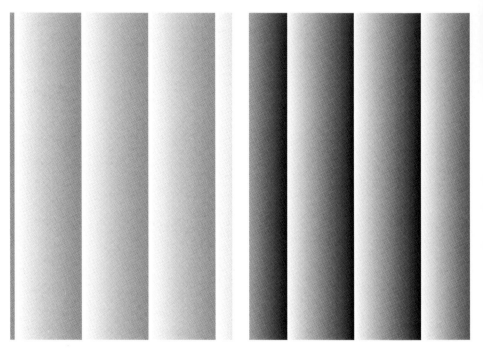

GRADATION TONE 1   GRADATION TONE 2

GRADATION TONE 3

GRADATION TONE 4

GRADATION TONE 5

GRADATION TONE 6

GRADATION TONE 7

GRADATION TONE 8

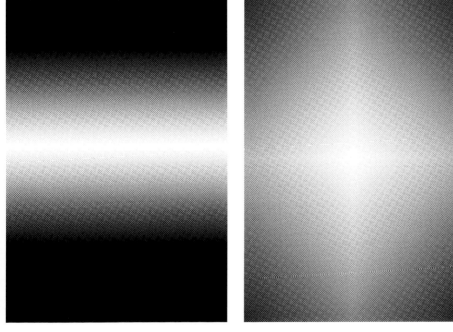

GRADATION TONE 9

GRADATION TONE 10

GRAYTONE 1

GRAYTONE 2

GRAYTONE 3

GRAYTONE 4

GRAYTONE 5

GRAYTONE 6 GRAYTONE 7 GRAYTONE 8

GRAYTONE 9 GRAYTONE 10

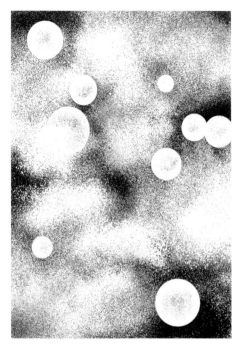

OTHER TONE 1

OTHER TONE 2

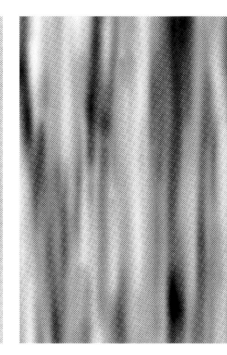

OTHER TONE 3

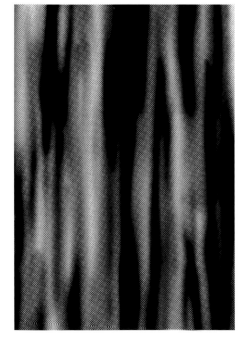

OTHER TONE 4

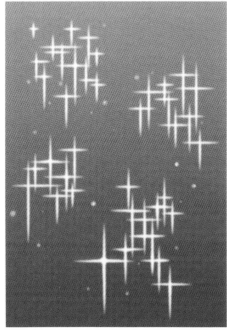

OTHER TONE 5

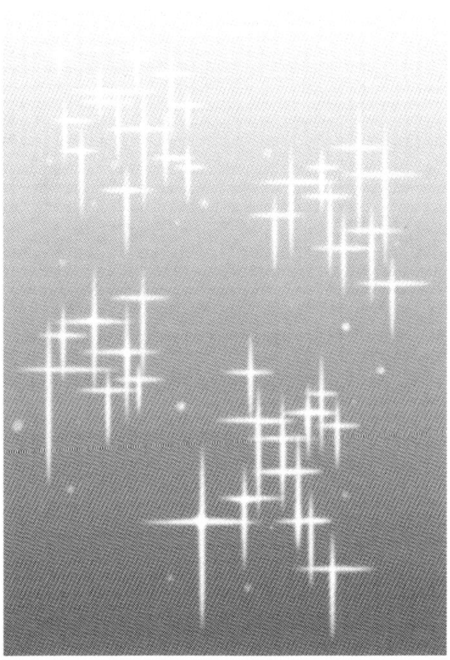

OTHER TONE 6

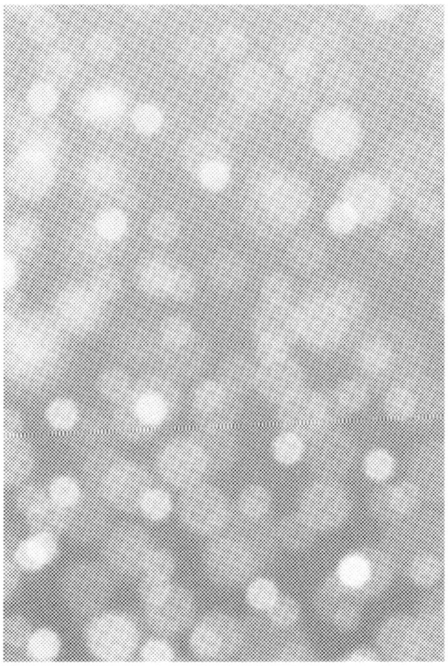

OTHER TONE 7

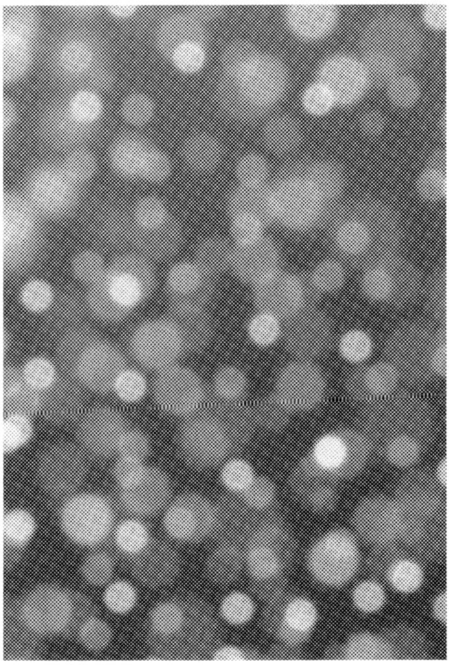

OTHER TONE 8

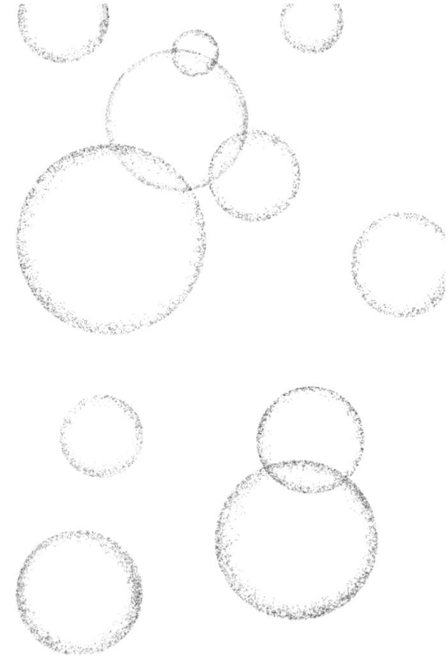

OTHER TONE 9

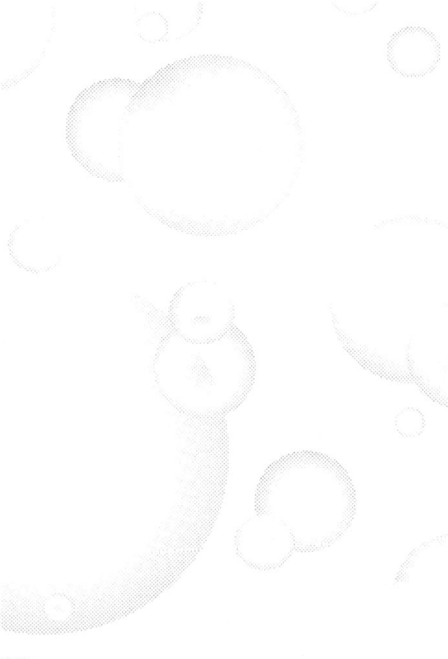

OTHER TONE 10

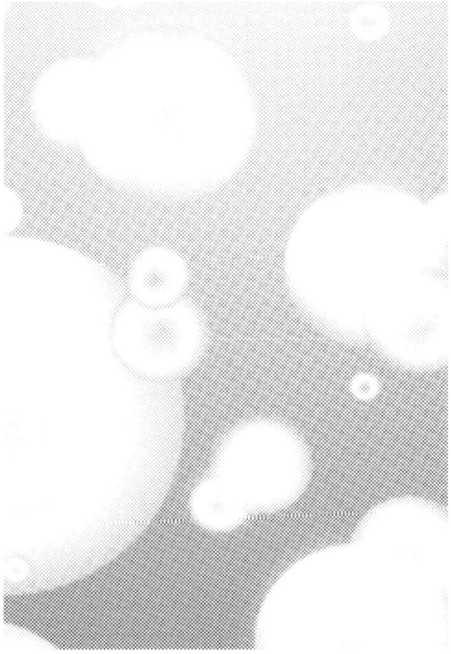

OTHER TONE 11

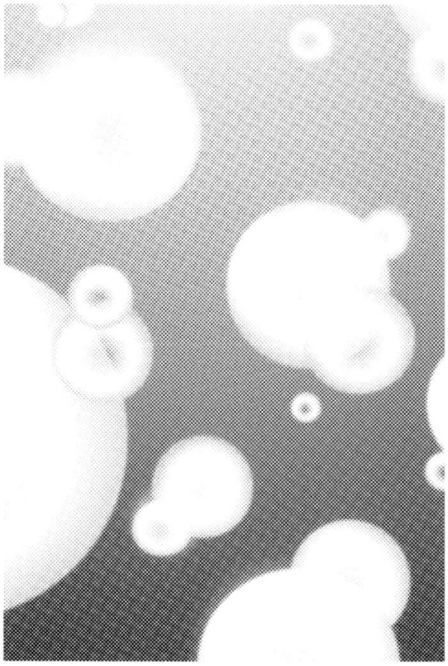
OTHER TONE 12

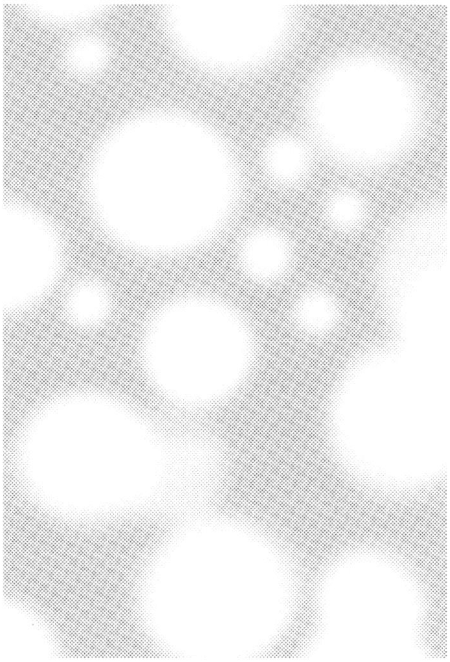
OTHER TONE 13

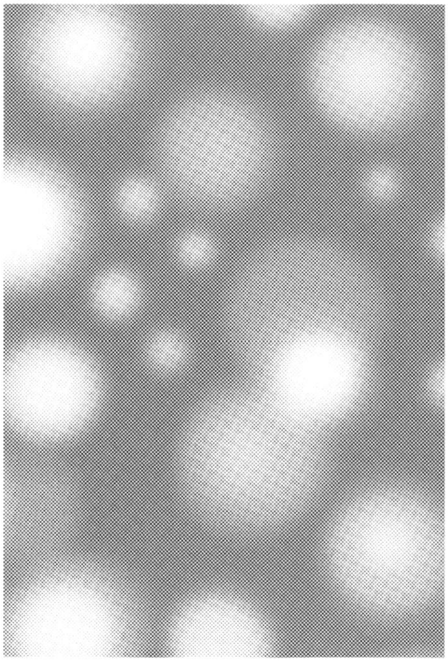
OTHER TONE 14

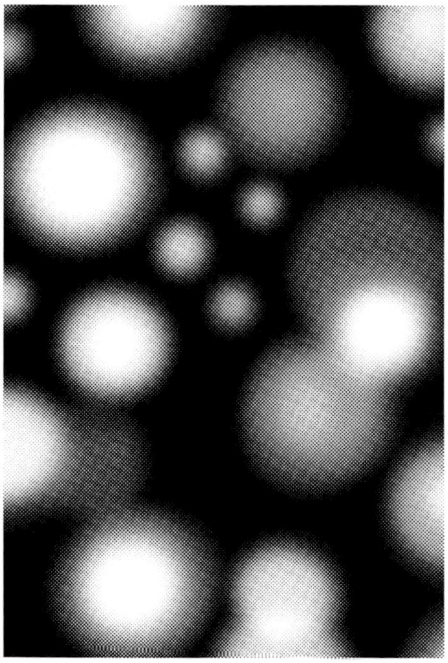
OTHER TONE 15

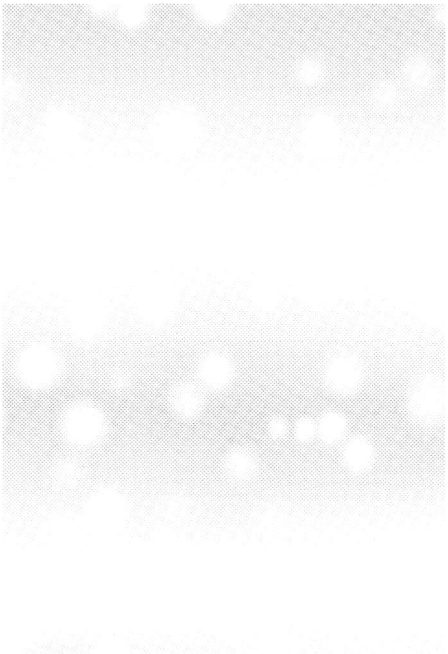
OTHER TONE 16

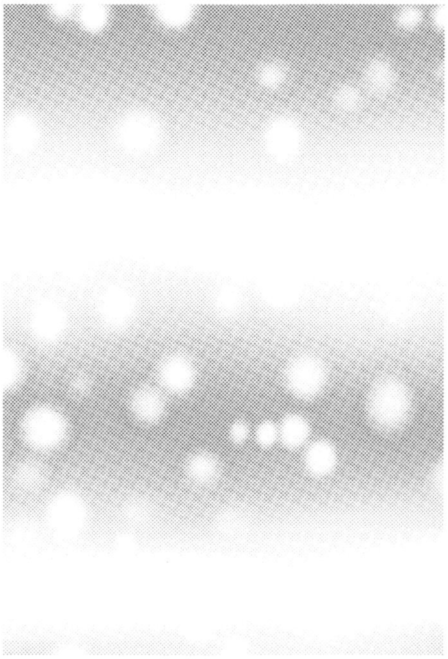
OTHER TONE 17

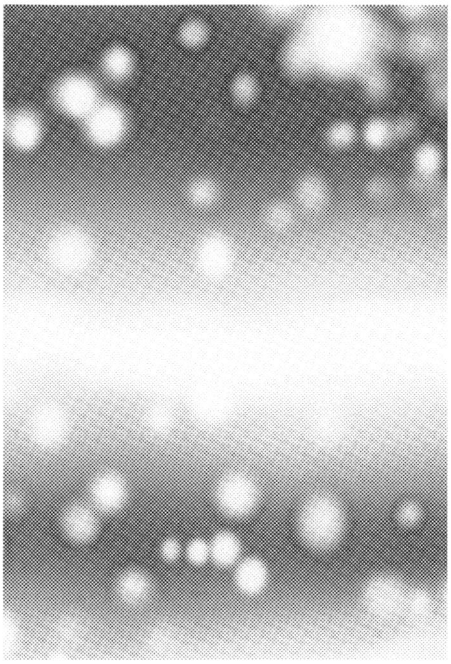

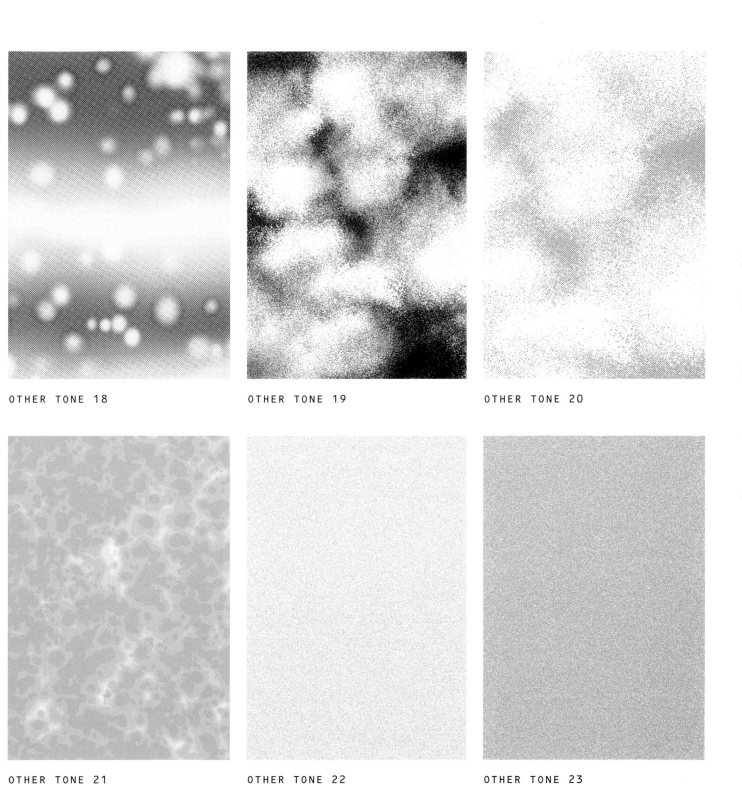

OTHER TONE 18

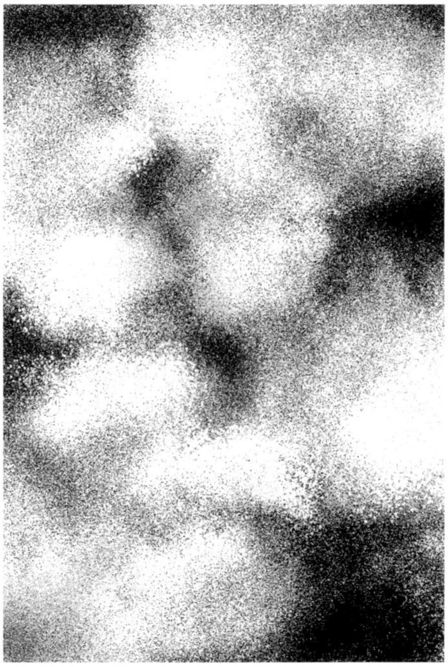

OTHER TONE 19

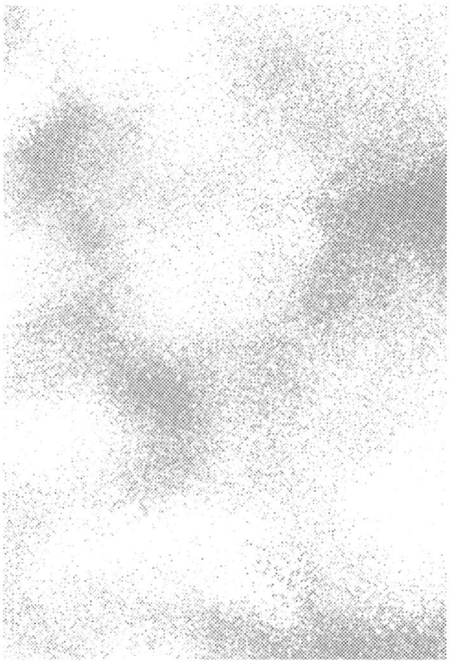

OTHER TONE 20

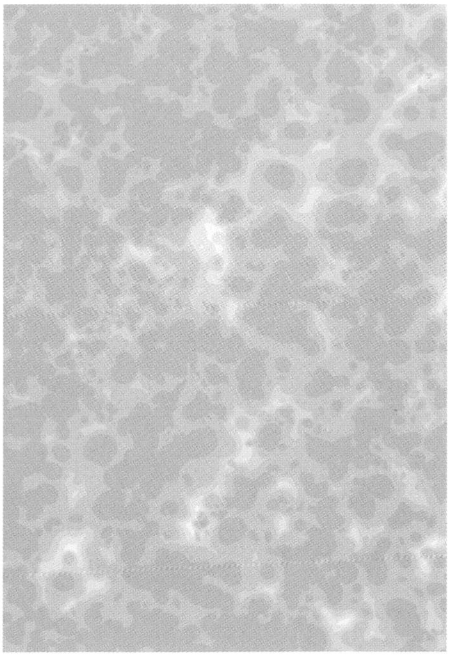

OTHER TONE 21

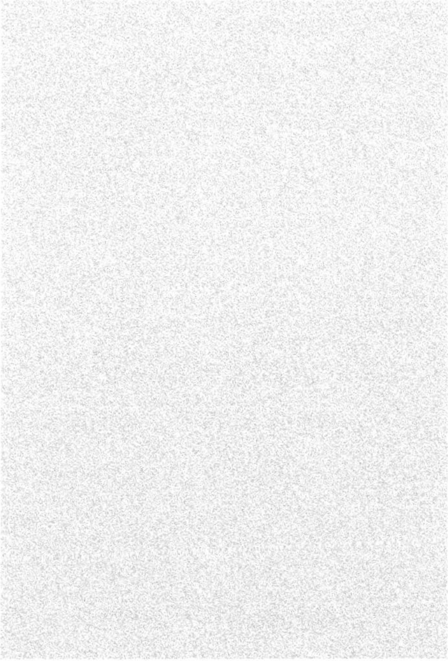

OTHER TONE 22

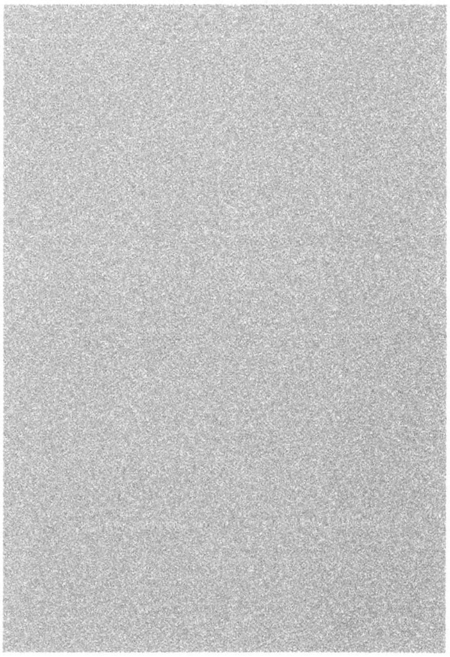

OTHER TONE 23

SHOYO

03 //
BACKGROUNDS AND ACCESSORIES

BACKGROUNDS PROVIDE THE SETTING FOR YOUR STORY.
IN TIME YOU MAY WANT TO CREATE YOUR OWN FROM
SCRATCH OR USING A PHOTOGRAPH. HERE ARE TEN
TO START YOU OFF, WITH SCENE SUGGESTIONS, AND
A GALLERY OF ACCESSORIES TO PEPPER YOUR STRIP WITH.

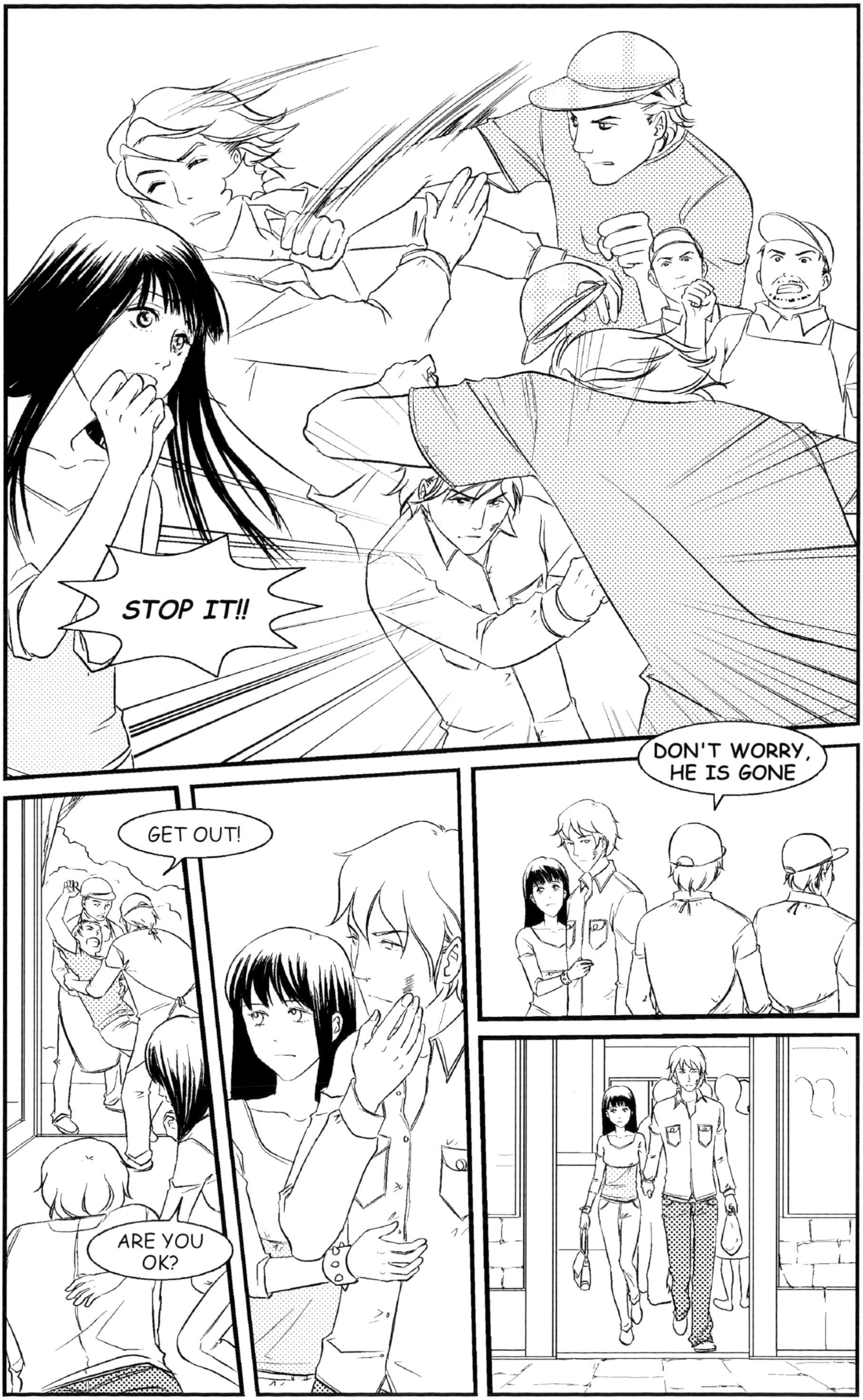
STOP IT!!
GET OUT!
ARE YOU OK?
DON'T WORRY, HE IS GONE

SHOUJO
BACKGROUNDS

INCLUDING BACKGROUNDS IN YOUR MANGA PAGES IS ESSENTIAL TO HELPING THE READER FOLLOW YOUR SHOUJO STORY. THEY ADD DETAIL TO PAGES, AND HELP DETERMINE THE SETTING AND SITUATION OF YOUR CHARACTERS. ESTABLISHING PANELS—THE FIRST TIME A NEW LOCATION IS SHOWN—WILL USUALLY BE RELATIVELY BIG, FEATURING LOTS OF THE BACKGROUND ARTWORK, WHEREAS SMALLER, CLOSE-UP PANELS COULD SHOW SMALL DETAILS WITHIN THE BACKGROUND, OR IN SOME CASES SIMPLY BE LEFT BLANK.

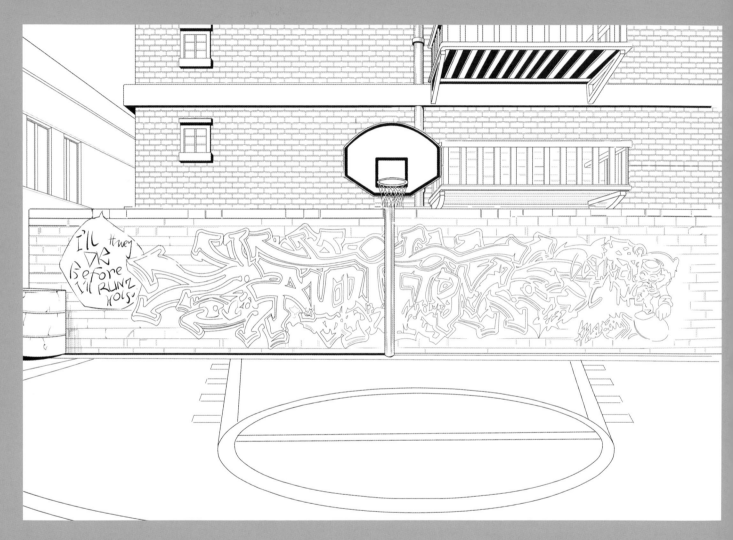

BASKETBALL COURT
The basketball court is perfect for an after-school showdown between two sporting rivals, or for a life-changing crime after dark.

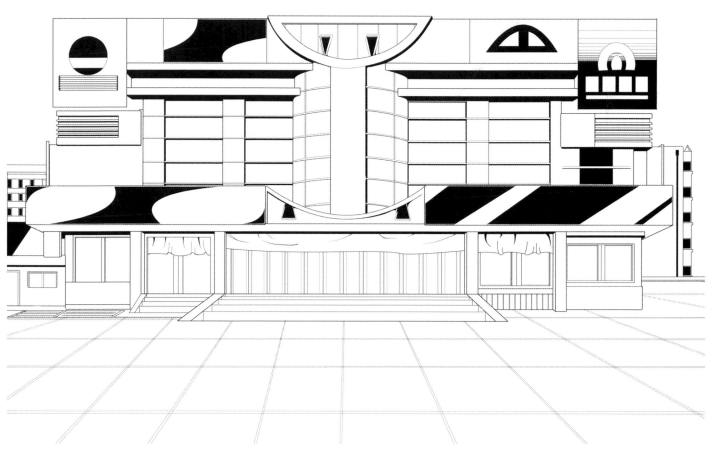

CINEMA

The cinema: ideal for a romantic date, a girls' night out, or perhaps it is where a character works over the weekend?

CLASSROOM

The schoolroom is empty now, but in minutes it could
fill with all manner of secret crushes, bitchy politics,
tortuous schoolwork, and dreamy substitute teachers. . .

PRINCESS BEDROOM

A bedroom fit for a princess: a private refuge. What keepsakes, diaries, and much-loved stuffed animals will get pride of place on the bed?

SHOUJO

SCIENCE LAB

Full of bubbling test tubes, sulphurous gases,
and runaway hormones, the science room brews
up everything from lab partner romances to
strength-giving super serums!

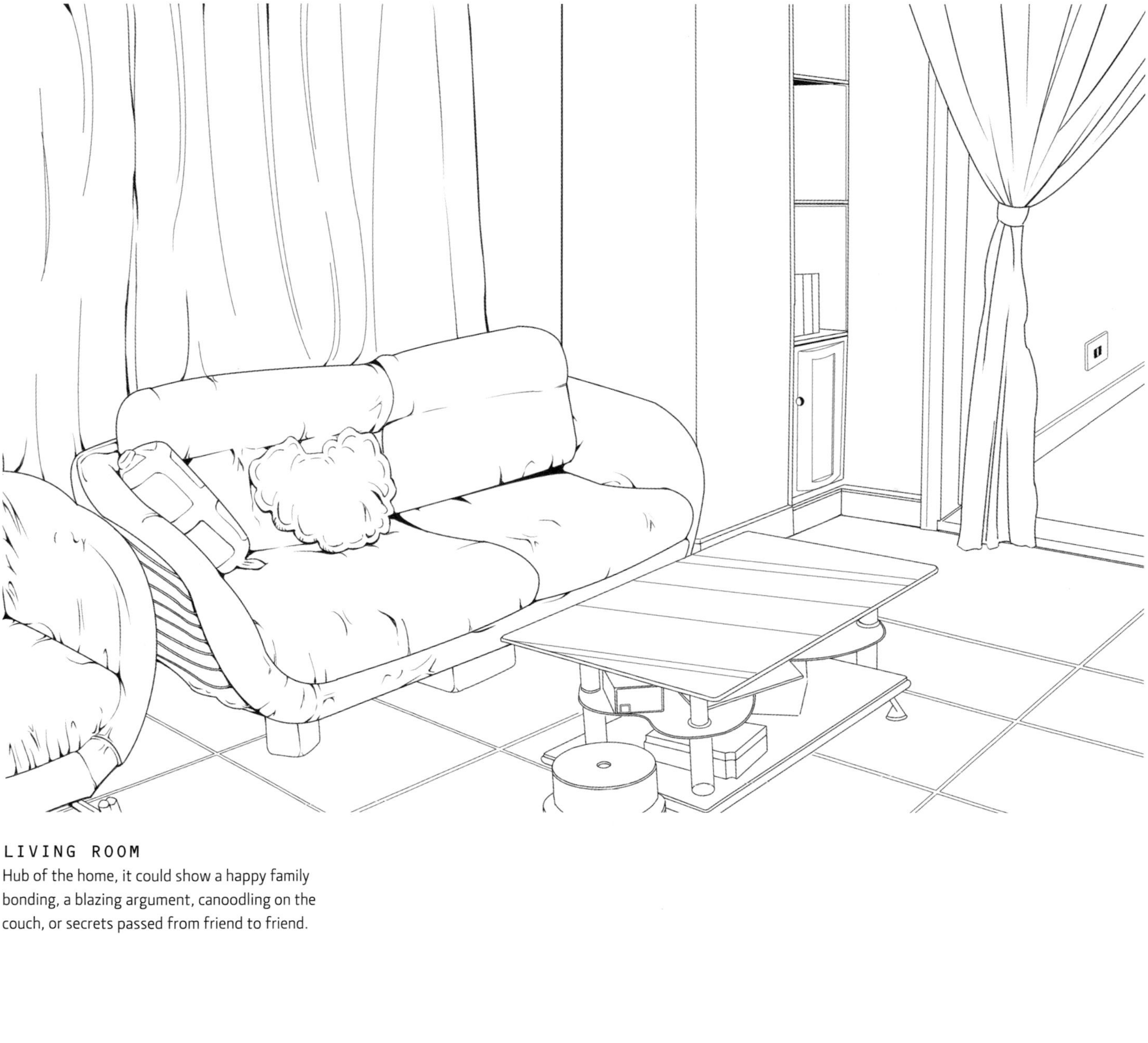

LIVING ROOM

Hub of the home, it could show a happy family bonding, a blazing argument, canoodling on the couch, or secrets passed from friend to friend.

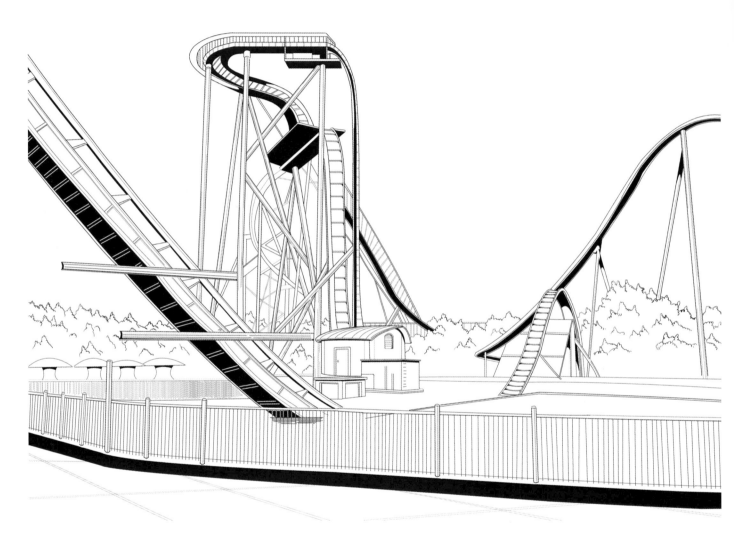

THEME PARK

First date? School trip? Cotton candy and stuffed prizes pop up wherever you look, and screams of roller coaster riders echo in the air.

EXCLUSIVE RESTAURANT
The nail-biting first meeting with a boyfriend's
parents, the location of the best birthday party
ever, or the entrance to a teenage spy ring. . .

CORRIDOR
The best gossip happens in the school corridor,
but this could easily be the hall of an apartment
block, hospital, or creepy old house.

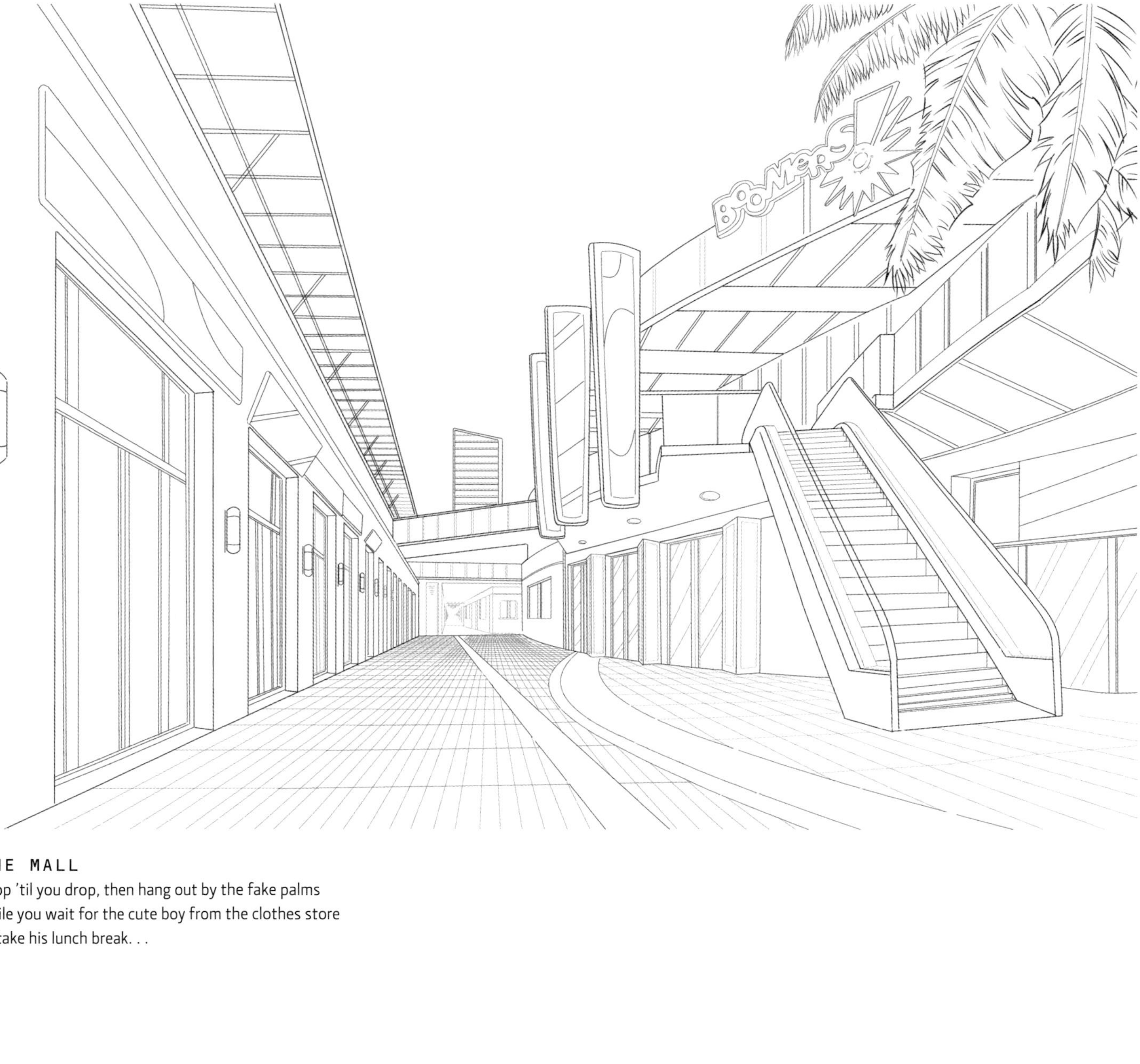
BOOMERS

THE MALL

Shop 'til you drop, then hang out by the fake palms while you wait for the cute boy from the clothes store to take his lunch break. . .

ACCESSORIES

NO ROOM—OR CHARACTER—IS COMPLETE WITHOUT IDIOSYNCRATIC TOUCHES THAT MAKE A PLACE LOOK LIVED IN AND A PERSON MORE THAN A BLANK SLATE. YOU'LL FIND MANY OBJECTS ON THE DISC TO ADD WARMTH AND PERSONALITY TO YOUR PANELS. FROM A MUCH-LOVED TEDDY BEAR TO AN UNTUNED GUITAR, A JUST-CHARGED IPOD TO A LONG-COOLED PIZZA; YOU'LL FIND IT ALL HERE.

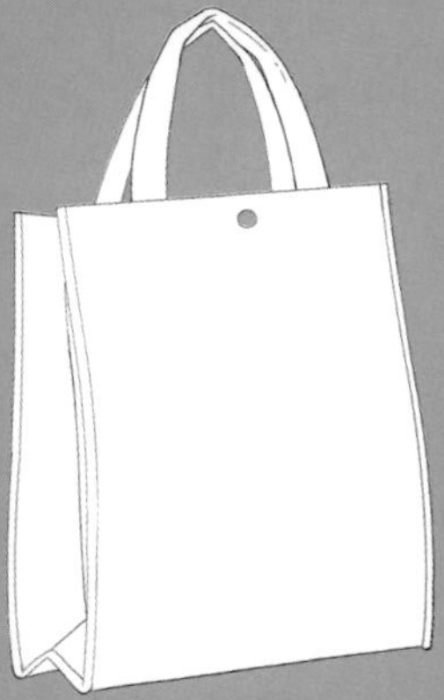
BAG

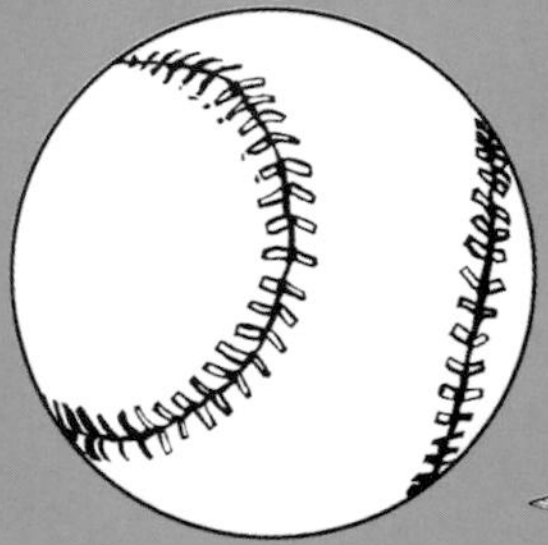
BASEBALL

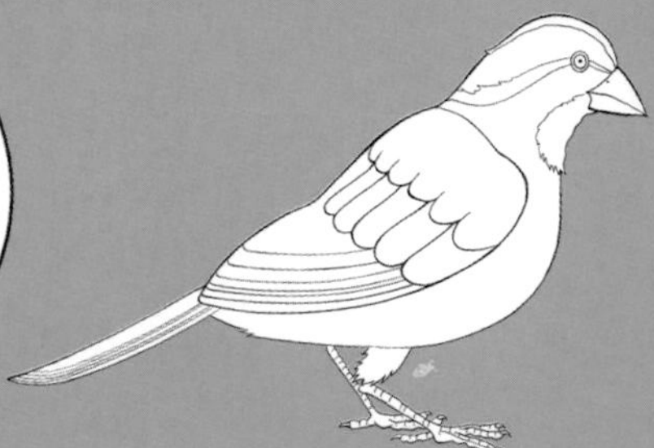
BIRD

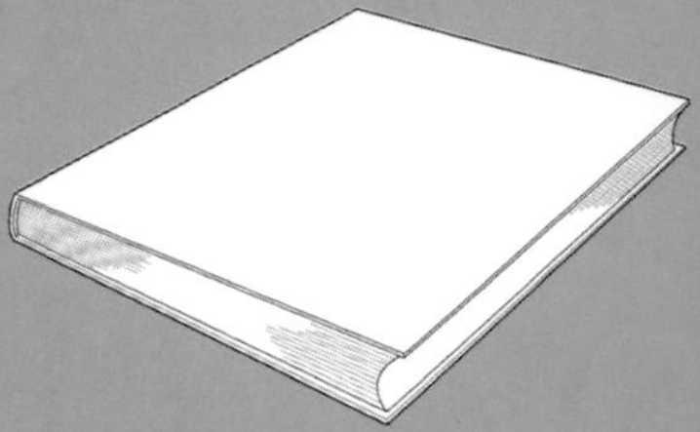
BOOK

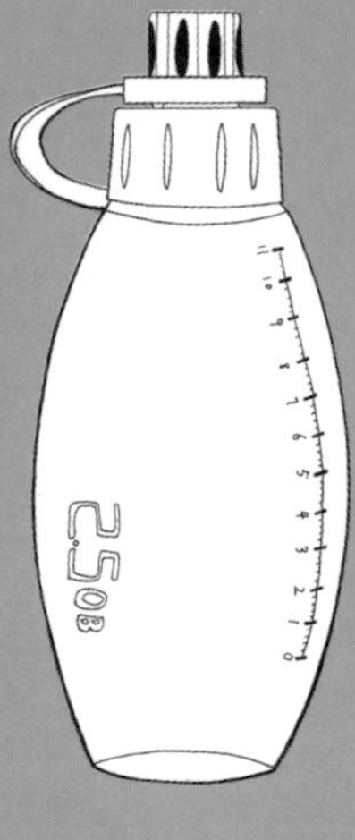
BOTTLE

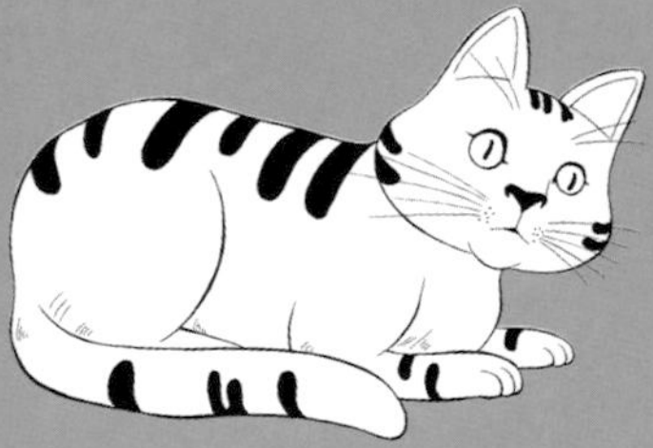
CAT

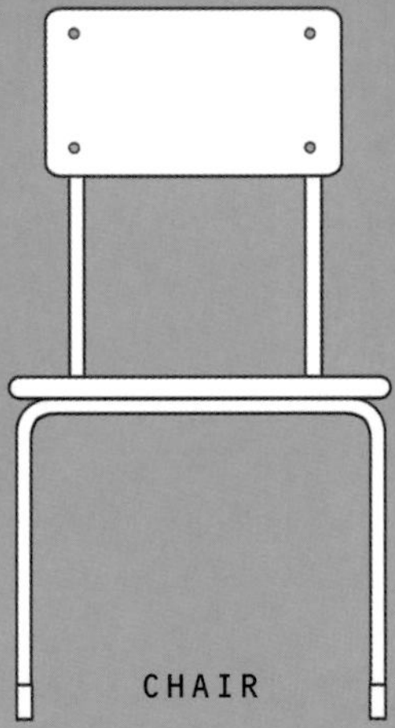
CHAIR

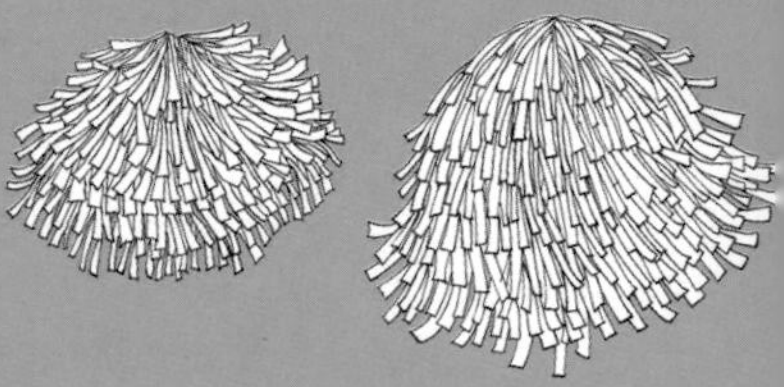
POM POMS

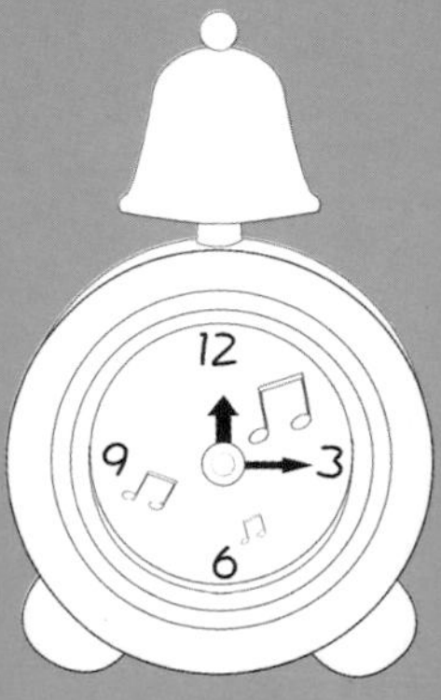
12
9
3
6
CLOCK

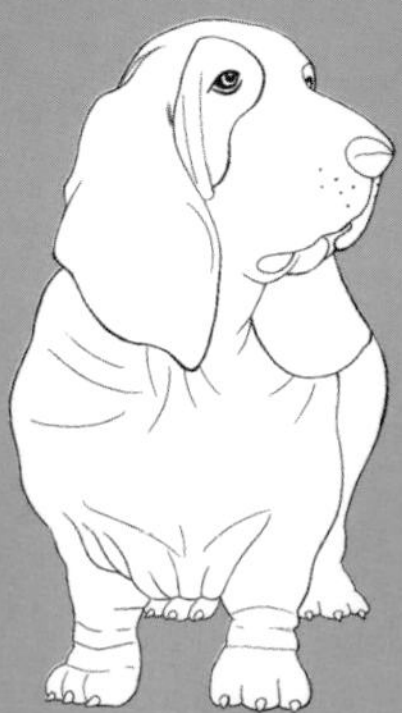
DOG

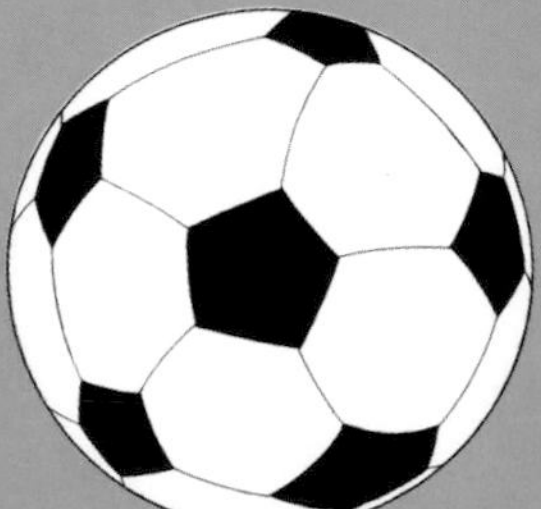
FOOTBALL

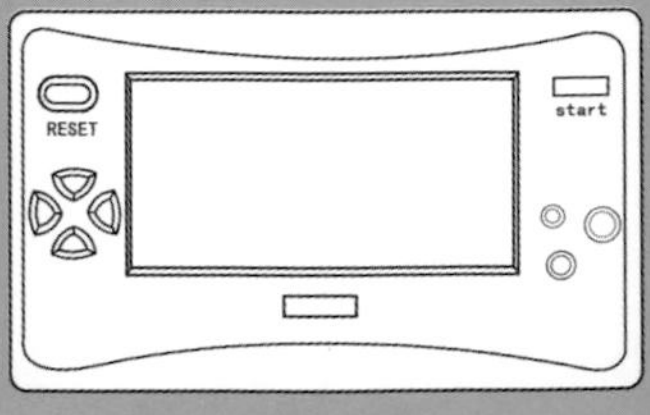
RESET
start
GAME CONSOLE

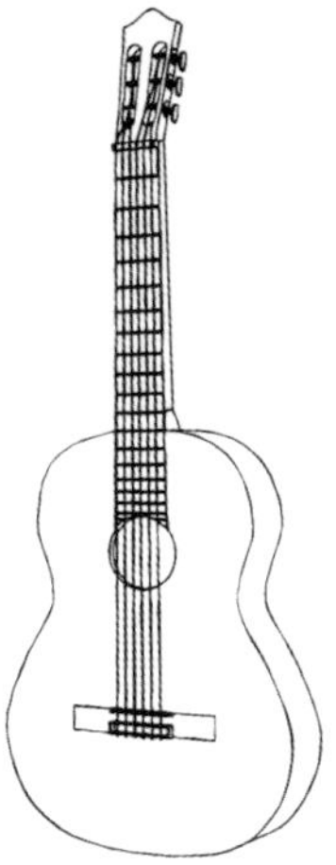

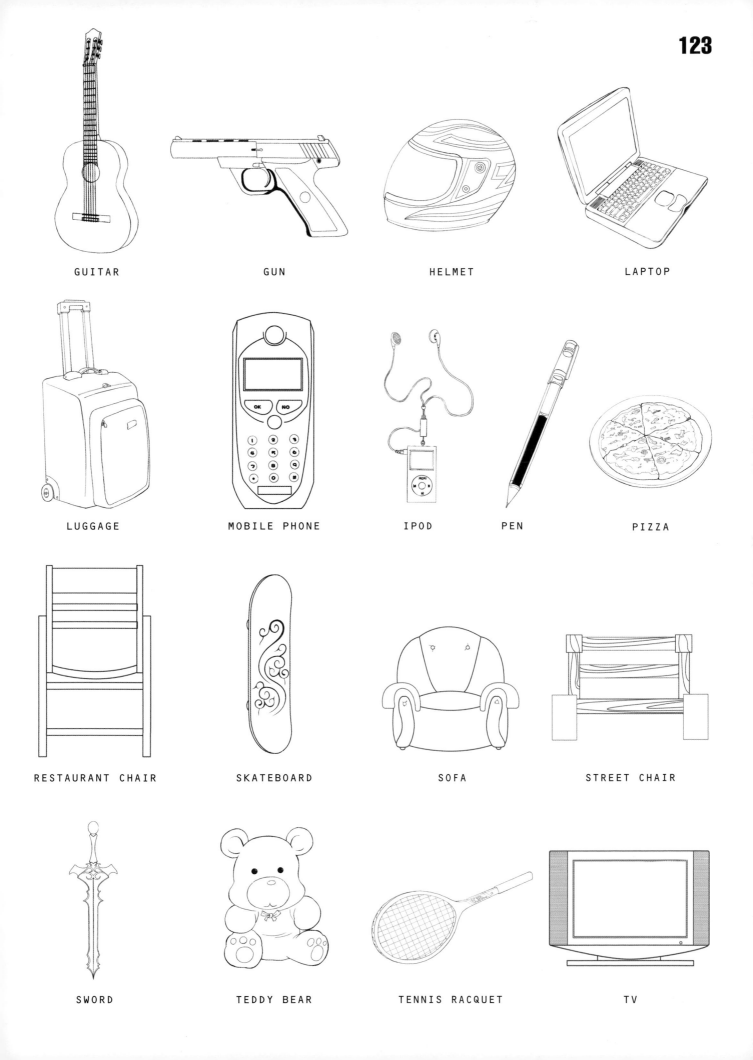

GUITAR

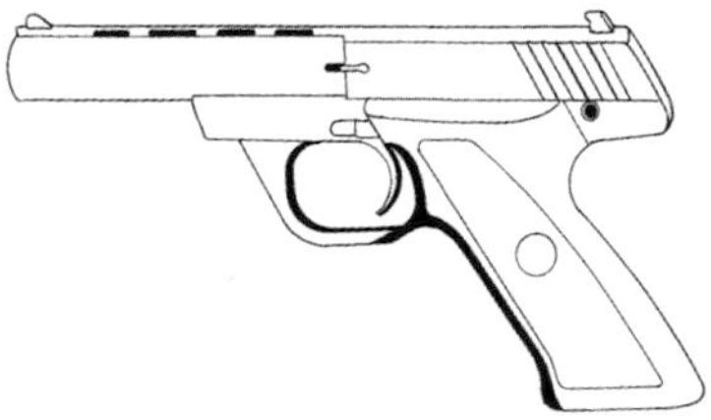

GUN

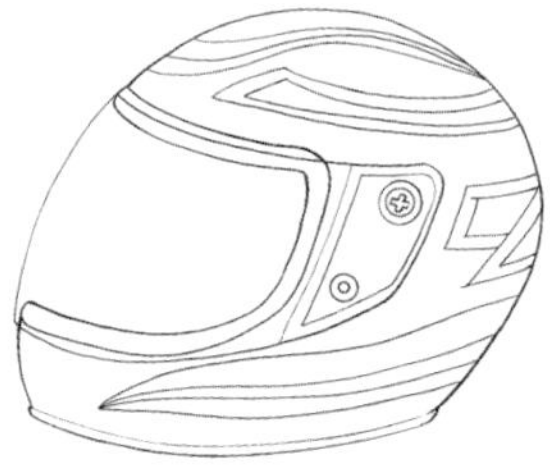

HELMET

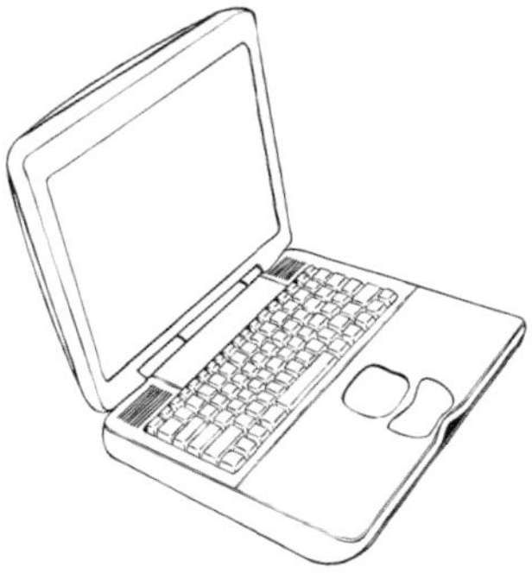

LAPTOP

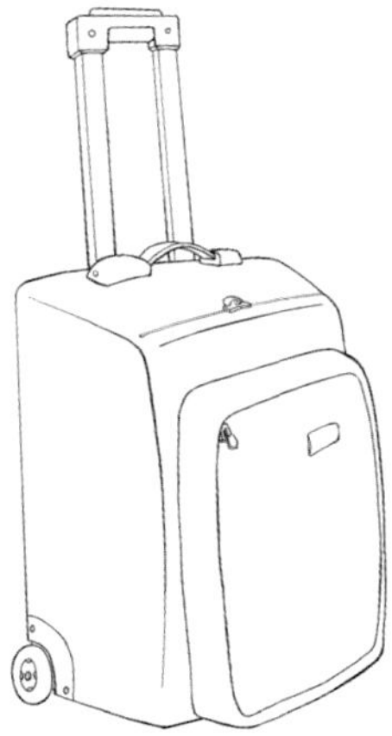

LUGGAGE

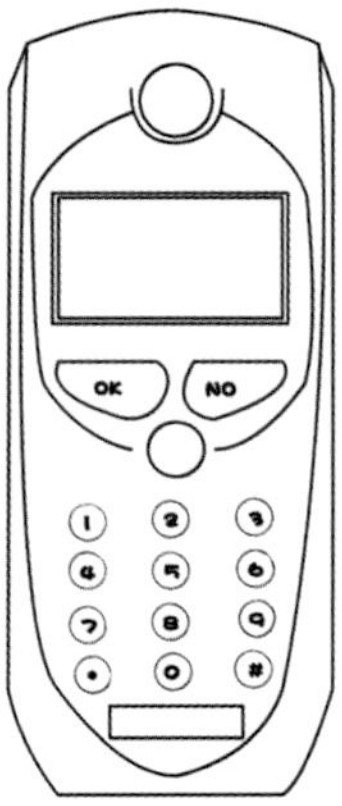
OK
NO

MOBILE PHONE

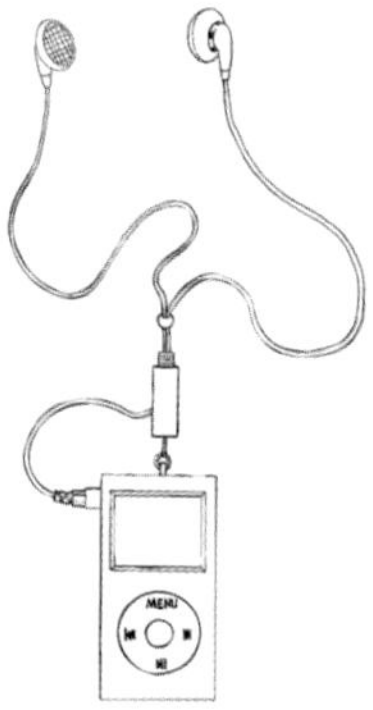

IPOD

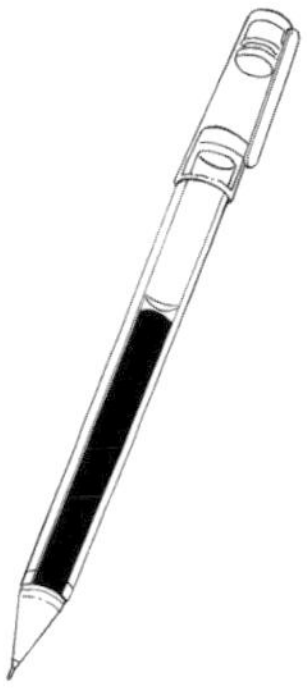

PEN

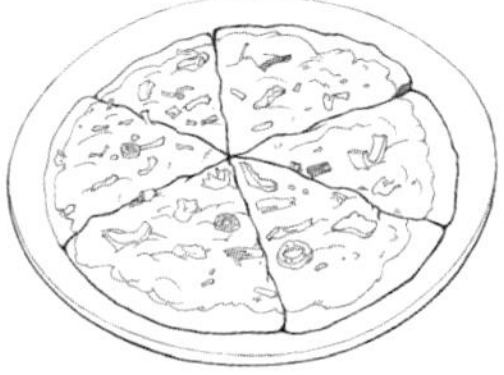

PIZZA

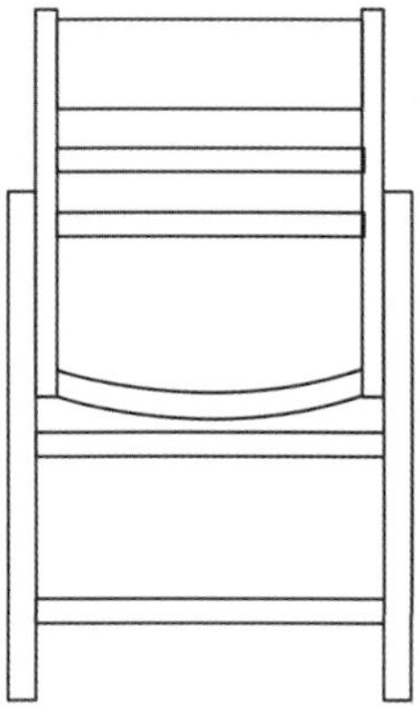

RESTAURANT CHAIR

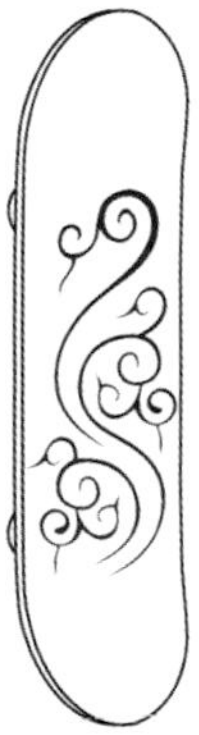

SKATEBOARD

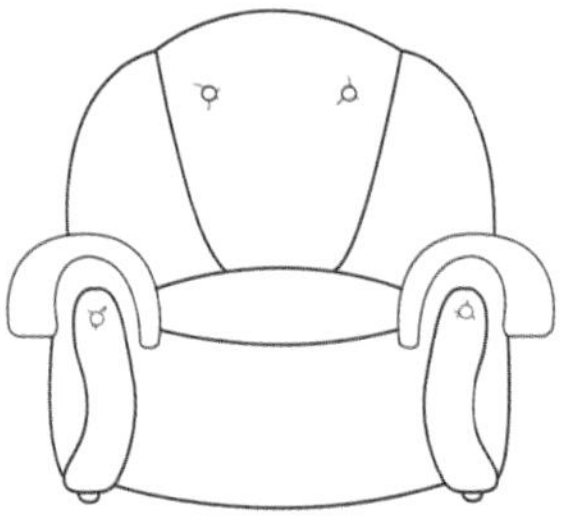

SOFA

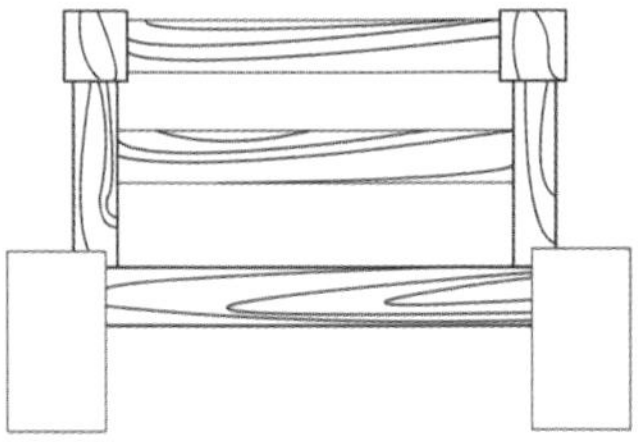

STREET CHAIR

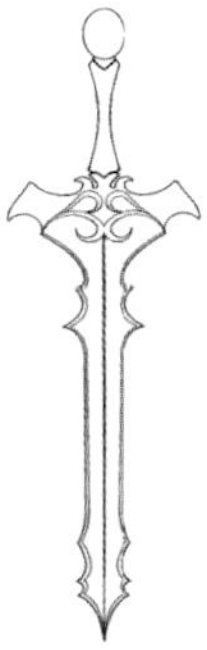

SWORD

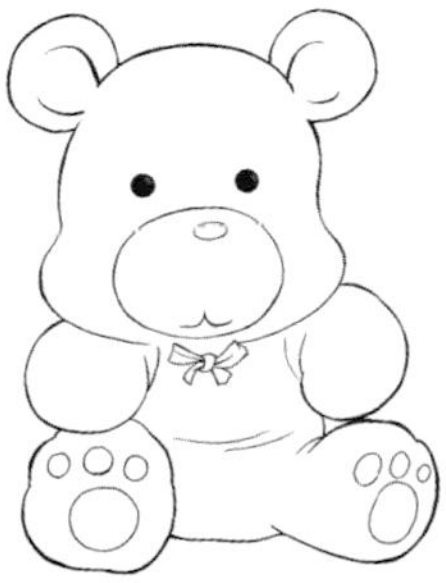

TEDDY BEAR

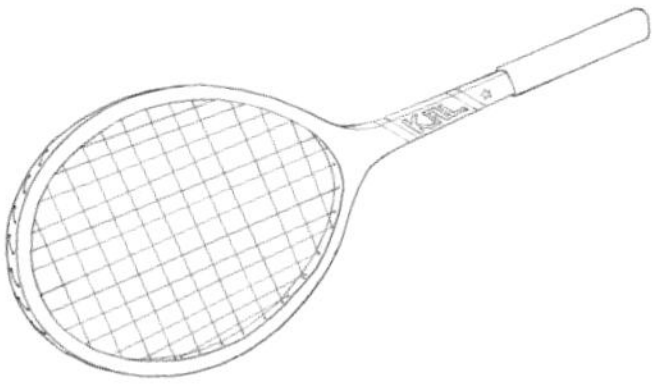

TENNIS RACQUET

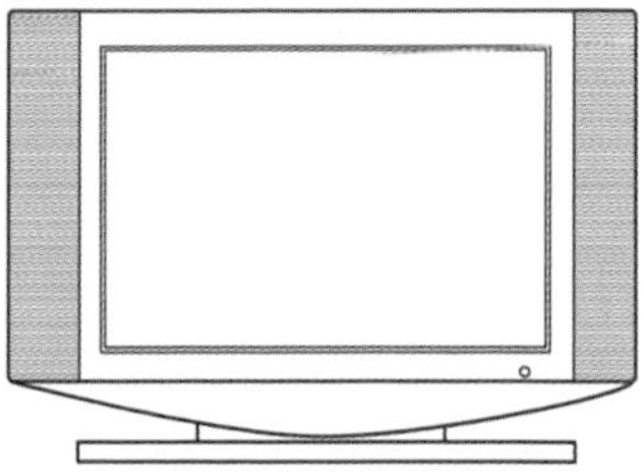

TV

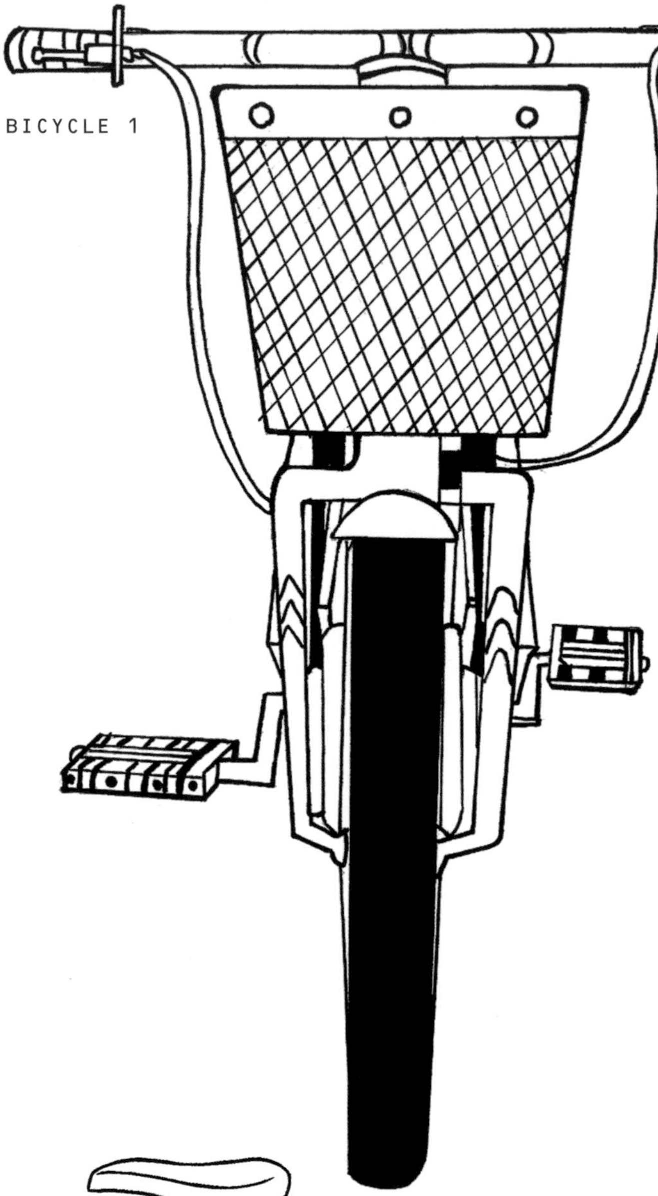

BICYCLE 1

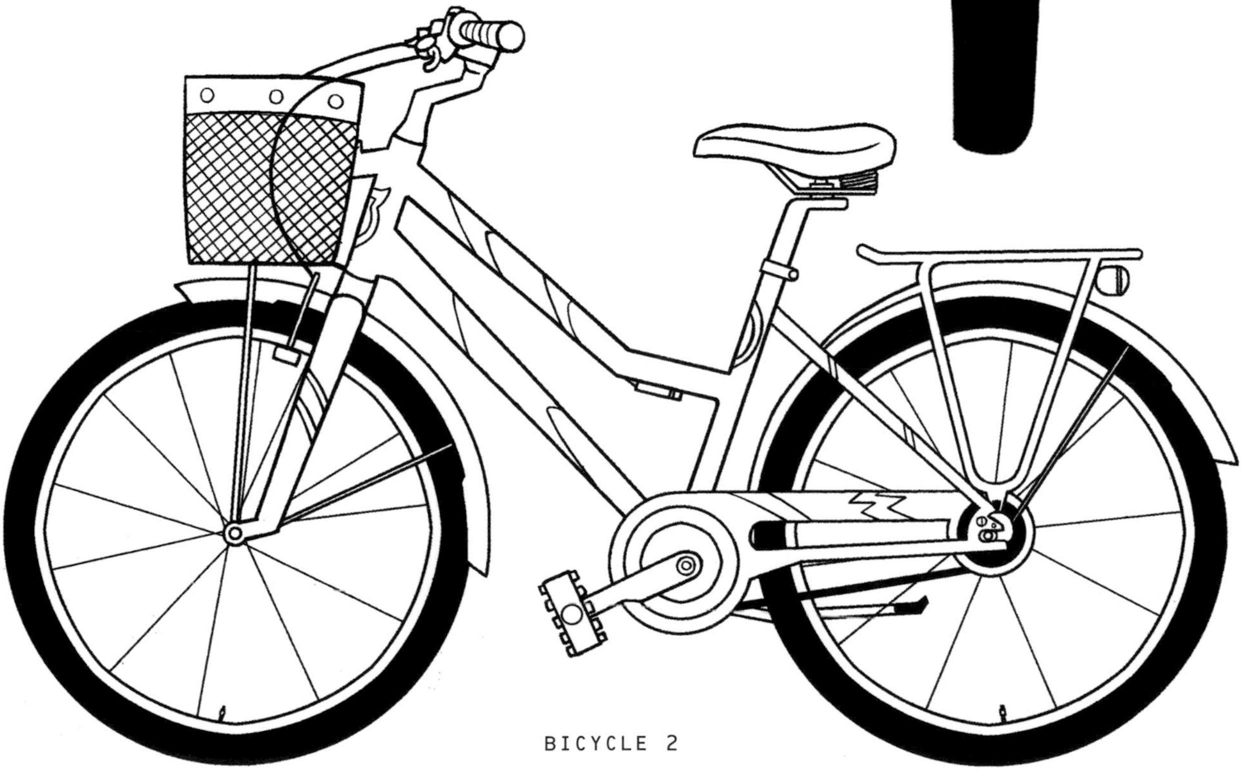

BICYCLE 2

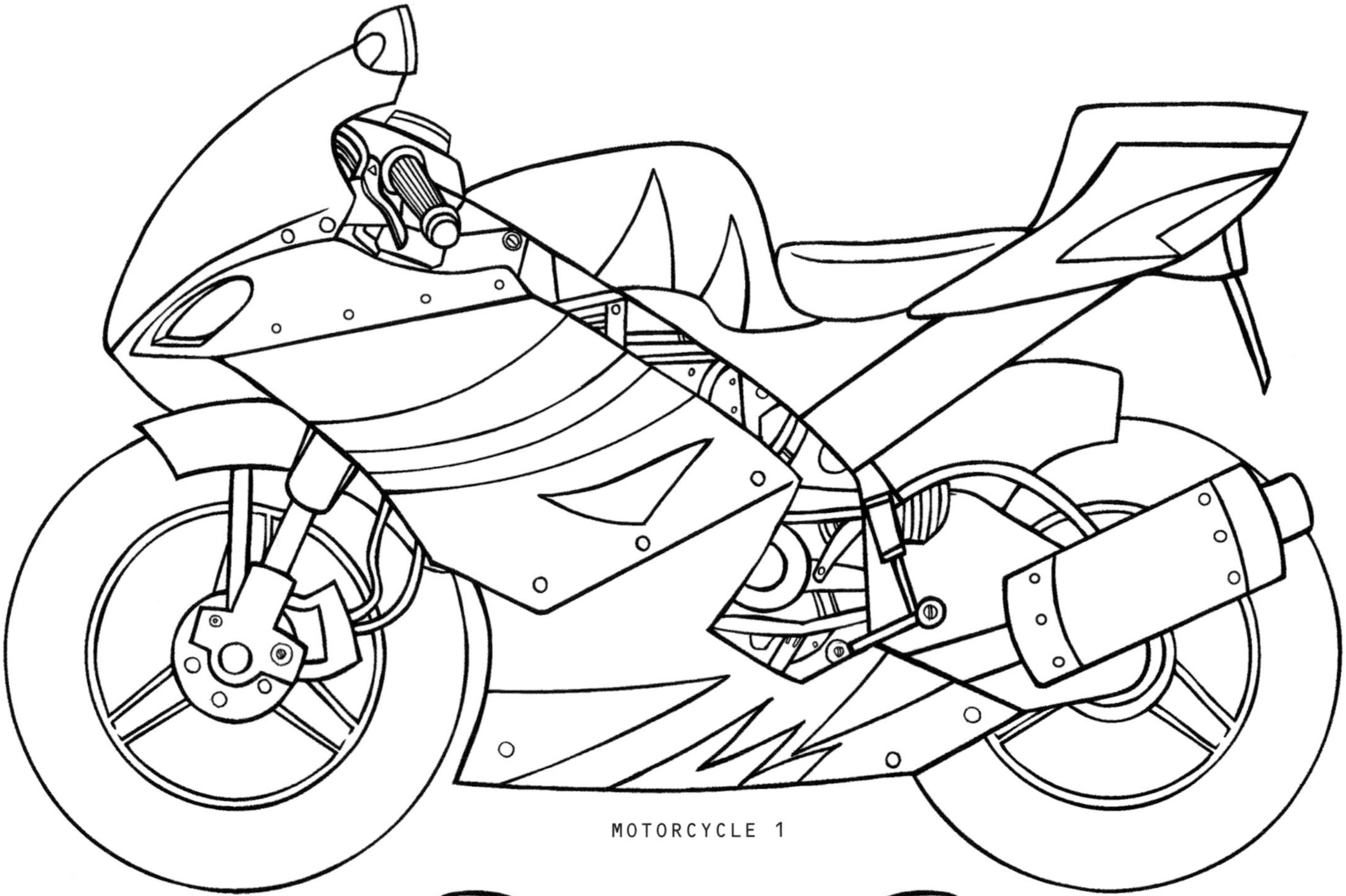

MOTORCYCLE 1

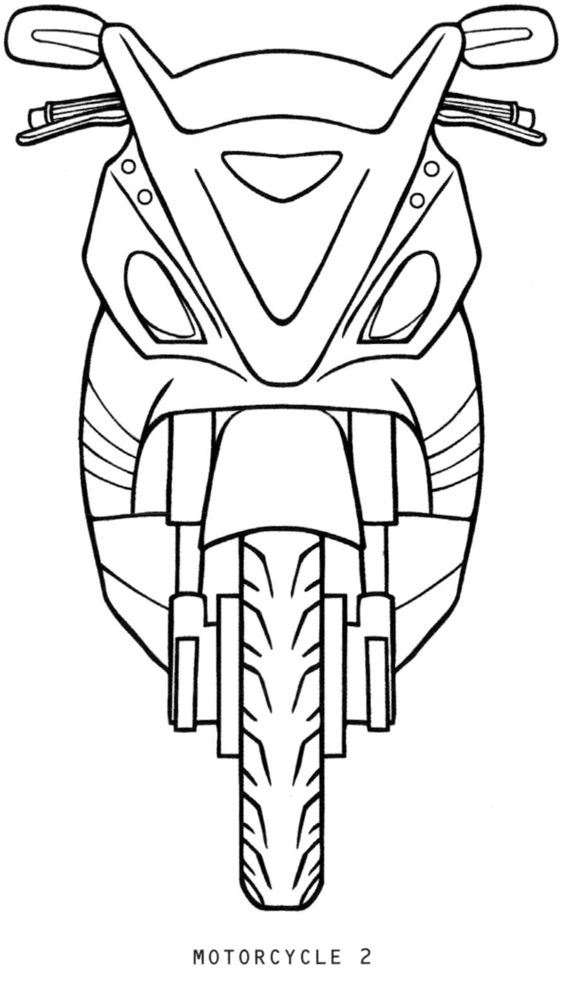

MOTORCYCLE 2

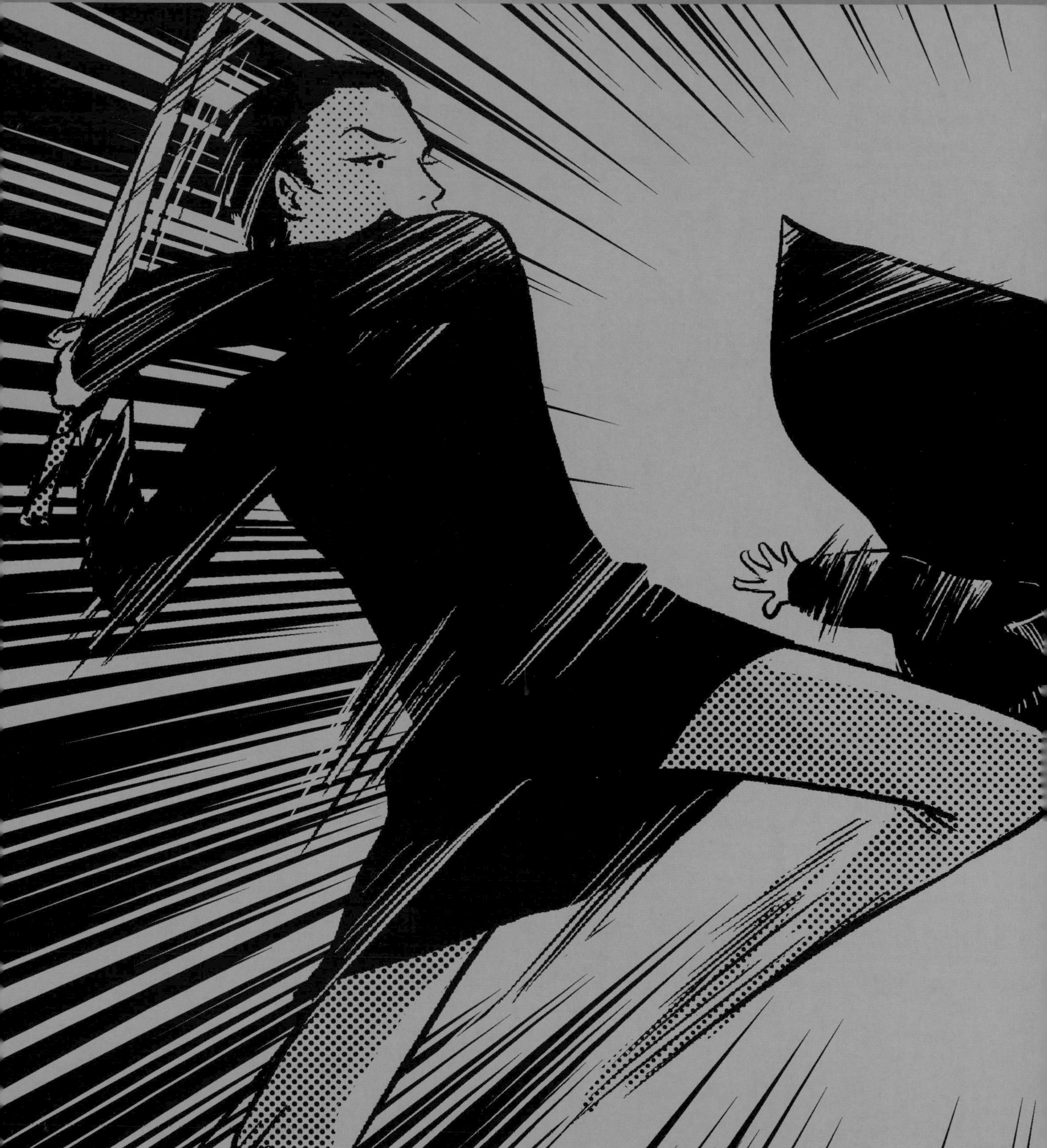

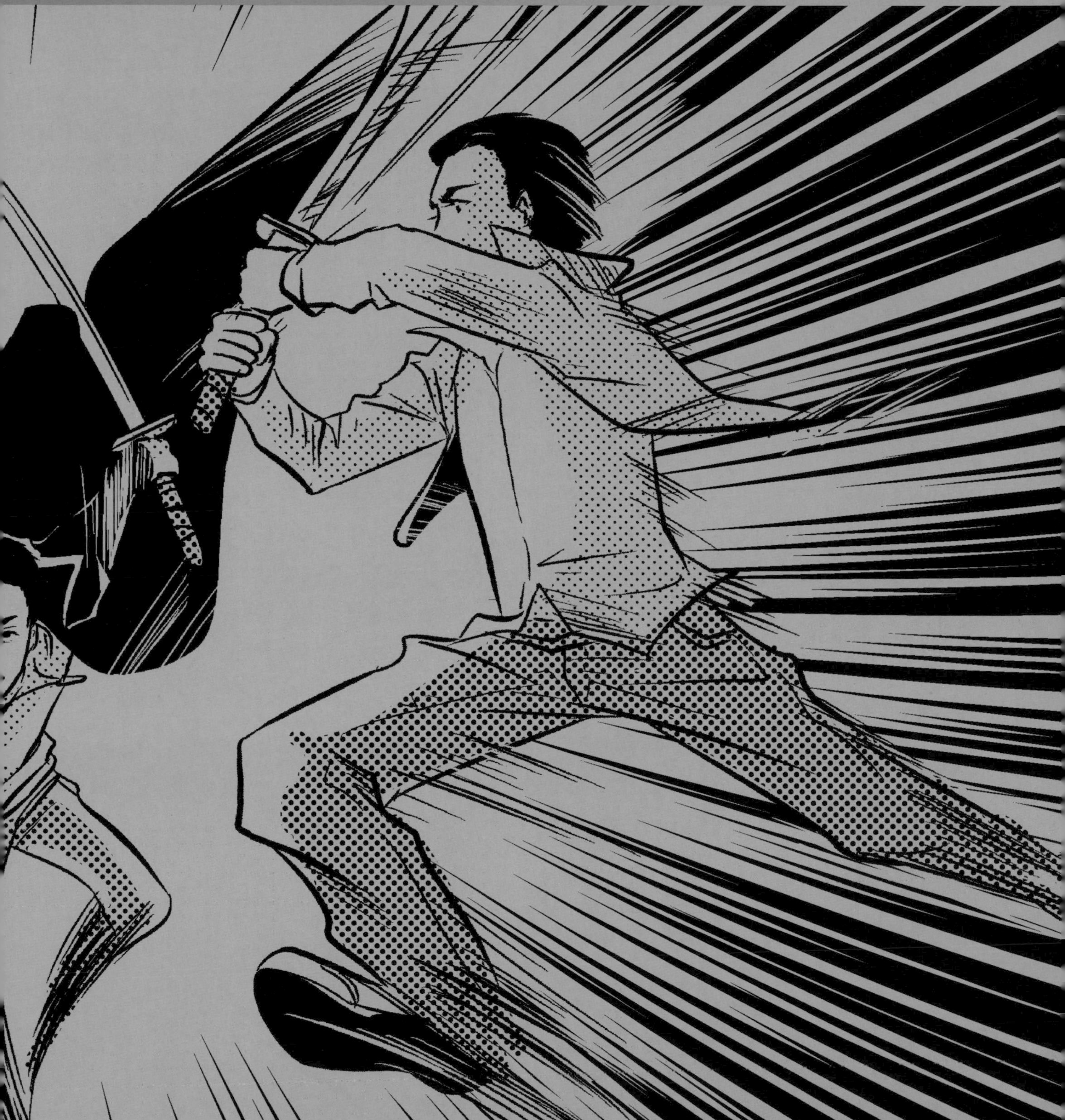

INDEX